Incentives to Pander

How Politicians Use Corporate Welfare for Political Gain

Policies targeting individual companies for economic development incentives, such as tax holidays and abatements, are generally seen as inefficient, economically costly, and distortionary. Despite this evidence, politicians still choose to use these policies to claim credit for attracting investment. Thus, while fiscal incentives are economically inefficient, they pose an effective pandering strategy for politicians. Using original surveys of voters in the United States, Canada, and the United Kingdom as well as data on incentive use by politicians in the United States, Vietnam, and Russia, this book provides compelling evidence for the use of fiscal incentives for political gain and shows how such pandering appears to be associated with growing economic inequality. As national and subnational governments surrender valuable tax revenue to attract businesses in the vain hope of long-term economic growth, they are left with fiscal shortfalls that have been filled through regressive sales taxes, police fines and penalties, and cuts to public education.

Nathan M. Jensen is Professor of Government at the University of Texas at Austin. He was previously an associate professor in the Department of International Business at George Washington University (2014–2016) and associate professor in the Political Science Department at Washington University in St. Louis (2002–2014).

Edmund J. Malesky is Professor of Political Economy and the Associate Chair of the Political Science Department at Duke University. He is a noted specialist in economic development, authoritarian institutions, and comparative political economy in Vietnam and has published extensively in leading political science and economic journals.

Business and Public Policy

Series Editor:
ASEEM PRAKASH, University of Washington

Series Board:
Vinod K. Aggarwal, University of California, Berkeley
Tanja A. Börzel, Freie Universität Berlin
David Coen, University College London
Peter Gourevitch, University of California, San Diego
Neil Gunningham, The Australian National University
Witold J. Henisz, University of Pennsylvania
Adrienne Héritier, European University Institute
Chung-in Moon, Yonsei University
Sarah A. Soule, Stanford University
David Vogel, University of California, Berkeley

This series aims to play a pioneering role in shaping the emerging field of business and public policy. *Business and Public Policy* focuses on two central questions. First, how does public policy influence business strategy, operations, organization, and governance, and with what consequences for both business and society? Second, how do businesses themselves influence policy institutions, policy processes, and other policy actors and with what outcomes?

Other books in the series:
Timothy Werner, *Public Forces and Private Politics in American Big Business*

Hevina S. Dashwood, *The Rise of Global Corporate Social Responsibility: Mining and the Spread of Global Norms*

Llewelyn Hughes, *Globalizing Oil: Firms and Oil Market Governance in France, Japan, and the United States*

Edward T. Walker, *Grassroots for Hire: Public Affairs Consultants in American Democracy*

Christian R. Thauer, *The Managerial Sources of Corporate Social Responsibility: The Spread of Global Standards*

Kiyoteru Tsutsui & Alwyn Lim (Editors), *Corporate Social Responsibility in a Globalizing World*

Aseema Sinha, *Globalizing India: How Global Rules and Markets are Shaping India's Rise to Power*

Victor Menaldo, *The Institutions Curse: Natural Resources, Politics, and Development*

Jeroen Van Der Heijden, *Innovations in Urban Climate Governance: Voluntary Programs for Low Carbon Buildings and Cities*

Liliana B. Andonova, *Governance Entrepreneurs: International Organizations and the Rise of Global Public-Private Partnerships*

Michael P. Vandenberg and Jonathan M. Gilligan, *Beyond Politics: The Private Governance Response to Climate Change*

Incentives to Pander

How politicians Use Corporate Welfare for Political Gain

Nathan M. Jensen
University of Texas at Austin

Edmund J. Malesky
Duke University, North Carolina

CAMBRIDGE
UNIVERSITY PRESS

University Printing House, Cambridge CB2 8BS, United Kingdom

One Liberty Plaza, 20th Floor, New York, NY 10006, USA

477 Williamstown Road, Port Melbourne, VIC 3207, Australia

314–321, 3rd Floor, Plot 3, Splendor Forum, Jasola District Centre, New Delhi – 110025, India

79 Anson Road, #06–04/06, Singapore 079906

Cambridge University Press is part of the University of Cambridge.

It furthers the University's mission by disseminating knowledge in the pursuit of education, learning, and research at the highest international levels of excellence.

www.cambridge.org
Information on this title: www.cambridge.org/9781108418904
DOI: 10.1017/9781108292337

© Nathan M. Jensen and Edmund J. Malesky 2018

This publication is in copyright. Subject to statutory exception and to the provisions of relevant collective licensing agreements, no reproduction of any part may take place without the written permission of Cambridge University Press.

First published 2018

Printed in the United Kingdom by Clays, St Ives plc

A catalogue record for this publication is available from the British Library.

Library of Congress Cataloging-in-Publication Data
Names: Jensen, Nathan M. (Nathan Michael), 1975– author. | Malesky, Edmund J., author.
Title: Incentives to pander / Nathan M. Jensen, Washington University, St Louis, Edmund J. Malesky, Duke University, North Carolina.
Description: Cambridge, United Kingdom ; New York, NY : Cambridge University Press, 2018. | Includes bibliographical references.
Identifiers: LCCN 2017048009 | ISBN 9781108418904
Subjects: LCSH: Tax incentives – United States. | Tax credits – United States. | Corporations – Government policy – United States.
Classification: LCC HJ2331.U6 J46 2018 | DDC 338.9/22–dc23
LC record available at https://lccn.loc.gov/2017048009

ISBN 978-1-108-41890-4 Hardback

Cambridge University Press has no responsibility for the persistence or accuracy of URLs for external or third-party internet websites referred to in this publication and does not guarantee that any content on such websites is, or will remain, accurate or appropriate.

Contents

Acknowledgments		*page* x
1	Introduction: The Global Competition for Capital Meets Local Politics	1
	1.1 Incentives over Time and Across Borders	3
	1.2 Political Pandering: Up and Down	5
	1.3 The Puzzling Use of Investment Incentives	8
	1.4 Organization of the Book	15
2	Theory of the Political Use of Investment Incentives	18
	2.1 Electoral Pandering	20
	2.2 The Use of Incentives by Elected Politicians	23
	2.3 The Open Secret: Anecdotal Evidence for Politicians' Awareness of Incentive Inefficiencies	25
	2.4 Even Good Politicians Can Enact Bad Policies	27
3	Incentives and the Competition for Investment Within Countries and Around the World	29
	3.1 National Incentives and Effective Tax Rates Around the World	31
	3.2 The Subnational Competition for Incentives	37
	3.3 Conclusion	39
4	The Economic Case Against Investment Incentives	41
	4.1 Farming Incentives: The Story of Google in Lenoir	41
	4.2 The Economic Arguments Against Incentives	45
	Are They Effective at Attracting or Retaining Investments?	46
	Can Governments Target Firms and Pick Winners?	48
	Do Incentives Generate Jobs?	49
	Are Jobs Worth the Cost?	51
	The Only Option?	54
	4.3 Illustration: The "Promoting Employment Across Kansas" Incentive Program	54
	4.4 Conclusion	57
5	Economic or Political Competition? Allocation and Oversight of US Incentives	58
	5.1 Local Competition and Incentives	59

vii

	5.2 Adapting Our Theory and Main Hypotheses to US Cities	61
	5.3 Research Design	66
	The Independent Variable: Elected Mayors	68
	The Dependent Variable: The Frequency and Size of Incentives	68
	Balance Between the Electoral Treatment and Control Groups	69
	Entropy Balancing	70
	Exogeneity in Institutional Selection	77
	5.4 Conclusion	81
6	**Money for Money: Campaign Contributions in Exchange for Incentives?**	**83**
	6.1 Campaign Contributions and Incentive Programs	84
	6.2 Analysis of Campaign Contributions and State Incentive Programs	86
	6.3 More on the Kansas City Border War	92
	6.4 Conclusion	94
7	**Political Pandering in the United States: A Survey Experiment on Incentives and Investment**	**95**
	7.1 The United States as a Laboratory	97
	7.2 A Survey Experiment of US Residents	98
	Ordered Probit Analysis	104
	Conditional Effects of Incentives	108
	7.3 What Do Voters Know About Incentives?	114
	7.4 Credit Claiming in the United Kingdom	116
	7.5 Conclusion	119
	Appendix	120
8	**Pandering Upward: Tax Incentives and Credit Claiming in Authoritarian Countries**	**122**
	8.1 Pandering Upward in Single-Party Regimes	125
	Varieties of Authoritarianism	125
	The Success of Single-Party States	126
	Meritocratic Promotion and Local Incentives in Single-Party Regimes	127
	8.2 Comparing Incentives Between Democracies and Non-Democracies	131
	Tax Policies by Type of Authoritarian Country	133
	Promotion and Upward Pandering	136
	Discussion of Cross-National Results	140
	8.3 Meritocratic Promotion and Pandering Upward: A Regression Discontinuity Approach in Vietnam	141
	Sharp Regression Discontinuity Specification	143
	Results of the Regression Discontinuity	152
	Robustness Tests	154
	A Closer Look at Incentives	154
	Summary of Vietnam Analysis	157
	8.4 Testing the Personalism Hypothesis in Putin's Russia	158
	Personalist Authoritarianism Under Putin	158
	Model Specification and Data	160
	Results	162

Contents ix

	Summary of the Russian Analysis	165
	8.5 Conclusion	166
	Appendix	168
9	**The Distributional Effects of Investment Incentives**	**179**
	9.1 Incentives Increase Tax and Spending Inequality	181
	9.2 General Patterns of Tax Inequality and the Use of Incentives	183
	9.3 Increasing Sales Taxes to Pay for Tax Incentives	188
	Descriptive Statistics and Bivariate Relationships	188
	Regression Analysis	190
	Qualitative Evidence from Legal Authorizations of Incentive Programs	192
	9.4 What Are the Fiscal Trade-Offs? School Districts and Economic Development Incentives	193
	9.5 Conclusion	196
10	**Potential Policy Solutions to the Pandering Problem**	**198**
	10.1 The Ineffectiveness of Clawbacks	199
	10.2 Can Transparency Improve Economic Development?	201
	10.3 Testing the Benefits of Transparency in the United States and Canada	205
	Testing Transparency About the Costs of Incentives in the United States	205
	Testing Transparency About the Costs of Incentives in Canada	208
	10.4 Conclusions	213
	Appendix Detailed Analysis of Clawback Programs in Missouri	214
11	**Final Thoughts**	**222**
	11.1 The Biggest Incentive Deal of All Time?	222
	11.2 Incentives for Economic Development	222
	11.3 Debating the Use of Incentives	223
	11.4 A Final Reflection on Theory and Evidence	224
	11.5 America and Beyond	229
	References	231
	Index	254

Acknowledgments

While the writing of this book started in 2012, our intellectual debts for this project date back many years. The foundations for this project began in a collaboration with Mariana Medina and Ugur Ozdemir when they were graduate students at Washington University in St. Louis. We acknowledge their contributions in the notes to Chapter 7, but their intellectual contribution has strengthened every aspect of this project.

Numerous other co-authors and research assistants provided support for this research. Matt Walsh provided the heavy lifting on the data organization for Chapter 5, but we draw on this incentives data throughout the manuscript. Mi Jeong Shin and Kathryn Sproule had important contributions to the data collection of Texas campaign contributions for Chapter 6. Bob Corvin and Michael Dickerson performed excellent data work for Chapter 7. Phan Tuan Ngoc and Edwin (Belton) Moore put together the data on promotions for analysis Chapter 8. A team of undergraduate and graduate research assistants have found stories, collected data, and provided intellectual feedback, all found throughout the book. We are indebted to Benjamin Crisman, Stephen Decker, Lillan Frost, Amanda Hayes, Alexander Hoyer, Katharine Sullivan, and Charles Warner. Phan Tuan Ngoc and Harunobu Saijo assisted with the index creation.

Over the years we have benefited from the generous comments of colleagues at speaker series and conferences, as well as the interviews Nate has conducted with economic development professionals in the United States and abroad. Thanks to Jude Hays, Witold Henisz, Randall Stone, Layna Mosley, Craig McIntosh, and participants at the Globalization and Governance Conference at Washington University, the Internal Political Economy Society Annual Conference, and the Yale International Relations Workshop for their valuable comments and suggestions on the theory and empirical analysis in Chapter 7. Thanks to Brady Baybeck, Randy Calvert, Jim Clinger, Bill Lowry, and Gary Miller for their comments and suggestions on Chapter 5 of the manuscript. Kimberly Nelson shared data on state laws governing city forms of

Acknowledgments

government. Adam Bonica provided useful suggestions for the campaign contribution data in Chapter 6. Andrew Kerner, John Reuter, and Rory Truex offered valuable advice on Chapter 8.

Primary funding for the survey experiments in this book is from Murray Weidenbaum Center on the Economy, Government, and Public Policy. The Weidenbaum Center funded two full waves of surveys through the Cooperative Congressional Election Survey, a survey in the United Kingdom through YouGov UK. The Center for New Institutional Social Sciences at Washington University provided support to purchase the incentive data used in Chapter 7. The Ewing Marion Kaufmann Foundation provided support for data collection and analysis for information on the Kansas City border war throughout the book. Insightful comments from Yasuyuki Motoyama and Jason Wiens helped improve our work in Chapter 4. A grant from the Washington Center for Equitable Growth contributed to analysis of the fiscal costs of incentives presented in Chapter 9. We are grateful to the United States Agency for International Development (US-AID) and the Vietnam Chamber of Commerce and Industry (VCCI) for allowing us to use firm-level data from the Vietnam PCI-FDI survey in Chapter 8. Thanks also to Alexander Klemm and David Szakonyi, who provided us with international and Russian data respectively for use in Chapter 8 as well.

Throughout the years we have benefited from numerous conversations with critics and supporters of economic development incentives working in government, business, and NGOs. These conversations not only helped improve the quality of our work, they also gave us the optimism that we are all joining in an effort to help promote fair and equitable economic development in our communities. This book is our contribution to this collective effort.

1 Introduction
The Global Competition for Capital Meets Local Politics

Kansas City, Missouri, may sound like an unconventional place to begin examining the dynamics of the global competition to attract investment. Despite the city's warm Midwestern feel and its location near the geographic center of the United States, it has recently become embroiled in intense economic warfare. The opponent in this fiscal battle is not a major US metropolis or a booming, emerging market like India or Brazil, but is actually the city's namesake – Kansas City, Kansas. Separated only by a porous, artificial state division, the two cities are locked in an intense border war for millions of dollars in investment generated by the relocation of foreign and domestic companies. The primary arsenal in the battle is the multitude of location-specific incentives targeted at foreign and domestic investors. What are these "incentives" that have fueled the conflagration and why did the two Kansas Cities rely so heavily upon them? These are the questions we take up in the pages below.

Throughout this book we use the broad definition of incentives to cover a wide range of policies targeted at individual firms, which critics refer to cynically as "corporate welfare." We base our definition of incentives on the United Nations Conference on Trade and Development (UNCTAD), which describes incentives as "measurable advantages provided by government to particular companies or groups of companies with the goal to force them to behave in some way."[1] In most cases, we examine incentives aimed at shaping the location of a firm's investment projects, which can include: a new project, an expansion of an existing plant, or the retention of an existing company that considered relocating to another administrative jurisdiction.

Incentives can be discretionary allotments, including "deal-closing funds," such as the Texas Enterprise Fund (TEF), which provides cash incentives to attract new investments. Other incentives can be statutory, providing incentives to any firm that qualifies for government support. In most cases, such as the Promoting Employment Across Kansas (PEAK)

---

[1] UNCTAD (1996, 11) cited in Tavares-Lehmann (2016, 17).

and Missouri Quality Jobs Program, discussed in the border war above and described in more detail in Chapters 4 and 9, the programs are a mixture of statutory requirements to qualify for incentives and discretion regarding which firms receive incentives and how much money they are worth. Only some firms qualify for incentives, and within this subset of firms, politicians ration the allocation of tax credits, cash, or other benefits. Central to our definition, however, is that these benefits are precisely targeted at some firms, and are not general economic policies which bestow benefits on all companies like broad-based corporate tax reductions or infrastructure rollouts.

As we discuss in more detail in Chapter 4, one of the most common types of incentives is providing tax relief to individual firms, while maintaining generally higher rates on the books. Such relief usually takes the form of exemptions from national taxes, common in developing countries to reductions in state and local taxes, which comprise the majority of incentives in the United States. Countries, states, and local governments also provide additional incentive types, including worker retraining grants, relocation funds, free or highly subsidized land, and infrastructure improvements.

Comparing these widely varying forms of incentives has its challenges, yet the common theme across all incentive programs is that government officials allocate scarce resources or forgo vital future tax revenue to attract, retain, or promote the expansion of a small number of firms. In the United States, competition across states, counties, and cities have led to a proliferation in the amount and an escalation in the volume of these programs.

The competition has grown so intense in the Kansas Cities that the twins were the subject of an exposé on investment incentives by the *New York Times* (Story 2012), which suggested that the area was one of the best examples in the United States of the socially costly competition for investment. Indeed, the article claimed that these incentives did little more than subsidize companies to shift back and forth across the border. Our own data analysis in this book finds that from 2010 to 2012, no less than sixty-seven companies in the Kansas City border war received a total of $312 million dollars in tax reductions and other targeted inducements, such as land clearance or infrastructure outlays, to either remain on, or relocate to, one side of the state line.

Counted among the border jumpers is Applebees for its 2011 decision to move its corporate headquarters and 390 jobs to Missouri from Kansas after receiving $12.9 million in investment from the Kansas City Development Corporation (*Wichita Eagle* 2011). Those 390 jobs were soon whittled down to ninety, however, as the family restaurant chain abandoned the Kansas City metro entirely for the warmer climate of Glendale, California, in 2015 (Davis 2015). Importantly for our arguments in this book, Glendale did not offer Applebees any incentives at all to induce this last move (Masunaga 2015). The city cut some red tape, but the relocation was entirely driven by a broader consolidation exercise of DineEquity – Applebee's parent company – which sought to move the marketing, operations, and culinary departments closer to those of the International House of Pancakes, DineEquity's other major chain (Davis 2015).

Applebees is one example of a broader phenomenon of sizable economic development incentives that appear to have little impact on firms' location decisions or longevity. Many of the "incentivized" firms in the border war were planning to expand their business anyway, and the majority of the "new" firms to the area simply shifted their mailboxes a few miles across the border. Civil and company leaders have signed a letter to both governors to stop the fruitless battle, but to no avail (Greenblatt 2011). The states of Missouri and Kansas continue to provide generous incentives to firms, despite scandals,[2] general criticism, and obvious uncertainty over the effectiveness these programs. James Sly, the mayor of Kansas City, Missouri, reflecting on the 2015 Applebees relocation, stated publicly that he hoped the company's exit would convince Kansas officials that the border war has only cost both cities revenue while having little impact on their economies (Davis 2015).

1.1 Incentives over Time and Across Borders

The Kansas City imbroglio is only one recent example of the politics of incentives. Investment incentives are sometimes more broadly referred to as place-based economic development policies. As we noted above, they differ from other tax and infrastructure policies in that they are targeted to individual firms, or some subset of firms.

For example, numerous US locations provide tax abatements from state and local taxes as a means of encouraging new businesses. Governments simply forgo potential revenue to encourage local economic activity by reducing corporate income tax (CIT) rates, forgoing tax penalties, or offering rebates on previous payments. Tax abatements, while common, are only one form of economic development. Tax holidays allow firms to avoid payment of taxes, most commonly CIT or property taxes, for a

---

[2] One example is the Mamtek scandal in Missouri, where an artificial sweetener plant was awarded millions in incentives from Missouri only to declare bankruptcy and default on their economic development bonds (Hancock 2011).

specified period of time while they start up operations. Another controversial incentive approach, tax increment financing (TIF), provides a subsidy, often in cash, and finances the payment through future tax revenues. These are similar to another incentive called industrial revenue bonds, whereby governments essentially issue debt to provide incentives to firms or subsidize firm-specific infrastructure or land clearance. Throughout this book we will provide myriad examples of the vast array of incentives offered by governments. Central to all of the incentives is that they are a type of private good that by design benefits favored recipients and excludes others.

Investment incentives are not new. The first documented investment incentive package dates back to 1160, when Italian local governments bid for a textile production facility (Wells et al. 2001). Fast-forwarding a few centuries, the first documented incentive in the United States was New Jersey's luring of Alexander Hamilton's manufacturing company in 1791 (Bernstein 1984). Yet, a concern remains that the implementation of incentives has grown in recent years in regards to frequency, cost, and the types of government offering incentives.

The United States has some of the most transparent incentive programs in the world, and the increasing use of sizable incentives is obvious.[3] Individual American states have also provided some of the globe's most generous incentive programs, including at least seventeen packages of over $100 million each over the past ten years (Thomas and Wishlade 2009). Many of these incentives have focused on luring auto producers, so it is fitting that one of the largest of these programs was Alabama's purportedly successful wooing of a Mercedes-Benz plant at the cost of over $200,000 per employee (Moran 1998). New laws are in the pipeline, with a number of US state legislatures debating further changes in incentive programs (Hickey 2013).

Less well known is the aggressiveness of cities and counties in offering incentives to firms. In 1999, 68% of US cities, and most US states, used their own financial incentives to attract capital. This number skyrocketed to 95% of US cities in 2009.[4] While the total number of incentives to firms probably peaked in the early 2000s, the rise of "megadeals" has further increased the resources spent on US incentive programs (Mattera et al. 2013).

---

[3] US states are generally subject to Freedom of Information requests on their incentive policies. Many of these states have elected to provide information about their incentive allocations in annual reports and on the websites of state economic development agencies. Local governments are less transparent, although a 2015 policy change by the Government Accounting Standards Board has the potential to dramatically increase the transparency of these incentives. We discuss this policy change in Chapter 9.

[4] We discuss this data source in more detail in Chapter 4.

Incentive use is not confined to the United States. Li (2006) systemically documents incentive programs with his analysis of fifty-eight developing countries. Similar to the United States, evidence shows that the global use of incentives is increasing over time.

An UNCTAD study (2002) demonstrates that thirty to forty *new* incentive programs are created each year across the globe. In one of the most systematic treatments on the topic, Klemm and Van Parys (2012) examine the difference between the statutory tax rate and the "best rate" that is applied to an incentivized sector or individual investment in a large sample of countries. Although the statutory corporate tax rates remained reasonably stable from 1996 to 2007, the difference between the statutory rate and the best rate stood at 5% in 1996 and increased to 8% in 2007.

Our own database of incentives, largely documenting US programs, averages over 3,000 packages per year. One of the larger deals outside of the United States was made by the Abu Dhabi government in 2012, when it offered a $100 million incentive deal to the bankrupt Digital Domain Media Group in an effort to establish a major film studio in the United Arab Emirates. In 2011, Nissan received a fifty-year, $5 billion tax credit for their investment in Rio. As we discuss later in this book, Boeing's incentive to produce the 777X in Washington State amounts to almost $9 billion. While these deals attract international attention, far more common are incentives offered in the range of a couple million dollars.

1.2 Political Pandering: Up and Down

What explains the use of incentives as an economic development policy? In this book we argue that incentives, while economically inefficient, give politicians the opportunity to *pander* to voters. We suggest that politicians and voters operate in asymmetric information environments, wherein policy-makers have a better understanding of the optimal policy choices than their constituencies. Tullock (2005, p. 231) famously argued that ignorance regarding highly technical policies, like economic development incentives, is rational for busy voters who never will experience the true costs of the giveaways. As he put it, "The representatives are normally much better informed than the voters, in fact better informed than the voters could be expected to be." In these situations, politicians have an incentive to pander by choosing the policies that are popular even if they are not in the voters' direct interests (Maskin and Tirole 2004; see also Caplan 2007).

In this book, we argue that incentives are the perfect pandering tool. If a firm is going to locate in a politician's district regardless, what better way for the politician to claim that he or she was pivotal in the decision than to hand over a check to the firm at a ribbon-cutting ceremony. If the firm is not going to move, no matter what, the politician might as well offer a huge incentive package to show voters that everything possible was done to attract the project.

Indeed, no other policy lever available to politicians can play these key credit-claiming and blame-avoiding roles in the eyes of voters – not even the factors that have been found to have the most sizable influence in statistical models of investment attraction. Proximity to sizable markets is important for attracting investors, but no matter how hard they try, the politicians representing the warring factions in the Kansas City border war cannot move their states any closer to Los Angeles. Politicians may advertise their support for educational reform, but the human capital that investors seek is in the eighteen- to forty-year age range. Changes in primary and secondary school standards will have little impact on human capital stock for an investor currently considering a move. Politicians are stuck with the labor force groomed by their predecessors. Infrastructure and local market size have the same problem. They are important for investment but require medium-term investments that cannot pay off quickly enough to claim credit for an immediate investor's decision. One tool in the box that can be used immediately is incentives. Whether or not they actually pull in investment, they serve a more important political purpose: an incentive directly attaches a politician's name to the new investment project.

Using survey evidence and actual allocations of incentives, we demonstrate in this book that politicians overuse incentives for electoral reasons and that offering incentives is a dominant strategy. It pays to offer incentives whether or not a politician believes that the investor is coming, and whether or not the incentives matter at all in the location decision.

Of course, our theory is not the only story. There are a number of possible explanations for the ubiquitous use of incentives, but upon closer examination, they all fail to provide critical pieces of the puzzle. To simplify, we can group these alternative explanations into two categories: (1) corruption and campaign contributions, and (2) a "race-to-the-bottom" competition for capital, whereby state regulations and taxes continually erode as they attempt to best each other in creating favorable investment environments.

The most popular explanation for escalating incentive activity is that corrupt politicians are simply exchanging campaign contribution dollars for hard-working taxpayers' money; however, our statistical analysis of the PEAK program suggests a different pattern. Only four of the sixty-seven companies provided contributions to the governors' reelection

1.2 Political Pandering: Up and Down

campaigns in 2010 and 2012; and in total, employees of these companies contributed only a tiny amount to all state-wide political races in Missouri and Kansas. While the average investment incentive was upward of $4 million, the average total campaign contribution from recipient firms was less than $3,000. This limited involvement of firms in the provision of campaign contributions is consistent with research that has found little evidence of quid pro quo exchanges of campaign contributions and favorable policies (Ansolahebere et al. 2003).

Despite statistical evidence, we cannot definitively rule out an exchange of incentive contracts for political favors. Interest groups can be creative in their approaches to financing campaigns in the United States, ranging from funneling money to parties or to governors' associations, or through various political action committees. There is also the possibility that the quid pro quo is not intended for an election campaign but for an elected politician's wallet. At least one study has found a relationship between a city's use of incentives and federal corruption convictions. It remains unclear, however, whether convictions are a sign of greater corruption or greater efforts to combat it (see Felix and Hines 2013). At the end of the day, there are numerous potential exchanges and not a lot of hard evidence for any one of them. Thus, we argue that an alternative political process is a more likely explanation for the incentive wars.

A second popular explanation is that the rising use of such incentives is an example of mobile capital that is pitting governments against one another in a race to the bottom, as localities continue to water down taxes and regulatory protections in an effort to lure the next marginal firm (Rudra 2008; Volden 2002). If this argument holds, then it must be that politicians find themselves in a classic prisoner's dilemma game, a reference to a stylized game were two rational accomplices in a crime cannot credibly commit to cooperate and end up implicating each other, even though cooperation would have ensured the shortest possible punishment. In the case of competition for multinational investment, the argument goes, rival politicians know that offering an incentive is irrational, but without a credible guarantee, they end up viciously competing against one another. The competition does not end at the water's edge, however, since subnational governments – states, provinces, and even cities – have jumped into the race, attempting to lure investors into their jurisdictions. Politicians supposedly offer these incentives because they have no other option. Failing to play in the fiscal game will lead to both major losses of potential new investment and the defections of existing firms.

One international example of this pattern is the United Kingdom's generous support of BMW. Britain's woes in auto production date back as least to the 1960s, when Chrysler purchased distressed carmaker Roots. In 1994, cash-strapped British Aerospace sold the Rover Group, maker of the famous Land Rover, to BMW. This sale was a problematic fit from the beginning, and BMW made threats about moving production to Hungary unless the British government provided a more generous aid package. A £152 million incentive package was authorized by the British parliament in 1999 in the hopes of retaining the company.

Yet, this race to the bottom is more complicated than seems at first blush. In a real race to the bottom, the United Kingdom would have done its due diligence and learned the specific size of the Hungarian program, and then matched it exactly or just marginally improved upon it, up until the point that BMW would change its mind. Instead, the UK government provided the incentive despite the lack of any evidence that Rover had actually contacted the Hungarian government or received any promises of incentives. Not only was this Hungarian offer a bluff, but it was the same bluff that the government fell for in 1975, when Chrysler threatened to leave: Chrysler received a £162.5 million incentive from the government and then divested two years later (Bailey and de Ruyter 2012, p. 15). And just like the Chrysler bluff, in early 2000, BMW announced it was planning on divesting from Rover.

The story provides two reasons to be suspicious about the race-to-the-bottom explanation. First, this story is not simply one of economic competition between countries to lure investment. In both cases, the investments, despite their generosity, could not change the minds of the companies to divest from their acquisitions; hard business calculations meant that the alternative investments were untenable with or without the incentive. This factor leads to the second issue. The same country making the same policy mistake twice, within the working memory of opposition party members and other policy elites, is extremely hard to explain away by myopia. To understand it, we need to look into the political calculations of the British policy-makers. Once we do, we see that political strategy is central to explaining these incentives.

1.3   The Puzzling Use of Investment Incentives

In broad strokes, the argument in this book is organized around documenting and answering three puzzles. Below, we provide a brief snapshot of these puzzles and how we answer. Each one of these puzzles could potentially be answered by an alternative theory; but only our theory of political pandering and credit claiming provides a satisfactory answer to all three questions.

1.3 The Puzzling Use of Investment Incentives

Puzzle 1: Why Use a Policy That Is Uncertain, Expensive, Distortionary, and Usually Ineffective?

Academic economists do not agree on much, but there is one area of apparent professional consensus: the broad use of incentives to attract investment is bad policy. Markusen and Neese (2007, p. 1) claim in their popular book on investment competition: "Incentive competition is on the rise. It is costly, generally inefficient, and often ineffective even for the winning regions." Their insight provides us with a starting point for the criticisms of incentive programs. In addition, considerable evidence in economics supports the ineffectiveness of tax incentives, which we outline in Chapter 2. A quote by Easson (2004, p. 63) summarizes the basic logic:

According to the conventional wisdom, tax incentives for investment – in particular for foreign direct investment (FDI) – are not recommended. That is the view held almost universally by theorists and by the international bodies that advise on tax matters. Tax incentives are bad in theory and bad in practice.

Perhaps most illustrative of the limited importance of incentives for firms is a study of incentives in North Carolina, which found that only 30% of executives from the companies that participated in an incentive program were aware that they had received such inducements (Jolley et al. 2015).

Even if incentives are important in some cases, the complication for economic development officials is that the evaluation of effectiveness of incentives requires the precise understanding of counterfactual logic, which asks the following: (1) Would the investment have come without the offering of incentives? (2) What are the benefits of the incentive to the state relative to the costs of providing incentives?

The first consideration is much more complicated than it appears on the surface. Take the example of foreign investment. The literature on multinational enterprises and FDI is based on models of market imperfections. Firms are not just comparing the after-tax return between sites; rather, firm-specific factors drive location decisions. For example, foreign firms often locate in order to better reach customers in the host country. Indeed, the predominant claim for why countries like the United States and China attract so much investment is that their large domestic markets pull in investment. Natural resource extraction also requires physical proximity. Other factors, such as labor costs, levels of human capital, and proximity of intermediate goods can affect investment patterns as well.[5] Given that taxes are only one element of a firm's investment decision, scholars have struggled to evaluate the relationship between firms and national tax policy. Yet the limited evidence suggests that the majority of these incentives are

---

[5] Dunning (1977) is the classic work on the topic.

funneled to firms that would have invested anyway, based on the structural factors outlined above. We document this evidence in Chapter 4.

Given the well-documented complexity of correctly assessing the effectiveness of incentive programs, we are skeptical of government officials' ability to price discriminate; offering some firms large incentives to swing their investment decisions and others no incentives is questionable. Our review of the literature on incentives finds that roughly two-thirds of incentive dollars are allocated to firms that would have invested or expanded regardless of any received incentives. Shockingly, we find almost the same "redundancy" ratio in original surveys in both Kansas and Vietnam. A supermajority of incentive dollars is going to firms that have already made up their minds to invest. Even in hindsight, well-trained scholars cannot document if taxes were essential for a firm to relocate. Can we really expect politicians to make real-time decisions on how pivotal incentives are to attracting a firm?

Even if we allow that governments can properly target incentives and that these packages have a direct impact on investment location decisions, incentives can still be problematic for host governments. Illustrating the classic "winners curse," the "winning" government is the one that offered the most incentives and therefore suffers most the burden of paying the highest cost for the investment (Easson 2004). As a result, a number of studies have documented how the size of many incentive packages actually leads to a net loss to communities, where the benefits of the investment are swamped by the huge fiscal cost of the incentives. Numerous renewable energy companies went bankrupt or laid off workers in the wake of the post-2008 global economic recession, providing some sensational news stories of failed incentive programs.

Finally, the use of incentives can lead to issues of adverse selection – that is, when governments attract investments that would not otherwise locate in the country. This may sound like the exact goal of government policy, but scholars have documented the disastrous consequences of many government policies to attract investment (Moran 1999). Firms that cannot profitably operate without subsidies will intentionally seek to locate in a district offering continuous support from the government (Moran 2002).

An alternative distortion that can be damaging to a country's development prospects is the tendency of incentives to attract multinational corporations that have the ability to be profitable relatively quickly and can therefore amortize the full value of tax holidays. Countries or states that rely on tax incentives may find themselves with a disproportionate number of low-end manufacturing and retail outlets rather than high-value-added, technology-based incentives that must invest in labor

1.3 The Puzzling Use of Investment Incentives

training and in research and development before turning a profit. The net result is that incentives may lead localities to surrender the positive spillover effects of high-tech investments in favor of FDI flows with limited long-term development effects.[6] A classic study of this problem by Grieco (1982) examines the bargaining relationship between the Indian government and computer manufacturers over time. While the core of the study documents this changing bargaining dynamic, a secondary story uncovers how early government policies led to the wrong types of computers being manufactured in India, which resulted in limited spillovers from the investment and India falling farther behind in personal computer technology.

Of course, we are not claiming that governments can never use policy levers to attract investment and promote economic development, but the evidence is considerable that the reliance on incentive programs is an ineffective mechanism in obtaining this goal. If this is the case, why are these ineffective programs so common?

Puzzle 2: Why Do Politicians Herald Incentives, Not Hide Them?

As we noted, a potential alternative explanation for incentives is the corrupt exchange for campaign contributions or bribes. This simple argument, commonly found in the popular press, is that investment incentives and subsidies in general either are driven by illegal government corruption or are legal means of obtaining campaign contributions. Politicians are thus engaged in a quid pro quo of sorts, where government money is used to subsidize investments at the taxpayers' expense as a means of raising campaign contributions. We directly address the possibility of the campaign quid pro quo, yet find little evidence for this pattern.[7]

An alternative yet equally troubling possibility is that politicians are using incentives to attract *some* new investment. Politicians write big checks for essentially every interested investor, swinging some investments in the process. The high costs of these programs are easy to sell politically if there is a "fiscal illusion," whereby voters only observe the programs' benefits (investment) while the costs remain hidden from them (see Wagner 1976).

---

[6] Equally problematic is that incentive-driven investment selects firms that are motivated to capture rents rather than to build efficient global production platforms. Reviewing the literature on the automotive industry's foreign investments, Moran (2005) shows that many automobile investments took advantage of incentives and protected markets, building small "boutique" plants that were too small to operate efficiently.

[7] See Chapter 6.

We are skeptical of both of these arguments since they require the assumption that politicians are hiding the full costs of these incentives. On the contrary, there is considerable evidence that governments actively promote their use of incentives.[8]

If these types of illicit deals were the driving motivation, why would politicians brag so openly about their involvement in public speeches, press releases, and documentation on their investment promotion centers? Certainly, they must believe that there is some benefit to be gained from directly addressing the public. At the time of starting this book project, the Missouri reelection campaign for governor was in full swing. Like many states, the issue of jobs was one of the most important factors in this swing state, and a centerpiece of incumbent Jay Nixon's economic development strategy was a series of incentive programs. On the governor's website, as part of his "Moving Missouri Forward" pledges, he included this outline in the second paragraph:

Getting Missourians back to work is Gov. Nixon's top priority. Under his Show Me JOBS Initiative, we will use a combination of small-business loans, strategic tax credits and other incentives to keep good-paying jobs here in Missouri – and to attract the high-quality, high-tech jobs of the future to our state.[9]

The website includes a link with information about the Show Me JOBS program. In the press releases section, the governor provides the normal links to positive information. In many cases, these are links to specific investments, expansions, or retentions of firms in Missouri.

One news summary gives an idea of the information contained. Titled "Gov. Nixon helps automotive parts supplier break ground on new $42 million production facility in Liberty,"[10] the article focuses on the jobs created and the size of the investment. This news article includes a quote from the company president, Tom Skudutis, explaining the support of the governor, as well as information on the special legislation that was passed in 2010 creating these incentive programs. The article ends by documenting the specifics of the incentives:

The state of Missouri helped make possible the expansion of LMV Automotive Systems in Missouri through the authorization of economic incentives. The Missouri Department of Economic Development authorized $2,045,733 in Missouri Quality Jobs and $1.6 million in Missouri BUILD program tax

---

[8] Our survey experiments in Chapter 7 show, however, that although voters reward politicians for offering large incentives, they are sensitive to the trade-offs. Thus, a politician can openly talk about a massive incentive that is bigger than the competitor's, but it becomes a liability if voters link it to either higher taxes or cuts in government spending.

[9] Office of Missouri Governor Jay Nixon (2016). Building Missouri's Future.

[10] Office of Missouri Governor Jay Nixon (2012).

1.3 The Puzzling Use of Investment Incentives 13

incentives. The company can redeem the incentives only if it meets the strict job creation and investment criteria of each program.

In addition, the state is awarding a $1.5 million Community Development Block Grant to the city of Liberty to fund infrastructure improvements around the new building, and $500,000 in training incentives to the company.

While we can expect this sort of rigorous documentation in academic studies, the consistent use of incentives in press releases by governors' offices around the country and in campaign materials suggests that politicians see the use of incentives as an asset, not a liability. We suggest that this is a clear example of credit claiming, where politicians tout the use of these incentives as a means of showing voters how government policy is affecting investment.

This is not to say that voters are insensitive to policy trade-offs. In our own survey experiments that we present throughout this book, we find that voters are much less supportive of incentive programs when they are framed properly as trade-offs between higher taxes or less spending on issues like education. As we note in Chapter 10, a major fight over the transparency of these programs led to public comments by actors on both sides of the debate, with educational institutions and other public-interested groups pushing for greater transparency in how these incentive programs limit future tax revenues. The other side – mostly represented by economic developers and associations of elected officials – contended that these incentive programs do not cost taxpayers because they are designed to grow the tax base.

Of course, politicians rarely publicize the trade-offs involved in generating the incentives, which is the point of the transparency movement. In sharp contrast, they merely publicize the total allocations as a way of attaching their names to new investment projects. This action, we demonstrate empirically, wins votes.

Our analysis is focused on the United States. Here, we can not only theorize how variation in electoral institutions shapes the motivations for economic development but also analyze detailed data on the use of incentives. The political context – including voter attributions of responsibility for economic performance – varies across countries, and we can only offer examples and conjectures on how various political factors actually operate outside of the US context. In our survey experiments,[11] we find clear support that offering incentives brings political benefits in the United States but less support for this theory in the United Kingdom. This result leads us to question under what conditions the pandering logic operates in other contexts.

[11] Presented in Chapter 7.

Puzzle 3: Why Do Authoritarian Regimes Offer Greater Incentives Than Electoral Democracies?

One illustrative international example of this type of credit claiming outside of the United States comes from Wells et al. (2001). Indonesia's incentive programs were first passed in a 1967 law, under the motivation of attracting investment and overcoming the high corporate tax burden in Indonesia. Wells et al. claim that Indonesia is an interesting experiment: Indonesia's government repealed its incentive program in 1984, yet there was little evidence of lost investment. Despite this lack of evidence, the government of Indonesia reintroduced investment incentives after the Asian Financial Crisis.

Why would the government reintroduce investment incentives despite evidence of their ineffectiveness? One explanation from Wells et al. is bureaucratic: the agency responsible for these incentives has no reason to administer these programs in a cost-effective manner. The other explanation pertains to the beliefs of voters and politicians. Wells et al. (2001, p. x) argue:

> there is the power of a good story, even if the story isn't true or is a special case. In particular, while hard evidence does not support the belief that Indonesia has lost any significant amount of foreign investment to other nations in the region because these other nations offer better incentives than Indonesia, it is nonetheless widely believed in Indonesia that there are major cases of "lost" investment.

What is especially interesting about this example is that the implementation and original repeal of incentives occurred in Indonesia during a period of authoritarian rule. Our theoretical model of electoral pandering cannot explain this case.

In the final substantive section of the book, we extend our work to an authoritarian context. We argue that a modified version of pandering, or credit claiming more precisely, can be at play even within authoritarian regimes. Our theory builds on the fact that local government officials in authoritarian regimes are not subject to direct elections. In most cases, these officials are dependent on central government officials for their political survival and promotion. We argue that this dependence can lead to a form of *upward pandering*, in which local government officials use incentives to take credit for investments in their districts.

In many authoritarian countries, government officials have career concerns that are linked to attracting investment. We therefore theorize that authoritarian institutions most clearly linked with meritocratic performance at the local level (single-party regimes) are associated with the highest levels of incentive use. These regimes have incentive behavior similar to that of democratically elected officials, whose motivations to pander (downward) lead to an excessive use of incentives. Ironically, the countries with the greatest inner-party accountability are associated with the greatest use of ineffective economic development policies.

1.4 Organization of the Book

Our argument is organized as follows. In Chapter 2, we articulate our theory as we draw on an array of literature, from American electoral politics to behavioral economics. Before turning to the specifics of our pandering story, we document the extensive use of incentives around the world in Chapter 3. In Chapter 4, we discuss the economics case against incentives that has been articulated by public finance experts. These first four chapters provide an overview of the problem and our theoretical explanation for the use of incentives.

The rest of the book is organized around the three puzzles above. We argue that our credit-claiming/pandering theory can explain all three. In Chapters 5 through 7, we employ a range of statistical tests, mostly based on surveys and natural experiments on US data, to test our pandering theory against the corrupt-exchange and prisoner's dilemma alternatives. In general, the findings are supportive of the notion that incentives are a tool for pandering and credit claiming.

In Chapter 5, we further explore the use of incentives by US municipalities. Using variation in form of government, we examine how directly elected mayors, as opposed to appointed city managers, vary in their use of incentives. Our main finding is that elected mayors are associated with substantially larger incentive offers and much weaker oversight of these programs.

That elected officials are more likely to offer larger incentives and to limit oversight of these programs is consistent with our pandering theory but might also be evidence for the role of private interests shaping elections. Elected officials could be exchanging incentive dollars for campaign contributions.

In Chapter 6, we provide an overview of the campaign contribution literature, casting doubt on the simple theory of incentives based on quid pro quo exchanges. Using original data from Texas, Kansas, and Missouri, we find no evidence consistent with such exchanges. These findings are more tentative than definitive; given the creativity of providing funds for campaigns, we can only claim that we do not see any clear evidence for a quid pro quo exchange. More important for our book project, we argue that we can directly test our theoretical mechanism, which isolates pandering from these other electoral mechanisms.

In Chapter 7, we test our pandering theory in a series of survey experiments in Canada, the United Kingdom, and the United States. Randomizing survey primes that provide information on whether or not a district received investments and then on the level of incentives offered, we can directly evaluate how voters reward or punish politicians for the use of incentives.

In the United States, results provide strong support for our theory. Voters reward politicians for attracting investment into their state, and these voters provide *additional* credit if the politicians used incentives to attract the investments. If an investor chooses to locate in a different state, the politician suffers an electoral punishment, but this punishment is reduced if the politician used incentives. Put in another way, offering large incentives allows a politician to reap extra benefits if the firm locates in the state and to avoid blame if the firm chooses a different investment location. Our findings are less clear in the case of the United Kingdom, which we discuss at length in this chapter.

Chapters 5 to 7 provide evidence for politicians' incentive behavior in developed democracies; it does not account for the proliferation of incentives in nondemocratic countries. Indeed, existing work suggests that authoritarian countries offer greater incentives than democracies (Li 2006; Klemm and Van Parys 2012). Thus, our third puzzle is how can our electoral pandering story explain the fact that incentives are higher in countries that do not have free and fair elections? In Chapter 8, we probe this question, demonstrating that the greater authoritarian incentives are entirely driven by a subset of authoritarian regimes, called single-party states, where imperfect quasi-meritocratic promotions generate an incentive to pander upward to central elites in order to claim credit for foreign investment projects that happened to show up in their provinces.

The Vietnamese and Russian cases provide unique opportunities to further test our theoretical extension into nondemocratic countries. In Vietnam, government officials have an official retirement age, which limits the professional opportunities for older government officials and tempers the motivations to pander to government officials by offering excessive incentives. Using this retirement age in a regression discontinuity design, we find that career motivations lead to greater use of incentives by government officials who have the opportunity for promotion and that this incentive use falls dramatically as government officials reach the point when they are too old for further advancement.

Russia provides evidence that regime change – with a movement away from meritocratic, directly elected governors to personalistic, appointed governors – has a dramatic impact on incentive use. In our analysis we track governors who were in power prior to political consolidation under

1.4 Organization of the Book

Putin and remained in power after the switch to appointed governors in 2005. We find that governors were much more likely to reform their incentive policies during periods of direct elections than under the personalistic system enacted by Putin.

Chapters 9 and 10 offer extensions beyond the major argument of our book. In Chapter 9, we study and test a less well-known problem with economic incentives – their contribution to economic inequality. To make the credit-claiming argument, we do not require the premise that incentives are detrimental, only the ability of incentives to provide positive economic benefits is highly uncertain for both politicians and voters. In Chapter 9, we return to the economic consequences of incentives, demonstrating that political pandering obscures their deleterious effect on distribution. We demonstrate that elected officials regularly pay for economic incentives with regressive taxation and spending policies that disproportionately affect the poor and middle class to fund their incentive programs.

Chapter 10 explores two potential policy solutions to incentive conundrum. First, we explore the use of clawback provisions as a way to safeguard taxpayer money. Clawback provisions police incentive programs by using the threat of cancellation and recouping of incentive payments or credits when firms do not live up to the incentive agreements. Secondly, we study efforts to provide greater transparency in the allocation of incentives, both on the specific firms receiving incentives and the fiscal costs to communities. We find very little evidence for the success of clawbacks, but fascinating evidence that transparency on the true effects of incentives thwarts their use as a political tool.

Chapter 11 concludes with an overview of our contribution and thoughts about how this work can be further extended beyond countries included in this analysis.

2 Theory of the Political Use of Investment Incentives

On December 1, 2017, the President Elect, Republican Donald Trump, stepped up to the microphone to triumphantly address a crowd of steelworkers and local elites in Indianapolis, Indiana. During his hard-fought electoral campaign against the Democrat nominee, Hilary Clinton, the Carrier gas furnace factory in Indianapolis played a prominent role. After the company announced that it planned to move manufacturing operations at the Indianapolis plant to Mexico to take advantage of the lower manufacturing wages there, the furnace factory employees became a mainstay in Trump's stump speech (Cohn 2017). Not only did Trump blame the prospective move on the policies of the previous Democratic administration, he promised to personally rectify it. "Here's what's going to happen," Trump said at the rally. "They're going to call me, and they are going to say, 'Mr. President, Carrier has decided to stay in Indiana.'" True to form, Trump was confident in the prognostication. "It's not like we have an 80 percent chance of keeping them or a 95 percent. 100 percent" (quoted in Paquette 2017).

Now, standing in front of the boisterous crowd in the afterglow of the election, the President Elect claimed credit for having saved all of the Carrier jobs that were slated to be moved. "They're going to have a great Christmas," Trump said to rabid applause (quoted in Cohn 2017). Thanks to a last-minute deal, personally brokered between Trump and Carrier's parent company, United Technologies Corp., Trump announced that 1,069 jobs would stay in Indianapolis for the next ten years and the company would invest $16 million in factory improvements. Trump crowed about the long-term benefits of his deal-making for the region, "And by the way, that number is going to go up very substantially as they expand this area," he said. "So the 1,100 is going to be a minimum number" (quoted in Cohn 2017).

More than Trump's charisma and negotiating prowess was necessary to alter Carrier's business plans. To overcome the costs advantage of the $3.90 per day minimum wage in Monterrey, Mexico (Carter 2017), state and local officials put together an extensive package of fiscal incentives, including business tax reductions and tax holidays, totaling $7 million. A clawback clause in the agreement nominally offered some protection to the state. If the company outsourced any jobs over the next ten years, it would have to pay back the allotment (Carter 2017).

From the start, there was some fuzziness in the numbers. The agreement called for a retention of 800 employees (730 factory workers plus supervisors and clerical staff) – not the 1,100 repeatedly cited by the President Elect. Chuck Jones, president of the United Steel Workers Local 1999, suspected that Trump was dubiously counting engineering positions that were never slated to be moved. "He lied his a—off," claimed a frustrated Jones (quoted in Paquette 2017). In May 2018, months after the spotlight of the election passed, United Technologies revisited its Carrier decision. The company announced that it would commence layoffs to reach its legal commitment of 800 employees remaining in the factory. The Monterrey move was back on, the company clarified, and 628 factory workers in Indianapolis would be laid off. 338 factory workers were immediately made redundant in June 2018 with a further 290 ironically slated to be cut just before Christmas on December 22 (Cohn 2017). Further irony was inherent in the company's plan for its $16 million investment pledge. According to company supervisors, this will be used for automating factory operations, and generating further labor savings in factory operations (Paquette 2017). Factory workers should therefore expect more layoffs to come.

While the Carrier story received international media attention, we demonstrate that the key features of the episode are not at all unique. In fact, generous tax incentives, political credit claiming, and dubious employment benefits are a mainstay of modern electoral politics. To be clear, our critique is not with the bosses of the Carrier factory or United Technologies Corp. It is a publicly held company, competing for survival in a fierce global market. They have an existential obligation to identify cost saving and pursue efficient operations. For us, the puzzle is why politicians would dole out such generous handouts of corporate welfare to companies with little evidence that it changes their ultimate behavior or actually contributes to economic growth and employment.

In Chapter 1, we introduced the perplexing use of location-specific incentives. As the ultimate Carrier decision to outsource indicates, this form of corporate welfare is ineffective, inefficient, and distortionary. We provide a more systematic accounting of these issues in Chapter 4. In this chapter, we focus on articulating the theoretical mechanism that motivates our book and that explains the clear political logic that leads to the overuse of incentives. In short, we provide a first stab at answering the puzzle of why politicians, like Trump, employ incentives so profusely when their effectiveness is so uncertain. In commenting on the Carrier incident, Michael Strain, the director of economic policy studies at the right-leaning American Enterprise Institute, eloquently summarized the core thesis of our book: "The president took the opportunity to position himself as the champion of American workers" (quoted in Paquette 2017). In other words, Trump used generous tax incentives as form of political pandering to claim credit for Carrier's decision. We expand on this theory in the following chapters, providing more details and a restatement of our hypotheses before our empirical analysis. Central to our work is the development of theory on how voters respond to incentives and how politicians over-allocate incentives and provide limited oversight for their use.

2.1 Electoral Pandering

It is well known that elected politicians can use government spending for reelection purposes. In American politics, a classic literature has examined how the allocation of federal spending shapes the ability of incumbents to survive in office (e.g., Ferejohn 1974; Mayhew 1974). Yet, important new work notes that this literature fails to link government spending to the specific mechanism by which it translates into electoral gain. Grimmer et al. (2012), building on work that has found that voters struggle to assign responsibility for federal spending, argue that crucial messages of credit claiming are central to gaining an electoral advantage.

This literature is the launching point for our theory, but we differ from previous contributions in that we are less interested in how incumbents credibly claim credit for government spending. Instead, we argue that the government spending itself is the way in which politicians signal effort to their voters. For example, much of the literature on pork allocation by political incumbents sees the attraction of dollars to subnational districts as an end in itself or focuses on how pork is used for various private or public goods. In this volume, we argue that this spending is also used to show that politicians exerted effort at attracting private investment. Thus, rather than delivering spending to a district, politicians use their spending on tax incentives to claim credit for the delivery of private investment projects to the district.

We are careful here to specify that they *claim* the delivery of investment rather than *achieve* the delivery itself. As we argue in Chapter 4, incentives are largely ineffective in shaping the investment decisions of private firms. Consequently, our work focuses on why politicians use inefficient, and costly, policies to take credit for luring investment projects.

Political scientists have known for a long that politicians will use economic policies not necessarily to maximize growth and investment but to

2.1 Electoral Pandering

maximize the probability of reelection.[1] Indeed, scholars have identified two benefits of this type of electoral accountability for economic policy outcomes: the ability to screen for high-quality candidates (the selection effect) and the ability to punish or reward incumbents (the incentive effect) (Maskin and Tirole 2004). But the use of economic policies to attract votes comes with costs – the most important being the pandering problem, whereby politicians choose popular policies that are contrary to voters' true interests (Canes-Wrone et al. 2001). Harrington (1993) has shown that voters' uncertainty regarding the efficacy of different policy choices combined with the incumbent politician's future intentions will trigger his or her engagement in pandering behavior. The key insight from the dense work on pandering is that even if the incumbent politician begins the reelection campaign with a strategy that depends on personal beliefs about the true effectiveness of a particular policy, reelection pressures create a bias towards policies that are less effective but more popular among voters. Thus, politicians who have a sincere concern about the welfare of voters and perfect information about the ineffectiveness of incentives may still choose the "bad" policy due to reelection pressures.

These observations help us understand a number of puzzles in the existing research on incentives. As we noted in Chapter 1, a growing economics consensus points out that (1) incentives are ineffective in luring investment to a particular location and (2) the large sizes of these incentives are economically suboptimal, sometimes representing a net transfer to investors.[2]

We argue that in order for politicians to pander, voters need not hold incorrect views about incentives; they need only to be uncertain enough about the policies' ultimate benefits so that a politician can persuade them in a campaign. This less stringent assumption means that two politicians can hold radically diverse positions regarding the actual usefulness of incentives for attracting investment, but both will still find it fruitful to employ them to attract votes in the next election cycle.

Combining these insights about attribution with the established theories of electoral pandering cited above, we derive the following hypotheses of how voters will respond to economic development incentives that are used by politicians to claim credit or to deflect blame when competing for investment projects.

---

[1] The political science debate cited above includes arguments about how veto players and levels of partisanship affect tax policy setting. Most recently, Plümper et al. (2009) demonstrate formally that corporate tax rates are constrained by domestic political considerations.

[2] For an overview, see Oman (2000).

First, while the actual attraction of investment projects undoubtedly influences voting, so can the act of offering incentives by demonstrating that a politician put forth effort to lure a job- or revenue-producing project into the state. Even if the ultimate economic effects of such tax policies are inefficient, the work on pandering has shown that politicians can make use of the policies to signal alignment with voter interests.

Our pandering theory rests on three assumptions. First, we must assume voters believe that incentives are an effective way to attract investment. This assumption is not controversial. American voters consistently believe that taxes are among the most important factors in attracting investment and improving economic performance. A 2012 Gallup poll, for instance, asked respondents an opened-ended question: "In your view, what is the most important thing that can be done to improve the economy." The first choice was the creation of more jobs (named by 28%), and the second was "Decrease taxes/improve tax breaks," listed by 11% of the sample (13% Republican/10% Democrat) (Newport 2012). Even more tellingly, in 2011, Gallup asked respondents what Obama could do to create jobs. According to the results, 85% favored "Providing tax cuts for small businesses, including incentives to hire workers," and 73% favored "Giving tax breaks to companies to hire people who have been unemployed for six months." Surprisingly, there was little difference between parties in the responses to these questions (Newport 2011). Voters perceive tax policy as the most import factor for attracting investment (Polimetrix 2005).

The second assumption is that voters must directly observe the offering of incentives. This assumption is challenging to document systematically, but we can find clear evidence for it in the reelection campaigns of US governors. Numerous governor campaign websites and press releases tout the use of incentives to attract firms. Far from hiding these incentive programs, governors advertise their use. One example is the frequent references to economic development incentives on the New York and New Jersey governors' websites:

- A June 2015 press release, for instance, titled "Governor Cuomo Announces $181 million to Fund Projects Generating Economic Opportunity in New York State," documents specific incentives offered to for-profit and nonprofit firms (New York State 2015).
- A December 2014 press release documented the $702.9 million allocated to support regional economic development (New York State 2014).
- Press releases from the New Jersey governor's office include pictures of ground-breaking ceremonies along with information on government support for the related projects. For example, a report on a ground-breaking ceremony for Axtria Inc. on February 26, 2016, included both a picture of

the acting governor attending the event and a clear claim of credit: "The expansion was made possible in part by a $3.65 million Grow NJ award that Axtria Inc. received in September 2015. This project is expected to provide the state with a net benefit of $32,450,399 over a period of 20 years" (State of New Jersey 2016).

For politicians to be able to use these incentives in order to take credit for investment, a third and final assumption is required. Voters must have imperfect information on how pivotal a specific incentive was to attracting a firm. Again, this assumption is not controversial because voters cannot observe the counterfactual of no incentive, and politicians and firms both have reasons to deceive about the importance of incentives for the firm. Politicians want to claim credit for the investment, and firms want to minimize their tax burden by maintaining a threat of exit. In short, these are three reasonable assumptions that would likely hold for any country, state, or city's investment promotion efforts.

In summary, politicians can effectively attempt to claim credit for investment through the use of incentives. Voters believe higher incentives are a good policy choice, yet they are unable to evaluate if incentives were pivotal in the attraction of a particular firm. Rather than punishing politicians for the overuse of incentives, voters are systematically more likely to reward politicians who enact incentives in connection with attracting investment. This leads to our first hypothesis:

Hypothesis 2.1 (Credit claiming): Voters are more likely to vote for incumbent politicians when firms were attracted with incentives than for incumbent politicians who attracted the same firms without incentives.

Taking this logic a step further, pandering allows politicians to escape blame for poor economic performance by claiming that they enacted the policies favored by voters and demonstrated visible effort in trying to improve the economy, even if the effort was ultimately unsuccessful. Pandering logic dictates that voters should be more willing to accept policy choices that are in line with their beliefs about appropriate policies.

Hypothesis 2.2 (Blame avoidance): Voters are more likely to reelect incumbent politicians who failed to attract firms despite offering incentives than incumbent politicians who failed to attract the same firms without incentives.

2.2 The Use of Incentives by Elected Politicians

The theory on how voters evaluate the use of incentives has clear implications for elected politicians' behavior. As we discuss in more detail in Chapter 5, voters care about attracting investment to their district but are uncertain of how exactly incentives use affects a firm's decision. Following the pandering literature, we argue that politicians may implement an overly generous incentive policy because voters believe that these incentives can be effective in attracting investment. Thus, politicians provide incentives to firms that allow them to take credit for investment that would have come regardless, or they use incentives to diffuse blame by offering incentives to firms that are unlikely to invest in the state. To the degree that this description portrays policy selection accurately, we present evidence in the empirical chapters that more vigorous electoral competition for politicians creates the motivation to disregard issue complexity in exchange for a candidate's more salient objective of signaling his or her alignment with voters' interests.

Voters' beliefs regarding the effectiveness of incentives are an important factor in explaining this finding. As we mentioned above, American voters consistently believe that taxes are among the *most important* factors in attracting investment and improving economic performance (Newport 2011). Regardless of whether politicians believe that incentives are effective, we argue that politicians are motivated to provide these incentives and that the law establishing how to select executives helps determine the generosity of these incentives.

Furthermore, one of the biggest influences on a politician's survival is the attraction of investment. Politicians who can marginally increase the probability of attracting investment view the extensive use of taxpayer incentives as an enticing strategy. Given the importance of economic development for any politician, elected or unelected, executives in any system benefit from the attraction of investment. In Chapter 5, we adapt this theory specifically to municipalities in the United States, but the logic for any executive is similar.

Thus, our first hypothesis in this chapter, again adapted in Chapter 5, examines how the reelection concerns of directly elected politicians shape the use of investment incentives. This hypothesis is built on the uncontroversial assumption (documented in Chapter 7) that voters have incomplete information on the motivations for a firm's investment decision. Voters can observe a firm's choice of an investment or of no investment, and they can read press releases from firms or politicians on that decision. They have no way of knowing, however, how important a government policy was for the ultimate location decision. Yet voters have knowledge and biases about what they believe is important for firms in general, or about individual investments in particular.

This feature of incomplete information is not unique to incentives, and thus our broad claim that politicians can harness this information asymmetry for electoral gain has deep roots in the political science literature. In

2.3 The Open Secret

our context, politicians can use information asymmetry to take credit for investment that comes to their districts by arguing that investment incentives were pivotal to attracting the firms. Conversely, politicians can reduce blame for not attracting investments by arguing that the government offered large investment incentives and thus made all efforts to attract investment. In both cases, we observe the use of incentives for electoral reasons. In Chapter 5, we argue that this approach leads to a logical overuse not only in the *number* of incentives but also in the size of incentives.

2.3 The Open Secret: Anecdotal Evidence for Politicians' Awareness of Incentive Inefficiencies

In the articulation of the theory above, we have dealt with only one side of the story of pandering and incentives – the reasons for the voters' receptiveness. Equally critical is the politicians' awareness that the relationship between incentives and economic growth is highly uncertain. After all, politicians may be merely misinformed and misguided, instituting policies that they believe will work, simply because they have no evidence to the contrary.

Consequently, we need to demonstrate politicians' awareness of the fact that the incentives that they offer have a limited ability to attract investment and that these incentives are often excessively costly even if they do attract investment. More directly, we must introduce a fourth assumption – that politicians disregard the uncertain effectiveness of incentives owing to the political benefits that come from them, regardless of their outcomes. This assumption differentiates our pandering story from an alternative explanation that local politicians are themselves ignorant of the true effectiveness of incentives. Although examples of over-reporting the benefits of incentive polices are illustrative of a pandering story (Gabe and Kraybill 2002 (Ohio); Utah Office of the Legislative Auditor General 2013), they do not demonstrate intentionality. Unfortunately, finding incumbent politicians willing to go on the record and admit that these policies are deeply flawed is nearly impossible.

Nevertheless, a great deal of revealing circumstantial evidence can be assembled regarding the "open secret" among politicians concerning the ineffectiveness of incentives. Perhaps the best evidence is that a number of current elected officials were openly skeptical of incentive policies prior to holding office. For instance, Michigan Governor Rick Snyder criticized tax incentives during his election campaign, only to continue to push for new incentives (now relabeled as "grants") once in office (Pluta 2013). According to our data, Michigan remained one of the most generous states in providing incentives to new businesses after the transition to his administration. In addition, New York Governor Andrew Cuomo, when pressed by reporters to discuss incentives, stated that "I believe there are instances where you can find it wasn't the smartest investment of money." Cuomo later walked back his statement, clarifying that he was not talking about a specific incentive deal (Mrozek 2013).

Furthermore, an enlightening burst of insight occurred in the Texas gubernatorial election, when former Attorney General Greg Abbott and Republican Chairman Tom Pauken vied to replace Rick Perry as the Republican nominee for governor. Abbot declared his dislike of Texas' incentives – the country's largest overall program – arguing that Texas needs to "get out of the business of picking winners and losers." His opponent quickly called him out for his hypocrisy, noting that Abbot formerly approved nearly all of Perry's incentives as Attorney General. He quipped, "It's nice that suddenly Greg Abbott is completely reversing himself and agreeing with me on some of these issues, now that he's a candidate for governor" (Collier 2013).

Finally, a revelatory incident regarding municipal incentives also occurred when *This American Life* and *Planet Money*, two programs on National Public Radio (NPR), teamed up to explore economic development strategies in a show called "How to Create a Job" (Glass 2011). The prologue was the host Ira Glass' interview with Missouri Governor Jay Nixon, during which Nixon admitted that he had attended an event to celebrate the hiring of a single employee at a Missouri T-shirt printer that was a recipient of the governor's incentive program.

However, in the third segment, titled "Job Fairies," the reporting took a more controversial turn. Two reporters visited a national convention of economic development officers in San Diego and chronicled the "boosterism" of municipal officials (Glass 2011). The tone of this piece mocked elected officials and economic development managers so sarcastically and derisively – accusing them of "spinning" and "lying" – that NPR was forced to issue an apology for the segment (Schumacher-Matos 2011). Despite the acerbic tone, the message was clear: the economic development agencies were actually creating a very small number of jobs by attracting investment from other US locations, and more importantly, they knew it. As the NPR ombudsman summarized, "even their local impact is negligible," and "their real interest may be to protect their own jobs" (Schumacher-Matos 2011).

2.4 Even Good Politicians Can Enact Bad Policies

In economics and political science research, terms such as "inefficient redistribution" and "white elephant projects" describe the common pattern of politicians selecting policies that are, at best, inefficient and, at worst, harmful for economic development. Our book is a contribution in this area, focusing specifically on investment incentives, but its implications extend far beyond a single policy area. In the concluding chapter, Chapter 11, we directly address some of the policy debates on the use of incentives policies and provide suggestions for other options for cities, states, and countries to create jobs and facilitate economic development.

The prevailing explanation for these types of policies tends to focus on a collusive relationship between firms and government officials. Whether it is through campaign contributions or outright bribes to government officials, politicians may be using public policy to line their own pockets. Firms are willing to play this game since it is the taxpayers and consumers who lose, and firms are rewarded handsomely through incentives, trade protection, non-bid government contracts, and so on.

While there undoubtedly is evidence for these nefarious exchanges between private capital and public officials, our project explores how bad public policy can be made specifically because it is *public* policy. Government officials, struggling to retain their jobs or secure promotions, are trying hard not only to achieve difficult-to-obtain goals such as employment creation and robust economic growth but to do so in a manner that allows them to claim credit for good outcomes, all while looking for opportunities to deflect blame from failures. Even the most casual observer of the political process – in literally any country – can attest to politicians taking too much credit and avoiding too much blame for policy outcomes.

While these stories of bribery or credit claiming are easy cases to make, it is much more difficult to identify to what degree public policy is distorted by these mechanisms. Indeed, credit claiming and blame avoidance can both be influencing policy, yet a political reformer or an activist NGO who is attempting to change the system needs to identify the main driver of these bad policies. Is it money that corrupts public policy, or voters' ignorance that leads to terrible policy decisions?

This book addresses a single policy area in an attempt to provide a clear theoretical argument and rigorous empirical tests of how activities that we call "pandering" influence incentive allocations. Yet this rigor comes at the cost of limiting the generalization of empirical results beyond the area of investment incentives. Unlike political pundits who have definite answers for everything, we claim ignorance of the importance of pandering in other policy areas, such as international trade and the signing of global economic agreements. We simply have not done the analysis to address this question, and we believe that proper policy evaluation requires attention to both theory and data.

Nevertheless, our theory *should* travel across other policy areas, and this book may then serve as a guide. Politicians in elected and unelected political systems alike want to claim credit and avoid blame. Our theory of pandering is a systematic and generalizable motivation, and one that can explain the use of the inefficient, ineffective, and downright bad public policy of investment incentives.

3 Incentives and the Competition for Investment Within Countries and Around the World

German auto producer BMW has been scrutinized over a number of its incentive deals. As we documented in Chapter 1, the company received a huge incentive from the United Kingdom in reaction to the threat of moving production to Hungary. In 1992, BMW also extracted one of the largest US incentive goodie bags to date – a blockbuster package of over $130 million – to move to South Carolina (Nash 2011). And in 2002, for their new production facility in Leipzig, Germany, the company received the maximum incentive that is allowed by the European Union: €360 million (Pries 2006).

In October 2012, BMW announced the opening of a new plant in Brazil. The story follows a familiar pattern: Brazil has a complex set of policies that taxes imported automobiles but exempts auto producers making cars in Brazil, a strategy it has long used to entice auto producers to the country. Another policy is to offer generous incentives that are targeted at specific firms. The above examples illustrate BMW's ability to negotiate major incentive deals in Brazil, the European Union, and the United States, despite the very different incentive programs and rules governing incentives.

This BMW story fits into a larger literature in political science and economics on the competition for international capital. Within the public finance literature, a number of influential articles model how governments, maximizing the utility of the representative household, set taxes in a world of mobile capital (see Tiebout 1956; Oates 1972; Wilson 1986; Zodrow and Mieszkowski 1986). Selfless politicians, in this world, have good reason to lower their rates of taxation to make their countries competitive for capital. Countries differ in their attractiveness for investment, thus not all states will end up charging the same tax rate, although this competition for capital will drive down tax rates and government revenues.[1]

---

[1] See Wilson and Wildasin (2004) for a review of this literature.

The normative implications from this literature largely rest on how one views the role of government. The competition for capital reduces governments' ability to provide public goods, such as education, roads, and national defense (Wildasin 1989). Alternatively, global competition can be a check on excessive government, forcing governments to maintain low levels of taxation and spending (Brennan and Buchanan 1980). To the chagrin of both camps, the use of special incentives for firms can be both a drain to governments and lead to further expansion of the state into economic affairs. Far from providing a level playing field for firms and leaving revenue for social programs, these incentive packages end up picking "winners" with taxpayer resources by giving some firms or sectors a cost advantage over rivals.

Academic work on the politics of incentive wars is scarce, although academics have been extremely interested in the broader forms of tax competition occurring across the globe. Political scientists have built upon the public finance literature, explaining corporate tax-rate establishment under different institutional settings and various partisan compositions of government. Their work has identified that statutory corporate taxes have converged across developed countries, yet the effective tax rates and corporate tax receipts have remained relatively stable over time (Swank and Steinmo 2002). Even though the published rates may have come down, firms' actual tax burdens show much more variation across countries.

The most compelling research on tax competition has focused on tax rate competition across countries. For example, Davies and Eckel (2010) model tax competition with heterogeneous firms, finding equilibrium tax rates that are excessively low. Such work builds on other classic public finance models that find that tax competition leads to low tax rates and an underprovision of public goods (Wilson 1986; Zodrow and Mieszkowski 1984).

Much of the political science research finds a muted response by politicians to this global tax competition. Hays (2003) and Swank (2002, 2006) both find evidence for tax policy competition; yet, the manner in which politics shapes tax policy makes this form of tax competition and diffusion more nuanced than the traditional "race to the bottom." Similarly, Basinger and Hallerberg (2004) find that domestic political institutions – specifically, the number of veto players in the political system and the partisan composition of government – temper tax competition. The short story is that domestic constraints limit this competition, leading governments to largely maintain their ability to tax capital at the national level.

The work on tax competition has largely focused on tax rates. Recently, however, a growing literature in economics has begun to address the growth of incentive competition in influencing firms' location decisions. Markusen and Neese (2007), in an excellent review of the findings, argue that there is considerable evidence for increasing competition across countries for investment. Regional studies also find increasing use of incentive programs over time. In their study of incentive programs in Africa, Keen and Mansour (2010) note that while corporate tax rates have held firm, despite concerns of tax competition, the revenue base has narrowed significantly due to the use of selective tax incentives. In their analysis, the most common form of incentives in Sub-Saharan Africa – tax holidays – are now provided by two-thirds of these countries, increasing from less than half in 1980. Most pronounced is the boom in special zones that offer firms exceptions on tax treatment.

In other cases, scholars have found that while the number of incentives has remained steady or declined, the generosity of these programs is on the rise. This pattern of more megadeals has been documented in the United States (Mattera et al. 2013). One of the highest quality academic papers noting this trend is Klemm and Van Parys' (2012) study of tax holidays in a sample of forty developing countries in Africa, the Caribbean, and Latin America. They find a declining trend in the corporate tax rate, the maximum length of tax holidays, and the total amount of permitted investment allowances. Attempting to square these results with previous research, they state, "An explanation for this may be that even though the number of tax holidays keeps increasing, their average length has shortened" (Klemm and Van Parys 2012, p. 398).

The evidence seems clear that the use of targeted economic development incentives is increasing around the world. Ultimately, documenting this trend is less central to our study than these programs' overall political logic. Nevertheless, to best understand why their proliferation poses a puzzle, it is important to get a sense of how they are employed in the global competition for investment. In this section, we take a brief tour of some of the incentive programs around the world to provide readers with a perspective on their global popularity.

3.1 National Incentives and Effective Tax Rates Around the World

Despite politicians' efforts to use incentives to take credit for investment, there are little systematic, cross-national incentive data available. For example, most governments offer at least some types of incentives, but the reporting of these incentive deals varies wildly across jurisdictions and can be extremely spotty. In part, this inconsistency has to do with both the institutions offering the incentives and the degree of regulation over the incentives' usage. Some of these incentives are reported by national agencies or collected by supranational bodies such as the European Union. Deals can be documented by individual companies or leaked to outsiders and then assembled by advocacy groups, which are often trying to combat their use. A large number of incentives may be negotiated off the books and go completely unreported. As we argue in this book, elections motivate politicians to publicize their use of incentives. Other government officials with lower electoral motivations for credit claiming may be less willing to reveal details on these programs.

One clever strategy for cross-national comparison is to limit analysis to only formal incentive programs, which are documented in a country's investment and trade laws, and to assess their generosity relative to a country's effective CIT rate. While this method has the advantage of allowing us to directly compare a large sample of countries on published tax rules, there are limitations. Special deals – struck with investors that are not subject to these rules – are not captured in these incentive deals. With that important caveat, in this section we present a picture of the use of incentives across countries using data generated by Alexander Klemm and co-authors on effective tax rates, inclusive of formal incentives.

Klemm and Van Parys (2012) outline a methodology of comparing the published statutory CIT with the effective CIT for the most favorable tax regime. Their data is based on information from cross-national tax guides for forty-five countries between 1996 and 2007. The authors present two numbers: an effective average tax rate (EATR), which is the average CIT a firm might expect to pay, and the best effective CIT, which is the lowest rate that politicians can legally provide when attempting to woo firms. This estimate is still a noisy one because, firstly, we don't know whether every new entrant was actually granted the incentive package, and secondly, government officials have been known to surpass the official guidelines. That said, the technique allows us to compare the ceiling (the statutory CIT) of the highest tax rate and the formal floor of the best effective tax rate. The difference between these two numbers is the effective tax incentive given to firms.

In Figure 3.1, we show how three tax rates – the median statutory CIT, the marginal effective tax rate for the newest entrant, and the best effective tax rate – have changed over time around the globe in the period covered by the Klemm and Van Parys (2012) data. Three things about the graph are noticeable. First, very little effort went into reducing the statutory CIT over the period, which stays about 30% throughout the period, dipping only to 28% in 2007. This observation is important because it illustrates that countries were not competing for investment by lowering taxes generally; they found it more fruitful to offer targeted

3.1 National Incentives and Effective Tax Rates Around the World 33

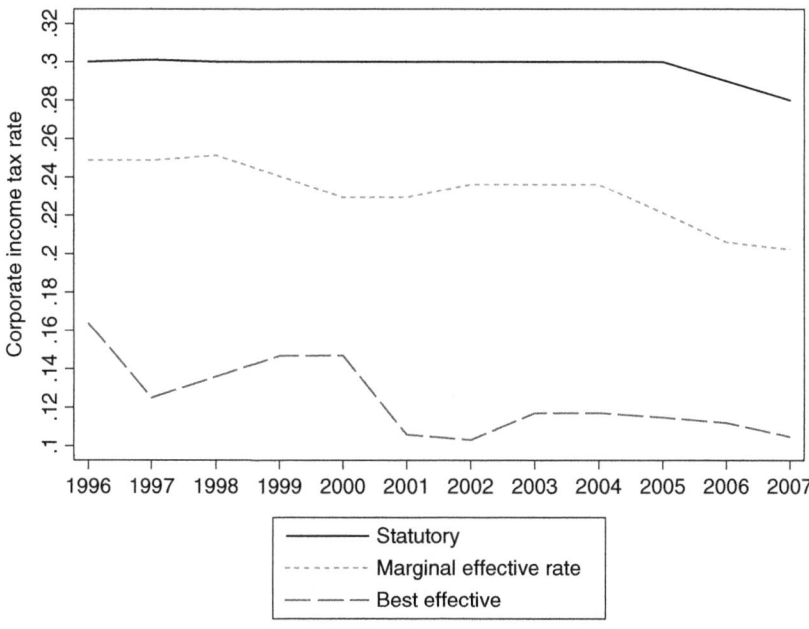

Figure 3.1 Median cross-national statutory, effective, and best tax rates over time.

inducements. Second, the gap between the CIT and the marginal effective rate – the rate paid by the latest entrant into the country – began to diverge over the period. In 1996, the implied tax incentive was about five percentage points, but by 2007, the gap increased to eight percentage points. A three-percentage-point change may not sound like a lot, but remember that it implies a $300,000 tax reduction on a $10 million investment.

The gap between the statutory CIT and the best possible tax regime, which many new entrants are certainly receiving, grew from fourteen percentage points to eighteen percentage points over the same period. This growth in the effective incentives is a clear indication that reliance on this tool is increasing around the world. Third, and equally important, the graph shows evidence that inequality can be exacerbated by political largesse, when some firms continue to receive the statutory CIT while favored or connected entrants are declared eligible for the best regimes.

In Figure 3.2, we plot the statutory corporate tax rate against the tax rate for the most generous incentive program over time for all the countries in the dataset. The clear message in the figure is that there is

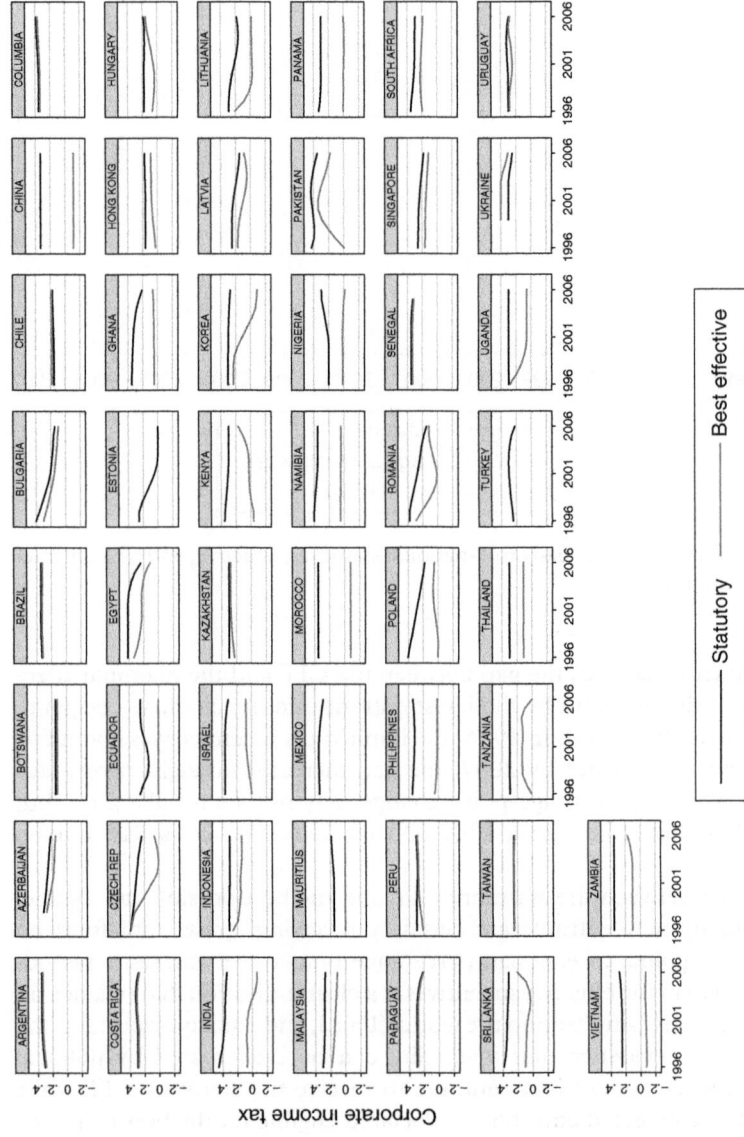

Figure 3.2 Actual cross-national statutory and effective rates by country (over time).

3.1 National Incentives and Effective Tax Rates Around the World 35

tremendous variation in both statutory tax rates and the effective rates taking into account incentives. Why are some countries relying on this tool, while others remain shy of employing it? In the remainder of this section, we discuss some of these countries in reference to this data.

We begin by discussing the small number of European countries in the dataset. The European Union has strong formal regulations governing the use of investment incentives.[2] European incentives, or "aid intensity," are governed by EU rules. Every seven years, the European Commission sets guidelines on the use of incentives, largely driven by a region's per capita gross domestic product (GDP). Wealthier countries and regions within those countries – such as Germany, France, and parts of the United Kingdom – can provide very little support for firms, whereas poorer regions can offer a host of incentives. Although wealthy countries in the European Union are more constrained, special policies for underdeveloped regions in rich countries also enable incentive usage.

The Klemm and Van Parys (2012) data excludes the wealthier EU countries but includes the following recent EU entrants along with other EU hopefuls: Bulgaria (joined the EU in 2007), the Czech Republic (2004), Estonia (2004), Hungary (2004), Latvia (2004), Lithuania (2004), Poland (2004), Romania (2007), Ukraine (not a formal candidate country), and Turkey (candidate country).

Although EU regulations limit the amount of incentives that can be offered, the European Union documents the regional aid that is used to attract "large investment projects" (European Commission 2016).[3] The Czech Republic is an example of a country that has a persistently high difference between its CIT and the best effective rates. The Czech Republic has been especially aggressive in luring auto production, offering incentives to manufacturing operations, including a €22 million grant and a €29.5 million tax exemption to retain the production of Skoda, a VW subsidiary, in 2008 and 2011.

Other countries – such as Hungary, Poland, and Romania – have seen some declines in the differences between their best effective tax rates and the CIT rate. Unsurprisingly, the declines are correlated with entry into the European Union. Despite this narrowing, many of these countries

---

[2] See Sinnaeve (2007) for a review.
[3] European auto brands alone have received sizable incentives over the past ten years from the wealthier EU countries. In 2004, Fiat received grants of €8 million, €33 million, and €47 million for investments in Italy. In the same year, Renault received two grants of €30 million and one of €33 million for investments in Spain. Renault obtained more grants in Spain: €45 million in 2005, €13 million and €32 million in 2006, and €17 million and €18 million in 2010. Peugeot received a €58 million grant for its investment in Galicia, Spain, in 2006. By comparison, Volvo and Volkswagen's €4 million and €9 million incentives for Spanish investments seem almost modest.

continue to offer large incentives, particularly in the automotive industry. Romania, one year after entering the European Union, provided a €25.5 million direct grant to Renault. Volkswagen and Fiat were granted €16 million and €26.99 million in incentives from Poland. Opel obtained €22.5 million in grants from Hungary in 2010, six years after Hungry joined the European Union.

Thus, the European Union's ability to police incentives is reflected in the Klemm and Van Parys (2012) data. Many of these EU entrants see a decline in the difference between the statutory rate and the best effective rate. Yet, wiggle room remains. Despite the EU rules on state aid, lucrative incentives have also been offered to iconic manufacturing companies throughout the European Union.[4]

European countries outside of the European Union may have less money, but they also have fewer rules on the provision of incentives. In 2012, at the crossroads of Europe and Asia, the Turkish government induced Hyundai to expand their production by offering special trade policy concessions on imported parts and a 5% rebate of their $607 million investment (Zaman 2012). These Turkish incentives are small compared to some of the large megadeal incentives offered in parts of Asia.

The government of Serbia (not included in the Klemm and Van Parys data) offered forty-five incentives from 2010 to 2012, including an enormous €250 million cash grant to Fiat, the Italian sports car manufacturer. Serbia awarded another €70 million in cash grants to three Italian clothing and footwear producers in 2012.

We round out our discussion of the countries in Figure 3.2 with a few examples from developing Asia. It is notoriously difficult to get detailed incentive data on China; nonetheless, we have evidence that in 2012 alone, the Chinese central government and its provinces offered four incentive deals in excess of $40 million to Chinese firms engaged in iron and steel production, heavy manufacturing, and energy. The specialized incentives are coupled with national incentive programs, which makes China the most extreme case in Figure 3.2 of firms with a high CIT and essentially zero effective tax rates for incentivized investment.

The Philippines is another example of a country that maintains a high CIT rate, yet provides generous incentives to investors. Many of these incentives are provided by the national government. For example, the Philippines Board of Investment provided JG Summit Holdings (a local

---

[4] Companies include Abbott Labs, Alcoa, Amazon, BP, Bridgestone, Caterpillar, Coca-Cola, Cadbury, Caesars Hotel, H&M, Dell, Dupont, Eli Lily, GlaxcoSmithKline, Hewlett-Packard, IBM, Intel, Johnson & Johnson, Merck, Michelin, Pfizer, Pirelli Tyres, Samsung, and Sony.

chemical company) a tax holiday for six years along with special tax allowances for wages and raw materials for their new $700–$800 million plant in Batangas City (Larano 2012).

Indonesia is an example of a country with a growing difference between the CIT rate and the best effective rate. One explanation is the use of tax holidays. In 2011, a joint venture of the Indonesian state oil company and Kuwait Petroleum Corporation secured a commitment from the Indonesian central government for a five–ten tax year holiday, plus future tax incentives for a refining facility on the island of Java.

These are just selective examples of countries from the Klemm and Van Parys data. Other countries – ranging from Israel to India to a number of African countries – all have tremendous differences between national tax rates and the effective rate paid nationally.

We should be careful about stretching this data too far, however. First, comparing effective rates with statutory tax rates raises a number of concerns. Tax rates on individuals and corporations are subject to numerous rules that can reduce the effective tax rate. Most common to corporate taxes are rules that reduce the tax base, most notably through depreciation allowances. Thus, some incentives (such as tax holidays) show up as a reduction in the tax rate, whereas others allow the firms to shield some of the tax base from taxes, leaving the rate unchanged. Finally, still other incentives – such as free land, infrastructure investments, subsidized capital, and cash grants – may have no impact on taxation but are clearly benefits to firms that are provided at the expense of taxpayers.

Another concern is that many incentives are not statutory and are created through either discretionary resources or special legislation that is enacted to incentivize a single investor. Such is the case with most of the incentives that we provided as examples above. Moreover, many investors are taking advantage of existing programs *and* have negotiated special deals from host governments.

Most importantly for our empirical analyses in this book, this descriptive data undercounts the use of incentives. It focuses on national-level incentives, but many federal countries – such as Argentina, Canada, Mexico, and the United States – provide generous subnational incentives. We provide a few additional examples and compare this incentive use with the data in Figure 3.2.

3.2 The Subnational Competition for Incentives

EU regulations governing state aid contrast with US incentive programs. Although the United States has recently created a national investment promotion agency (SelectUSA, selectusa.commerce.gov), it largely facilitates contacts between firms and subnational governments. A number of high-profile federal incentive programs exist, but they are largely geared towards promoting investment in specific industries, such as the Clean Energy Loan Guarantee Program. Most US incentives are provided by state and local governments, and remain largely untouched by federal law.

The United States is not covered in the Klemm and Van Parys data, but it is an excellent starting point for discussing the use of subnational incentives. As we document throughout much of the book, the United States is perhaps the most extreme example of a country in the Organization for Economic Co-operation and Development (OECD) using incentives for investment. The vast majority of these incentives are provided by states and local governments.

Canada is another country that is not included in the data in Figure 3.2. Compared to US policies, those of Canada are far more restrictive. Nevertheless, although some Canadian provinces ban specific types of incentives, our data reveals that over 400 packages were allotted by Canadian provinces and cities from January 2010 to April 2013. The vast majority of these incentives are provided by the two largest provinces: Ontario (170 incentives) and Quebec (147 incentives). Three of these deals top C$100 million, including C$304 million for shipbuilding in Nova Scotia, C$142 million for Toyota's expansion in Ontario, and C$132 million for the upgrading of a paper mill in Quebec. Unlike many US incentives, the majority of Canadian incentives are in the form of subsidized loans.

Mexico is similar to its North American neighbors in the use of subnational incentives. In Figure 3.2, Mexico is lacking data on national incentives. But Mexico provides generous incentives at the state and regional levels. IncentivesMonitor[5] has identified 58 total incentives from January 2010 to March 2013. Forty of these incentives were offered to firms locating on the border with the United States. The largest incentive was a $400 million loan to Chrysler for a Fiat 500 Minicar manufacturing facility in Mexico City, slated to employ 400 workers. In 2011, following a competition between Guanajuato and Jalisco, Honda Motors chose Celaya, Guanajuato, as a site for its third automobile plant in Mexico. In exchange for a plant projected to employ 3,200 workers, Honda received financial incentives – including an interest-free loan – valued at just under $50 million.

Evidence that the Klemm and Van Parys (2012) data understates incentive use in a number of countries is even more extreme for Brazil.

---

[5] IncentivesMonitor.com

In Figure 3.2, Brazil looks like a country that provides very few incentives since CIT rates are similar to the best effective rates. But Brazil is actually the textbook example of a country with intense subnational competition for investment. Thomas (2011) provides a concise overview, noting that since 1990, Brazilian states have engaged in intense incentives wars, often over major automobile investments. The most shocking of these incentives wars was Ford Motor's investment in Bahia, after the company had announced that seven Brazilian states were finalists for the investment. The final incentive package, allocated by one of the poorest regions in Brazil, amounted to over $1.4 billion (Thomas 2011, p. 115). Thomas argues that federal government limits on these incentives have been largely unsuccessful, often due to state governors' creative uses of packages that may nonetheless comply with federal law (Thomas 2011).[6]

What is especially striking about the Brazilian incentive wars is that many states are providing firms with inducements that clearly violate federal law – a pattern we observe in other states including China, Russia, and Vietnam (see Chapter 9 for an analysis of Russia and Vietnam). Although states are given autonomy over their tax policies, offering incentives – including a common VAT rebate used to attract investment – requires authorization by the National Council on Fiscal Policy. This process is an especially difficult one, given the political polarization in Brazil and the requirement of the council's unanimous support (Paiva et al. 2012). Most states simply bypass this process and offer the VAT rebate anyway.

3.3 Conclusion

Thus, this brief tour of incentives, guided by comparative data, has illustrated the pervasiveness of incentives across countries and across time. The actual use of incentives, however, varies across countries.

Examination of this topic requires care when measuring incentives and modesty when claiming generalizability. This evidence is easiest to document when evaluating the most transparent of countries and much more difficult in the case of authoritarian regimes. Regardless, it is clear that most countries use some form of firm-specific incentives.

---

[6] Rodríguez-Pose and Arbix (2001, p. 145) provide details on Brazilian incentives to auto producers. The authors argue that these incentives have included, among others, donations of land, investment in infrastructure, state and local tax breaks, and highly subsidized loans. Renault's 1999 investment in São José dos Pinhais is an early example of these policies. The company received 2.5 million square meters of land along with infrastructure improvements, including a railway terminal and a dedicated area in the port. This deal included interest-free loans up to $300 million denominated in local currency, with no repayment for ten years (Rodríguez-Pose and Arbix 2001, p. 146).

What is less clear is the variation across countries in the use of these tools. Cross-national data provides some clues to incentives use, but as we documented in Section 3.2, in this data many federal systems are coded as providing few incentives, despite common knowledge of their excessive use. As we will argue later in the book, the United States is relatively unique in the widespread use of state and *local* incentives.

Other than providing some evidence of the widespread use of incentives, precise comparisons of their generosity across countries are not necessary for our project. In our empirical analysis throughout our book, we examine incentives within a single country, exploiting subnational variation to help explain the political use of incentives. But before we test the theory that we built in Chapter 3, we provide evidence in Chapter 4 that incentives are indeed an economically inefficient policy and that they require a political explanation for their use.

4 The Economic Case Against Investment Incentives

The use of incentives is a subject of intense controversy. In the previous chapters, we briefly discussed the potential problems with investment incentives and our own theory on their overuse. In this chapter, we defend the core premise of our political theory on incentives, documenting incentive programs' systematic flaws by illustrating the downside of the proliferation of incentives. We begin by telling the story of Google in Lenoir, North Carolina, reflecting on the cost the small town paid to convince the Silicon Valley giant to locate a server farm there. Next, we summarize the lack of empirical support for the benefits of incentives in the existing economics literature. Finally, we perform our own analysis of the impact of the major Kanas incentive program on job creation.

The overall conclusion of the chapter is that there is no clear evidence for incentives as an effective economic development tool. Indeed, despite their widespread proliferation throughout the world, one academic study after another has shown them to be ineffective, inefficient, or distortionary. Given the large empirical literature and numerous documented examples of wasted resources, politicians, especially those in the United States, must be aware that incentives are no silver bullet for economic growth. At the very least, politicians must be aware of that their efficacy is highly uncertain when they affix their name to the dotted line.

4.1 Farming Incentives: The Story of Google in Lenoir

One highly criticized example of incentive use happened in Lenoir, North Carolina, a rural town of 18,000 located in the beautiful Blue Ridge foothills. Widespread dismay met Lenoir's wooing of a Google "server farm." These multi-million-dollar high-tech investments are often claimed to provide opportunities to generate well-compensated jobs in relatively poor regions of the country. Unfortunately, as documented in a *Business Week* story titled "The High Costs of Wooing Google," the costs often outweigh the benefits (Byrnes and Cowan 2007). Google was provided with up to $212–$260 million in incentives (predominantly property tax exemptions) over thirty years for a proposed 210 employees; a tax break of over $1 million per employee ($33,000 per employee per year). Given that average income at the facility was planned to be $48,300 per year, which to Google's credit is twice the local income in the county (Patton 2007), this would appear to be a pretty good deal.

Controversy about this investment stews, however, because Google's operations remain secretive, with few positive spillovers to the local community. It is helpful to keep in mind that Google was converting abandoned warehouses for a server farm. A more capital-intensive venture would be harder to find. What Google needed most was space to house computer servers that would store data and provide off-site data processing for its search engines and YouTube videos. This is why Lenoir was so attractive. A thriving furniture-manufacturing center in the post–World War II era, the Lenoir area was home to the Broyhill, Bernhardt, Kincaid, and Fairfield furniture companies. Until the 1990s, most of the city's citizens worked in the industry. In the 1990s, however, Lenoir was hit by the trends of changing consumer tastes and the benefits of off-shoring. As companies moved production overseas, the operations in Lenoir found it difficult to compete and eventually closed down. The city was left without its employment base but possessed a very attractive combination of empty space and warehouses – a perfect place for Google to house its servers and be positioned for future growth, according to Enoch Moeller, Data Center Operations Manager (Miller 2013). In addition to space, furniture factories demand a large amount of electricity and running water. Data centers have similar demands, so the basic infrastructure was in already in place to be up and running quickly (Gura 2012).

It was clear that Lenoir made sense for Google, even more so after the generous incentive package, but did Google make sense for Lenoir? Perhaps the most vital version of this question is simply to ask how many of the proposed 210 jobs would actually go to Lenoir citizens? It should have been clear from the outset that very few long-term positions would be available to locals. To be sure, there would be opportunities in the initial construction of the facility, and maybe opportunities for security guards and equipment maintenance. At the ground-breaking ceremony on April 19, 2013, Google announced that most of the 150 current employees were hired locally (Frazier and Henderson 2013). Yet, Google did not release information on the terms of employment or positions – and that matters. The most critical and highly paid employees at a server farm are technicians with the ability to run and operate the servers as well as the programming ability to manage the extensive data flowing through at any given second. Not surprisingly, these are also the employees with the greatest opportunities for long-term careers at Google.

4.1 Farming Incentives: The Story of Google in Lenoir

Figure 4.1 shows a screenshot of the job opportunities that Google placed on Glassdoor.com, a search site for tech industry jobs, in 2014. How many of these highly qualified technicians would Google find in a town of 18,000 former furniture manufacturers? With due respect to the hard-working people of Lenoir, the answer was very few. "That person who is no longer working in a textile mill, that's not the person you're going to find working in a research plant," said Michael Walden, an

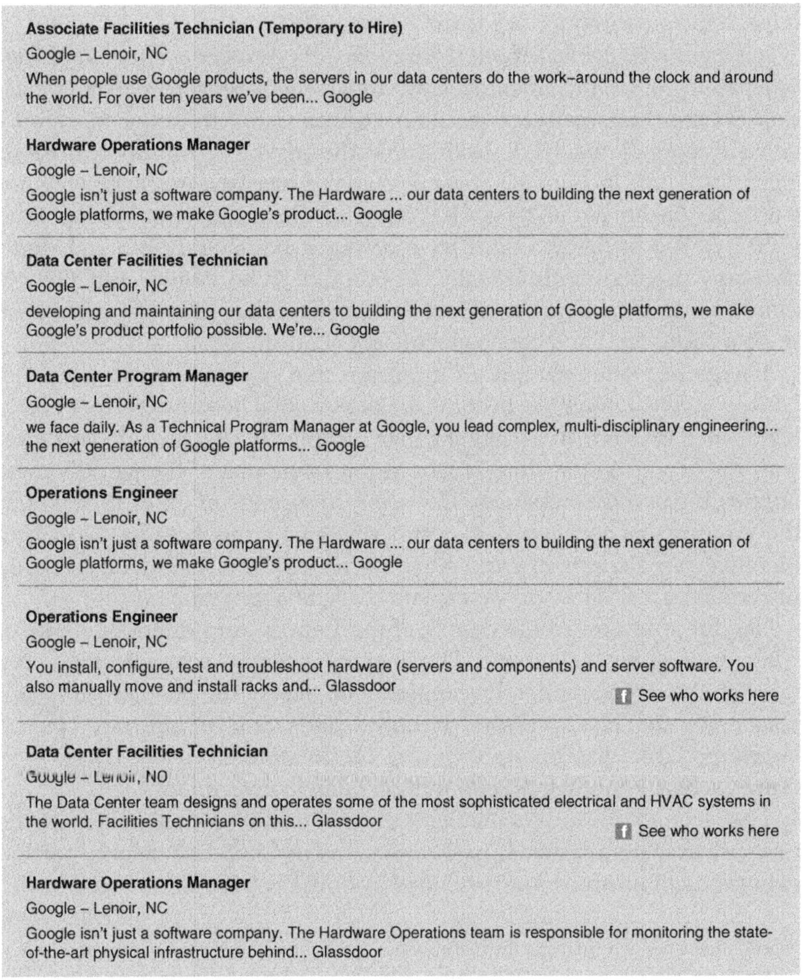

Associate Facilities Technician (Temporary to Hire)
Google – Lenoir, NC
When people use Google products, the servers in our data centers do the work–around the clock and around the world. For over ten years we've been... Google

---

Hardware Operations Manager
Google – Lenoir, NC
Google isn't just a software company. The Hardware ... our data centers to building the next generation of Google platforms, we make Google's product... Google

---

Data Center Facilities Technician
Google – Lenoir, NC
developing and maintaining our data centers to building the next generation of Google platforms, we make Google's product portfolio possible. We're... Google

---

Data Center Program Manager
Google – Lenoir, NC
we face daily. As a Technical Program Manager at Google, you lead complex, multi-disciplinary engineering... the next generation of Google platforms... Google

---

Operations Engineer
Google – Lenoir, NC
Google isn't just a software company. The Hardware ... our data centers to building the next generation of Google platforms, we make Google's product... Google

---

Operations Engineer
Google – Lenoir, NC
You install, configure, test and troubleshoot hardware (servers and components) and server software. You also manually move and install racks and... Glassdoor
　　See who works here

Data Center Facilities Technician
Google – Lenoir, NC
The Data Center team designs and operates some of the most sophisticated electrical and HVAC systems in the world. Facilities Technicians on this... Glassdoor
　　See who works here

Hardware Operations Manager
Google – Lenoir, NC
Google isn't just a software company. The Hardware Operations team is responsible for monitoring the state-of-the-art physical infrastructure behind... Glassdoor

---

Figure 4.1 Screenshot of Google jobs in Lenoir on Glassdoor.com (2014).

economics professor at North Carolina State University. "Most of those workers end up in lower-paying service jobs" (Carlstrom 2012). A few twenty-somethings were able to re-tool and win jobs, but older furniture employees had difficulty mastering the skills needed: dismantling hard drives, learning computer lexicon and basic coding, and understanding Linux, the Google operating system (Langfitt 2009). Visiting the town in 2012, American Public Media's *Marketplace* reporter David Gura chronicled abject disappointment in the city. One of his interviewees put her frustration with Google succinctly: "Personally, I can't see that it has done anything for our town" (Gura 2012).

It is easy to be cynical about the Lenoir story, but few politicians voiced opposition to the incentive deal. Although the mismatch between local skillsets and the investment should have been visible from the onset, only one city councilman, T.J. Rohr (now the mayor pro tempore), voted against the tax incentives, arguing that the incentive package was not worth it. As he put it to Zach Patton of Governing.com at the time (2007), "We probably could have driven a better bargain ... I don't have any problem with Google. Who could? Who would? But Google didn't come here because of our incentives. They came here because there's cheap land and cheap electricity" (Patton 2007).

This is just one example of a pattern that is visible throughout the United States. Lenoir has become the poster child because its story neatly juxtaposed a rural town struggling to overcome the effects of globalization with the promise of a white knight in the shape one of the world's most famous high-tech companies. However, thousands of cities throughout the country have engaged in some version of this activity – offering lucrative tax abatements and holidays to investors based on a highly uncertain payoff. How do we explain this global phenomenon?

Careful attention to the details of the Lenoir story offers one clue of where to look for the answer. The final tax incentive schedule was voted through the city council in December 2006, just in time for the campaign season for the 2007 mayoral elections and some of the city council elections. This was an opportunity for incumbent David Barlow to claim credit for landing a $600 million Google investment.[1]

The electoral incentives highlight the role of subnational politics in the investment incentive game. As we discussed in Chapter 3, a large portion of investment incentives are provided by both the central government and

---

[1] Lenoir has a council-manager form of government. In this case, the mayor was able to pass the Google incentive through the council, although not without dissenting members. Our empirical evidence in the next chapter highlights that these incentives are even more common and usually more lucrative under alternative forms of government that vest mayors with more power.

subnational authorities. In the United States, however, states and cities largely control the policy levers necessary to attract investment, with the federal government having a secondary role. Many states have even gone as far as establishing offices in foreign countries; by 2002, US states had established 175 foreign offices to promote trade and investment.[2] Analogous to competition between countries, governors of US states have become increasingly active in attempting to woo foreign capital by using tax incentives to distinguish their states from competitors (Davies 2004).

Most US states have also simultaneously increased taxes, slashed spending, and offered highly lucrative financial incentives to entice new firms. A critic of tax incentives, then South Carolina Governor Mark Sanford defended a $900 million tax credit for a proposed Boeing production facility by highlighting the new jobs that this policy would generate in South Carolina. The District of Columbia, Virginia, and Maryland engaged in a bidding war for Northrop Grumman's new corporate headquarters, offering millions in upfront incentives and tax credits.[3] In the midst of a budget crisis, Louisiana Governor Jindal further expanded corporate tax incentives to attract investment. Indeed, all fifty states now offer some form of incentives to lure investment (Davies 2004).

This use of targeted incentives to firms is difficult to justify on economic grounds. Fiscally strained governments offer lucrative tax treatment to firms, yet numerous studies have documented that these incentives have limited influence on the investment decisions of businesses or are too generous relative to the ultimate economic benefits. As summarized by the Tax Foundation, "[s]tates often overpay, granting such generous tax abatements that their already resident taxpayers must pitch in more just so that state 'economic development' officials can make headlines rolling out the red carpet for a newcomer" (Ahern 2010). And it is not just states. As the Google in Lenoir story illustrates, in many cases, relatively small cities and municipalities are also active in offering economic development incentives.

4.2 The Economic Arguments Against Incentives

Are these incentives effective at their stated goals? A cursory review of major newspapers teems with other examples of location-specific incentives. Many stories tout the economic benefits of such expenditures, but

---

[2] Le et al. (2003), cited in Bobonis and Shatz (2007).
[3] The company selected Fairfax Country, Virginia, for their headquarters.

the sums involved in attracting these firms can be eye watering. For instance, Kia Motors' recent decision to invest in Georgia came with a $258 million incentive program, amounting to $195,000 per direct job created (Chapman 2001).[4] Of course, lifting the large sticker prices of incentives is not an argument against them. Proper analysis requires a cost-benefit analysis of their costs versus the objectives that politicians hope to achieve. In this section, we provide a review of the state of economics literature in regard to whether incentives are worth the cost. We organize our review around five questions:

- Are they effective at attracting or retaining investments?
- Can governments target firms and pick winners?
- Do incentives generate jobs?
- Are jobs worth the cost?
- Are incentives the only option for generating economic development?

Are They Effective at Attracting or Retaining Investments?

The extreme cases cited thus far could mask a more efficient use of incentives. Perhaps incentives can be successful at luring new investment. After all, classic work on the relationship between state taxes and the location of foreign investment suggests that state taxes affect the distribution of investment (Hines 1996).

Most academic evidence, however, suggests that investment incentives have little impact overall on the location decisions of firms. In summary of the preponderant view of incentive programs, Easson (2004, p. 63) writes:

According to the conventional wisdom, tax incentives for investment – in particular for foreign direct investment (FDI) – are not recommended. That is the view held almost universally by theorists and by the international bodies that advise on tax matters. Tax incentives are bad in theory and bad in practice.

Three studies have been particularly important in establishing this claim, because of their rigor. Wells et al. (2001) use the repeal of Indonesia's tax incentive programs to demonstrate that they had very little effect on firms' decisions to move. Bronzini and de Blasio (2006) find that the primary impacts of Italian tax incentives were on the timing of investments. Incentives did not attract new firms or even increase the size of investments. Rather, incentives motivated investors to simply delay or expedite their entry decisions to take advantage of subsidies.[5] They also conjecture

---

[4] Similar accounts of incentive use are documented by Moran (1998) and Thomas (2011).
[5] The ability of firms to anticipate tax policy changes complicates the analysis of the implications of incentives. This anticipation is a feature of Auerbach and Hines (1988).

4.2 The Economic Arguments Against Incentives

another effect – that that the subsidized firms' investments may have crowded out the investments of non-subsidized firms. In a study of German manufacturers locating in the United States, Bobonis and Shatz (2007, p. 39) find that incentives have "little influence over the location of FDI." None of the three analyses concludes that incentives do not matter at all; rather, they most likely matter at the margins and are by no means the primary determinant of investment location choice.

Reflecting on the work above and other contributions, Klemm and Van Parys (2012) argue that they do not provide a clear answer on the broad impact of incentives because most previous work has been based on single-country studies that are difficult to generalize. As rigorous as the above studies were, how much can one learn from analyses of Indonesia, Germany, and Italy with widely different tax structures and economic contexts? Klemm and Van Parys (2012) thus provide an aggregate analysis of forty developing countries, finding no relationship between incentives and gross capital formation. This implies that the localities offering them do not receive significantly more investment than a comparison group of localities not offering them. They conclude, "there is little empirical evidence on the effectiveness of tax incentives to attract investment" (Klemm and Van Parys 2012, p. 365).[6]

Rigorously testing the impact of incentives is complicated, requiring a difficult counterfactual. What would have happened in the absence of the incentive program? Would the investor have come anyway? Would the same jobs have been created? One clever research design that might resolve the problem of nonrandom assignment is to examine how an unexpected budget shortfall, leading to a reduction of incentives (or their cancellation), affected investment. In a study of research and development incentives in Italy, de Blasio et al. (2015) use a regression discontinuity design around such a shortfall to examine how a shock to a program's funding affected innovation and investment. They find that a dramatic decrease in research and development funding has no real impact on investment, leading them to conclude that this incentive program was not effective in spurring innovation.

The general point is clear. There are considerable statistical challenges to examining how incentives affect investment, but the overwhelming evidence suggests that incentives have a very modest impact on most investment location decisions.

---

[6] Kenyon et al. (2012) extend the analysis beyond corporative income tax policies to property tax incentives in the attraction of investment. They also find little effect – "between 2004 and 2009, labor accounted for 21.8 percent of total costs for the manufacturing sector, and property taxes accounted for 0.3 percent" (pp. 23–24) – and provide a number of illustrative examples on how property tax incentives have no influence on location decisions.

Can Governments Target Firms and Pick Winners?

Given the general consensus on the ineffectiveness of incentives, why are they used so frequently? One explanation is that they become a mechanism to harness capital for economic development, but that they are focused on particular investments. By targeting specific firms for incentives, governments can price discriminate between different firms, often overcoming barriers like poor infrastructure (Morisset and Pirnia 1999). These upfront investments can generate positive spillovers that help the country, state, or local governments to attract future investment.[7] Novel research by Greenstone and Moretti (2003) is supportive of this notion, finding that a sample of "million dollar plants" in the United States led to substantial increases in wages and property values, with little evidence of fiscal stress on local government.

However, Easson's (2004, pp. 66–67) review of the literature on incentives provides reason to be cautious. By his estimate, "tax incentives are a decisive factor in no more than 20 percent of FDI decisions, although this proportion undoubtedly varies widely from one country to another and from one type of investment to another." James (2009, p. 13) reviews a number of studies on the effectiveness of incentives and presents a sobering summary:

> For example, a FIAS study on Thailand found that 81 percent of investments would have been made even without incentives. In Jordan, Mozambique, and Serbia, 70 percent or more of investments would have been made anyway, so incentives were redundant. Overall, redundancy levels are quite high for investors.

Looking beyond the potential benefits of investment and attracting firms to a specific location, our survey highlights the complications in providing incentives to firms. If it holds that incentives can be used effectively, one must also believe that governments have the capacity and interest to price discriminate, administering incentives based on an economic cost-benefit calculation.

There is little evidence that such discrimination take place. A 2012 review of US state economic development programs by the Pew Center on the states reveals that these programs mostly have little capacity, or interest, in evaluating incentives offered by state governments. Only twelve states have rigorous reviews of incentive programs, while an additional twelve states reviewed major incentives but did not utilize this data for public policy decisions. The majority of states (twenty-six) provided no systematic review of incentives.

---

[7] The classic study of agglomeration effects is Marshall (1920). For work on FDI and agglomeration see Head et al. (1995, 1999) and Barrell and Pain (1999).

Do Incentives Generate Jobs?

Throughout this book project, we focus on the political use of incentives. Importantly, however, incentives are thought to serve economic development purposes. Surveys of US economic development professionals find that job creation and the generation of future tax revenue are the ultimate goals of these incentives. In this subsection, we review the academic literature on whether incentives generate jobs both in the United States and in a select set of other countries.

A small body of academic work has examined the relationship between incentives and job creation globally, with studies largely concluding that incentives have little impact on job creation.[8] This includes evidence from individual countries as diverse as Brazil (Rodríguez-Pose and Arbix 2001), Indonesia (Wells et al. 2001), and Italy (Bronzini and de Blasio 2006). In a review of the literature, Zee et al. (2002) warn that although the evidence for these policies is inconclusive, they seem to create opportunities for rent-seeking and corruption.

The academic literature focusing solely on US incentive programs is not as clear cut, offering more mixed evidence. In an extensive overview of over 300 studies on the topic, Buss (2004) notes the literature's many conflicting results. A few studies have found a positive relationship between economic development spending (including incentives) and employment growth (Goss and Phillips 1994). Others conclude that the majority of work points to the inefficiency of tax incentives on labor markets (Peters and Fisher 2004). Looking at non-tax incentives, Patrick (2014) even identifies a slight *negative* impact on medium-term employment, and no impact on long-term employment. Finally, recent work has argued that the employment benefits of incentives are conditioned by underlying attributes of the economy (Reese 2014).

Even if incentives have an effect, they are most likely marginal in the decision-making process. Numerous studies on incentives and tax policies in general find that incentives are rarely the main factor in shaping investment location or expansion decisions, as shown in Bobonis and Shatz's (2007) study of German manufacturing operations in the United States. Instead, incentives are often what firms look for to sweeten the deal after they have already made a decision about where they want to be. Thus, incentives are not especially effective in luring new firms to a region. In a review of the literature, Bartik (2005) argues that attempts to

---

[8] One exception is a study of Alberta's job training incentives. Gattiker (1995) finds that worker training incentives, which are general and not firm-specific, had a large positive net benefit for the community. For work on the relationship between state and local taxes and employment see Phillips and Goss (1995).

attract new firms leads to incentives that are excessively costly relative to their long-term gains.[9]

Although summaries of the literature point to concerns about the use of incentives, focused studies on a single state or metropolitan region find results all over the map ... literally. Ammunition for those arguing against incentives is available. Studies of incentives in Ohio (Gabe and Kraybill 2002) and Michigan (Hicks and LaFaive 2011) found that incentives had no positive impact on employment. By contrast, for those wishing to find supportive evidence, job tax incentives (and property tax abatements) were thought to have a positive impact on employment in the Atlanta metro region (Bollinger and Ihlanfeldt 2003). In an analysis of 540 manufacturing firms in the Appalachian region, incentives affected the initial location choice, but did influence decisions to expand (Walker and Greenstreet 1991).

More nuanced conclusions are also available that argue that incentives are conditioned by underlying levels of unemployment. Although in many contributions, the recommendations are contradictory. For example, Goss and Phillips (2001) examine incentive use in Nebraska, suggesting that incentives are most effective in areas with higher levels of income and lower levels of unemployment. By contrast, Wassmer and Anderson (2001) argue that incentives should only be used to generate employment in the highest unemployment areas.

Much of the debate takes a broader approach, studying not just the impact of individual incentives, but enterprise zones that have the ability to offer targeted incentives to those who locate within their jurisdiction. Again, the evidence is mixed and it is hard to draw a definitive conclusion that such zones are working. Some work, of course, has identified positive effects. Busso et al. (2010), for instance, find that enterprise zones in six metro regions had a major impact on job creation and local wages. Bondonio and Greenbaum (2007) offer positive but nuanced conclusions, showing that the commonly found null impact of incentives fails to account for the complex dynamics of new establishments and firm deaths. They show that enterprise zone programs can, in fact, have positive impacts on receiving firms, but many of these net benefits are offset by non-incentive firms failing.

The preponderance of evidence on enterprise zones, however, is quite negative. Oakley and Tsao (2006) on federal zones, Neumark and Kolko (2010) on Californian zones, and Smith (2016) in a meta analysis of literature all conclude that enterprise zones have no significant influence

---

[9] Fox and Murray (2004), focusing on large investment projects, argue that incentive wars for investment provide few net benefits to communities.

on employment and a very limited impact on the local economy as a whole. Hason and Rohlin (2011) find that enterprise zones do generate employment, but at a cost per job as high as $2.9 million. Perhaps the evidence can best be summed up by the title of one of the most influential works on the subject, "Why Are State Policy Makers Still Proponents of Enterprise Zones? What Explains Their Actions in the Face of a Preponderance of Research?" by Greenbaum and Landers (2009). In the provocative piece, the claim that there is little evidence that these programs are successful and that policy-makers support for these programs must be driven by special interests.

At the end of the day, while there are some studies illustrating the positive employment effects of incentives, there is no clear evidence that incentives work and the preponderance of evidence points to high levels of redundancy and inefficiency.

Are Jobs Worth the Cost?

The next piece of the evaluation of incentives requires a cost-benefit analysis. Certainly, very generous incentive programs will be successful in inducing a few firms to relocate or expand. These programs will generate some jobs, but the fundamental question is whether the employment benefits are worth the costs. In other words, are incentives an effective economic development strategy? An important economic argument against incentives is that they are often excessively large and therefore lead to economic inefficiencies. This claim has been made by a number of academic studies.[10] LeRoy's (2007, p. 187) discovery of a $275,515 incentive to retain a single Dairy Queen job is an extreme example of an unfortunate pattern.

While this simple accounting of dollars per job provides prima facie evidence for this excess, a more systematic study requires the counterfactual of the net impact of incentives after taking into account their full multiplier effect.[11] The conventional wisdom on tax holidays, one of the most common forms of incentives, is nicely summarized by Keen and Mansour (2010, p. 577):

The main dangers of tax holidays, in any event, lie in their potential damage to revenue – a potentially low "bang-for-buck" in terms of additional investment

---

[10] See Head et al. (1999), Morisset and Pirnia (1999), Blomstrom and Kokko (2003), and Buettner and Ruf (2007). Numerous examples are provided by Moran (1998) and Thomas and Wishlade (2009).
[11] See Glaeser (2001) for a review.

generated per dollar of revenue forgone – and the risks to governance they can pose.

Research, such as that conducted by Buettner and Ruf (2007), confirms this, showing that incentives often appear excessive relative to their direct benefits. In an extensive review of the literature, Morisset and Pirnia (1999) find that tax incentives cannot overcome major obstacles to investment, such as poor infrastructure, and that the costs often exceed the benefits. Blomstrom and Kokko (2003) agree that while scholars have documented the positive spillovers of FDI, government incentive policies to maximize these spillovers are inefficient. In fact, Head et al. (1999) conclude that the costs of incentives are often large enough to offset any gains from investment. Based on similar evidence, Rodríguez-Pose and Arbix (2001) argued that financial incentives used by Brazil to attract automobile investment are a waste of government resources.

Subnational development agencies appear to be aware of this problem and, in some cases, may have distorted figures to make the costs seem less egregious. The Pew Center, for instance, provides some evidence of economic development agencies using deceptive practices to make incentives seem less costly on a per-job basis. In the 2012 review of US state incentive programs, the center notes:

> States have found that a high-quality evaluation can yield a dramatically different result than a less thorough one. For example, in Minnesota, the Department of Employment and Economic Development estimated that each job created through the state's Job Opportunity Building Zones (JOBZ) program cost about $5,000. After a more rigorous evaluation, the Legislative Auditor's office calculated a per-job cost of between $26,900 and $30,800. (Pew Center on the States 2012, p. 7)

A related concern is that incentive programs can lead to major economic distortions. In 1998, *Time* magazine ran a series of articles on government incentive programs, with a specific focus on one agribusiness company, Seaboard Corporation (Barlett and Steele 1998). Seaboard was the recipient of tens of million dollars of incentives from Minnesota ($3 million), Kentucky ($23 million), Kansas ($10 million), and Oklahoma ($100 million). Seaboard was lured to investment locations based on incentive programs and encouraged local governments to upgrade infrastructure and other public goods specifically for the company, only to pack up shop when offered greater incentives elsewhere. The article continued by revealing how Seaboard left locations highly indebted with infrastructure that was no longer needed after the company's exit.[12]

---

[12] An egregious example of incentives as a questionable job creation strategy comes from the often-denigrated incentives for film and TV production. The movie *A Landscape of Lives* collected £2 million from the UK government as part of their film incentives, only to be

4.2 The Economic Arguments Against Incentives

In addition to ineffectiveness and inefficiency, there are many indirect costs of incentives (James 2009), which include the costs of administering incentives and the possible distortions to firms' decision making. These distortions can include pushing investors to shape activities to qualify for incentives – for example, over-investing in capital equipment or, in some cases, even delaying investment while waiting for an incentive offer. As noted by James (2009, p. 20):

> This process can require considerable time and money from investors. Investment climate surveys in Jordan, Mozambique, Nicaragua, and Serbia have found that obtaining incentives delayed projects or raised costs for about a fifth of investors. Some delays lasted more than a year.

A final, and perhaps obvious concern, is that incentive policies in one city, state, or country can have consequences for other governments. For example, firms may negotiate exemptions from taxation and then use transfer pricing to funnel profits to tax-exempt locations from other locations that could be taxed.[13] Firms can also play governments off each other, either threatening to leave or relocating a few miles down the road to capture incentives.

In no place is this clearer than the border war around Kansas City. According to a study by the Hall Family Foundation, the incentive war in the Kansas City area resulted in companies employing 3,200 workers as they relocated across the border from Missouri to Kansas, and companies employing 2,800 workers as they relocated in the other direction (Eligon 2013). Over $200 million has been spent since 2009 by both states but with very few new jobs created; the border war is the very essence of a zero sum game.

Above, we have provided a wide array of examples of potential abuse of these incentive programs, but we carefully note that they are illustrative. Rigorous research must examine these programs, often taking into account the major differences across programs to establish how effective these programs are in creating jobs. Nevertheless, as we noted in our review of the academic literature on the topic, there is a large body of evidence that allows us to question the effectiveness of these policies. In Section 4.3, we provide an analysis of a single program, providing evidence on the ineffectiveness in generating jobs.

---

found out as a complete fraud. There was no movie. After the five producers were investigated by the British authorities, the company quickly produced an ironically titled movie with one letter change: *A Landscape of Lies*. Despite this last-minute attempt to comply with the rules for the incentive program, the producers were sentenced to twenty years of prison for fraud.

[13] See James (2007) for examples.

The Only Option?

These incentive programs remain, despite the plausible economic case against their use. Is it because investment-hungry governments have few other options to attract footloose capital? What do scholars recommend in their place? In a volume on FDI and development, Moran et al. (2005, p. 382) conclude that

> [i]nstead of competing to match whatever tax treatment was available from other jurisdictions, developing countries could devote more of those resources available for investment promotion to overcome imperfections in the supply of information, make infrastructure improvements, and launch education and training initiatives that can benefit foreign and indigenous firms alike.

Despite these clear alternatives for systematic programs for investment promotion, firm-level incentives remain. In the rest of this book we explain why firm-specific incentives are the favorite economic development tool for politicians. In the next chapter, we look at city-level incentive programs in the United States and show a striking pattern that is consistent with the political use of incentives.

4.3 Illustration: The "Promoting Employment Across Kansas" Incentive Program

Thus far, this book has provided diverse examples of incentives and has made conjectures about the impact and the politics behind their use. However, the main contribution of this book is academic, in that we build theory and harness empirical analysis to examine the use of incentives. While our focus is mainly on the politics behind the use (or overuse) of incentives, one of the main premises for our argument is that under many conditions these incentive programs are inefficient (and often ineffective) ways to build local economies. We justify this assumption through our review of the existing literature and an original analysis of a single incentive program in this section.[14] To do this, we return to the Kansas City Border War that we discussed at the beginning of the book.

From 2006 to 2011, Kansas allocated just short of $1 billion in incentives across a number of state economic development programs (Legislative Division of Post Audit 2014). These incentive programs have a number of goals, but as the names suggest, employment creation is central to many of them, including the flagship Kansas incentive program, PEAK.[15] We obtained detailed data on the program through

---

[14] Further analysis of this program can be found in Jensen (2017).
[15] Although the background information on PEAK applicants is exceptional, PEAK has many similarities to other state programs. For instance, PEAK provides an incentive to

4.3 Illustration: The "Promoting Employment Across Kansas" 55

public records requests, ranging from the timing of the proposed job creation to the names and email addresses of the managers who applied for the PEAK incentive. In addition, this program, administered by the Kansas Department of Commerce and the Kansas Department of Revenue, was one of two programs evaluated as part of the Kansas Post Audit Committee, providing additional information on the program.[16]

In our own work, presented in more detail in Jensen (2017), we use a rigorous set of statistical procedures to address selection bias and endogeneity (Hainmueller 2012; Hainmueller and Xu 2013). We find that firms that received PEAK incentives create an average of one more job per firm than non-recipients. For comparison, our public records request on the PEAK program revealed that this same set of firms proposed creating an average of 124 jobs (natural log of 4.83) and received an estimated benefit of just under $2.53 million. The jobs associated with the PEAK program are not only incredibly small for the vast amount of resources expended, they are well below the expectations set by the firms in their applications. In short, once we account for selection bias into incentives, we can identify *no* impact of incentives on employment.

We complemented our statistical analysis with an original firm-level survey of PEAK recipients. Using a public records request on the PEAK program, we identified 105 PEAK incentive applicants.[17] The key set of questions is the counterfactuals on what the firms would have done without the PEAK incentive. We asked two direct questions to applicants. First, we asked if the firm would have left the state of Kansas without a PEAK incentive, providing three possible answers (yes, no, unsure).[18] Next, we asked whether the firm's expected employment without a PEAK incentive would have resulted in fewer or the same number of employees.[19]

The main takeaway from this survey – revealed by the answers to both of these questions – is that a large percentage of the incentives appear to be redundant. Only five managers (out of twenty-four) indicated that they

---

encourage employment creation by firms in Kansas (i.e., retaining up to 95% of the payroll withholding taxes of eligible employees).

[16] Legislative Division of Post Audit (2013).
[17] Our response rate was 23%. This response rate is similar to Cycyota and Harrison's (2006) average response rate of 32% from 231 studies from 1992 to 2003, and Baruch and Holtom's (2008) average response rate of 35%. See Jensen (2016) for additional details.
[18] We fielded the following question: "Without the PEAK incentive, would your company have left the state of Kansas?"
[19] We fielded the following question: "Without the PEAK incentive, would your company have hired fewer employees or the same number of employees?" We report more extensive details on the survey methodology and results in Jensen (2017).

Table 4.1 *Comparing firms receiving PEAK incentives to other firms in Kansas: Coarsened exact matching (CEM)*

	CEM	CEM	EBAL	CEM
	Model 1	Model 2	Model 3	Model 4
PEAK	0.066	0.088	0.212	−0.021
	(0.216)	(0.216)	(0.216)	(0.322)
Constant	2.616***	2.484***	3.334***	2.703***
	(0.004)	(0.007)	(0.011)	(0.239)
Sector	No	Yes	No	No
N	297,544	79,752	147,883	144

Note: The dependent variable is the natural log of total establishment employment in 2012. Models 1, 2, and 4 present CEM using a dummy variable for the status as a subsidiary and the natural log of pre-PEAK employment. Model 3 presents entropy balancing (EBAL).
*** $p<0.01$

Table 4.2 *Results from a survey of PEAK recipients*

	Background information			
	Yes	No	DK	%
Company headquartered in Kansas	19	5		0.79
Company seeking incentives for expansion	14	10		0.58
Company seeking incentives for relocation	10	14		0.42
Company seeking incentives for retention	6	18		0.25
Efficiency of the PEAK program				
Application process was very or somewhat efficient	17	7		0.71
Would definitely or probably recommend program	22	2		0.92
Questions on the PEAK program				
PEAK benefits greater than other state offers	10	5		0.67
Would have left Kansas without the PEAK program	5	7	11	0.22
Would have hired fewer workers without PEAK program	5	11	7	0.22

Note: Yes and No columns count the number of responses fitting into each category. Note that the questions on expansion, relocation, and retention are not mutually exclusive. "DK" is the total "Don't Know" response for questions that offered this option. See Jensen (2017) for more details on the question wording.

would have left Kansas without the PEAK incentive program. However, this question on relocation is a difficult one since some of the firms were applying for PEAK incentives for expansion. Our second question is a more comparable measure of the impact of PEAK incentives. Again, only five out of twenty-four firms claimed that they would have hired fewer workers without support from the PEAK program.[20]

In summary, our analysis of the PEAK program adds original data to a literature already expressing skepticism of the effectiveness of incentives. Using matching estimated to reduce selection bias, we find no clear evidence that these incentives created jobs, and the survey evidence suggests that roughly two-thirds of firms that accepted PEAK incentives claim that the program had no impact on their investment or employment behavior.

4.4 Conclusion

The Google-Lenoir anecdote discussed in this chapter provides a vivid illustration that many incentive programs fail to pass the simple test of an association with positive growth in economic activity. This is not an isolated example. As we reviewed in this chapter, a voluminous body of research has pointed to the ineffectiveness of incentives. Incentives are often excessively costly and often not necessary (or redundant) for investors.

We further illustrate this point with our own original analysis of the PEAK incentive program. Consistent with previous work, we find that incentives have no impact on job creation. In a survey of PEAK recipients, the majority of investors stipulated that PEAK had no impact on their employment decisions.

These three pieces of evidence – the Google example, the previous scholarly literature on incentives, and our original analysis of the PEAK program – lead to the conclusion of the ineffectiveness of incentives. However, even more important for policy-makers, we make the case that incentives are costly for cities and states in Chapter 9.

Given the very limited benefits of these programs, as we argued in Chapter 2, the key to understanding economic development programs is to look at the *political* benefits of offering tax incentives. The remaining chapters of this book focus on the political decision to offer incentives, despite the knowledge of their ineffectiveness.

---

[20] Four percent of respondents were unsure.

5 Economic or Political Competition?
Allocation and Oversight of US Incentives[1]

Chapter 4 demonstrated that the primary political justifications for incentives do not withstand empirical scrutiny. There is very little evidence that these targeted giveaways attract new firms or create jobs. In fact, the bulk of evidence is in exactly the opposite direction. More likely than not, the incentives appear to be redundant, given to firms that were highly likely to have invested anyway. Moreover, in the minority of events where incentives do appear to sway corporate decision making, governments tend to overpay, surrendering far more in future tax revenue than is justified by the jobs created. Finally, these overpayments have consequences. As we demonstrate in Chapter 9, incentives have pernicious distributional consequences. They are correlated with both more regressive taxation and lower expenditures on public services such as education. In fact, as we show, the legislation authorizing many of these incentives explicitly requires that they be paid for through arguably regressive measures.

For these reasons, most tax experts and economists agree that investment incentives are bad policy. At the very least, it is fair to say that it is highly uncertain that the purported benefits will materialize and they impose real trade-offs for incumbent politicians. This brings us to the major motivating question of this book. Given their questionable benefits, why do politicians offer them? Indeed, why have we seen an escalation in the size and scope around the world? As we argued in Chapter 2, we believe that they key reason is that the political logic of corporate welfare outweighs their economic logic. Incumbent politicians, who value reelection, have clear motivations to use incentives to claim credit for luring investments into their jurisdictions. Beginning with this chapter, this portion of the book provides a set of empirical tests of our major theoretical claims.

As one might expect from our credit-claiming theory, incentive patterns appear to follow the electoral calendar. This pattern is generalizable across countries. Take, for example, Quebec's general election that was held in September 2012, following the parliament's dissolution in August

---

[1] This chapter presents material from Jensen et al. (2015).

2012. While there is no smoking-gun evidence that the government was providing more generous incentives in the run-up to the election, the descriptive data fits the pattern. Although the number of incentives offered in 2012 and 2011 was similar (thirty-eight and forty-two, respectively), the size of these incentives increased dramatically from an average of under $3 million in 2010 and under $5 million in 2011 to over $9 million in 2012. The incentives in the first half of 2013 (when our data ends) fell back to the pre-election levels of just over $5 million.

Perhaps this correlation is merely spurious. Fortunately for us, not all Canadian provinces are on the same electoral calendar. If incentives in all provinces peaked at the same time as in Quebec in 2012, such a finding would falsify our logic. A rough and ready comparison is Ontario, which held its general election in October 2011, a year earlier than Quebec's general election. Ontario demonstrates an even clearer relationship with the electoral cycle, with the government offering many more incentives during its election year (seventy-two) than during the preceding (forty-seven) or following (thirty-four) years. The size of these incentives is equally striking. In the year before the general election, the average incentive was $1.62 million, and in the year after, $3.16 million. During the election year, the average was over $6 million, implying a 400% increase from the previous year.

This motivating example illustrates the potential for political budget cycles in Canadian subnational incentive policies. In the next section, the United States provides an excellent case to examine how electoral pressures shape incentive use.

5.1 Local Competition and Incentives

While the competition for foreign direct investment is global, we have argued in the previous chapters that the United States is an excellent laboratory for studying the dynamics of competition.[2] In Chapters 1 and 2, we suggested that the proliferation of incentives in both the United States and Canada was seemingly associated with the electoral calendar. It is a provocative discovery, and a rigorous design is required to firmly test the electoral logic presented in Chapter 2. Specifically, we need to demonstrate that politicians facing electoral pressure are more likely to employ incentives.

As we indicate throughout the book, incentives are a global phenomenon, so a cross-national test is tempting. Unfortunately, such a test runs

---

[2] Some countries limit the subnational use of incentives, and the European Union has used regional aid rules to substantially reduce the size of investment incentives (Wishlade 2008).

into a common problem in political economy research. Countries differ in numerous important ways, making it difficult to isolate the difference in electoral competition from other principal factors that may also affect the employment of incentives (i.e., composition of government, presence of snap elections, labor relations, industrial policies, integration into international organizations). An alternative strategy is to look within the United States at individual governors' actions. This approach also seems promising at first, until one realizes that today, almost every state in the country has generous incentive packages, so the dependent variable has little variation. Again, causal identification is a problem here. To operationalize electoral pressure, we would probably want to focus on the timing of a state's election or on the strength of the incumbent's party. But lots of state-level policies may vary with the electoral calendar – such as infrastructure rollouts or civil service hiring – and the incumbent's strength may be a function of tax policy, the very thing we wish to test.

To truly feel comfortable that electoral pandering is generating the use of incentives, we essentially need a laboratory where identical economic decision-makers are randomly assigned to one of two groups: a treatment group that gets a dose of electoral pressure or a control group where the executive is shielded from pressure. We would need these economic decision-makers to be similar in every way possible (i.e., size of jurisdiction, wealth of population, education, geographic location), so the only thing that varied was the exogenous dose of electoral pressure. Only through a head-to-head comparison with a plausible counterfactual can we really be confident that our pandering theory is correct.

As international political economy scholars, our natural inclination was to search the world for the exact natural experiment we needed; hopefully, some country somewhere was experimenting with electoral institutions. We never thought that the best research design for our project was going to be found in the United States – literally, in our hometowns. Although we have focused our discussion on countries and US states in the previous chapters, many US cities and counties offer location-based incentives. In a survey of US city and county managers in 1999, 68% of localities used some form of incentive program. This number increased to 95% in 2009. In all, US local governments spend approximately $46.8 billion per year on location incentives to attract foreign and domestic investors, and to retain existing investment (Thomas 2011).

Oversight of these programs lags behind their implementation (Thomas 2007). Many of the state incentive programs are opaque, providing little information on allocation decisions. For the US city- and county-level programs, a survey conducted by the International

City/County Management Association in 2009 finds that only slightly more than half (55%) of locations have mandatory qualifications for receiving incentives, while 28% did not perform any cost-benefit analysis at all. Criteria for incentive qualification included the number of jobs created and the amount of capital investment. State programs have more oversight, but considerable variation remains in their reporting and performance requirements (Caplan and Associates 2009). This lack of information makes it difficult to distinguish if these programs are created for sincere economic development uses or by self-interested politicians, harnessing public capital for their own political or pecuniary gain.

In this chapter, we test our theory that these incentive programs are politically motivated. Building on previous research, we test how electoral motivations can drive incentive use and oversight.

5.2 Adapting Our Theory and Main Hypotheses to US Cities

We utilize the United States as a laboratory to test the broader forms of tax competition that we see across countries. Unlike many countries that limit the ability of subnational units to compete for investment, US states have free reign. Essentially, every state has at least one agency devoted to attracting financing, often with a menu of available incentives.

This chapter departs from debates on the economic costs and benefits of incentives, which were discussed earlier in the last chapter, and instead explores the political motivations for offering them. Although policymakers are clearly interested in the economic growth and direct employment benefits associated with firm investment, we argue that different electoral institutions generate alternative motivations for leaders, which, in turn, influence their use of incentives.

In a world of perfect information and fully loyal agents, electoral considerations would have a limited effect on an incumbent politician's decision to provide incentives. Policy-makers and citizens would completely understand the effectiveness of incentives, and everyone's preferences over the policy decision would align. In this scenario, whether the politician is elected directly or indirectly should make little difference in terms of the policy outcome (Deno and Mehay 1987; Persson et al. 1997).[3]

---

[3] We build on a larger literature in political science on the role of appointed versus elected politicians. For example, Huber and Gordon (2004) explore elected versus appointed judges, and Tavits (2009) examines the relationship between directly elected executives (presidents) versus appointed executives (prime ministers).

In many cases, however, politicians and voters operate in asymmetric information environments, wherein policy-makers better understand the optimal policy choices than their constituencies. Tullock (2005, p. 231) famously argued that ignorance regarding highly technical policies, like economic development incentives, is rational for busy constituents who will never experience the true costs of the giveaways. As he put it, "The representatives are normally much better informed than the voters, in fact better informed than the voters could be expected to be." In these situations, politicians have an incentive to "pander," choosing the policies that are popular even if they are not in the voters' direct interests (Maskin and Tirole 2004).[4]

Following Harrington (1993) we argue that voters have an intrinsic interest in economic outcomes (e.g., attracting investment) but have inadequately formed beliefs about the effectiveness of policies (e.g., incentives) in achieving these outcomes. In addition, consistent with Canes-Wrone et al. (2001), politicians may implement a policy that they suspect is inefficient economically to signal their alignment with the voters' purported interests. In our policy example, politicians provide incentives to firms that allow them to take credit for investment that would have come regardless, or they diffuse blame by offering incentives to firms that are unlikely to invest in the state. To the degree that this description portrays policy selection accurately, we present evidence that more vigorous electoral competition for the post of municipal executive creates the motivation to disregard issue complexity in exchange for a candidate's more salient objective of signaling his or her alignment with voters' interests.

Voters' beliefs regarding the effectiveness of incentives are an important factor in explaining this finding. Cross-national studies on the impact of incentives in attracting investment are scarce; equally rare are cross-national studies investigating the effect of individual beliefs about the role that tax policies play in investment attraction. Given this paucity in the research, we make no claims about the external validity the analyses in this chapter, which would require us to provide evidence in support of this key assumption.

But in the context of this natural experiment – incentives in the United States – we have considerable evidence to justify this key assumption. American voters consistently believe that taxes are among the *most important* factors in attracting investment and improving economic performance.[5]

---

[4] See also Caplan (2007).
[5] As we noted in Chapter 2, a 2012 Gallup poll, for instance, asked respondents an open-ended question: "In your view, what is the most important thing that can be done to

5.2 Adapting Our Theory and Main Hypotheses to US Cities 63

Regardless of whether politicians believe that incentives are effective, we argue that politicians are motivated to provide these incentives and that the law establishing how to select local executives helps to determine the generosity of these incentives. Indeed, in Chapter 7 we will show that politicians are not punished electorally for using these expensive policies and are even awarded additional credit for them.

Furthermore, one of the biggest determinants of a politician's survival is the attraction of investment. Politicians who can marginally increase the probability of attracting investment view the extensive use of taxpayer incentives as an enticing strategy. Although political leaders in mayor-council and council-manager systems both benefit from attracting new investment, previous research shows that announcements of an incentive program's success in enticing new firms to locate in a jurisdiction (or in expanding existing firms) generate direct electoral benefits and essentially no political costs (Jensen et al. 2014). These electoral benefits provide politicians in mayor-council systems with more reasons to offer generous incentives. Professional executives in council-manager systems may still provide financial incentives, but their principals – usually elected city councils – have better information about their effectiveness than the average voter. Thus, the ability of politicians to "overpay" for investment is greater in mayor-council than in council-manager systems.

Thus, our first testable hypothesis in this chapter focuses on how electoral institutions affect the actual allocation of incentives. Again, we are careful not to over-claim about our study's external validity. Our theory on the electoral motivations for incentive use is general, but subnational variation in electoral institutions and in the power of local governments in local economic development is rare. Nonetheless, our key contribution is to show how electoral motivations shape incentive use by comparing politicians under direct electoral pressures with appointed officials.

The logic is as follows. Voters do not have the ability to directly observe the factors that affect firms' location decisions, but they do have priors on the policy levers that are most effective in attracting investment. Local politicians can exploit both this information asymmetry and these priors

improve the economy?" The most common response was the creation of more jobs (28%), and the second most common, given by 11% of the sample (13% Republican/10% Democrat), was "Decrease taxes/improve tax breaks" (Newport 2012). Even more tellingly, in 2011, Gallup asked respondents what Obama could do to create jobs: 85% favored "Providing tax cuts for small businesses, including incentives to hire workers," and 73% favored "Giving tax breaks to companies to hire people who have been unemployed for six months" (Newport 2011). On the question of attracting investment, 70% of US respondents believed that tax incentives were a very important determinant of firm location choice (Ansolabehere 2010).

by using incentives to claim credit for new investments in the politician's district or to lessen blame when firms decide not to come to the district, or even to leave it. More specifically, if firms locate in their municipalities, politicians can point to the incentives as the main policy levers used to attract the investments. In addition, if the firms do not locate in their municipalities, the politicians can point to generous incentive offers as a means of ducking responsibility for not attracting the investment. Given that voters believe incentives to be an effective policy, politicians can pander to voters by using these policies even if politicians truly believe that they are ineffective or too costly.

The need to deflect blame as well as to claim credit means that some politicians are more likely to offer incentives and that these incentives have the potential to be excessively large. This is the case because the politician is attempting to demonstrate his or her efforts as well as take credit for the potential investment attraction. Thus, headline-grabbing numbers are important because the politician must be seen as trying to win in a competition with alternative locations. Therefore, voters could view low incentive offers relative to competitors' offers as half-hearted; in other words, as if their hometowns did not have "skin in the game," as Ken Hagan, a county commissioner in Florida, put it when describing why his county needed to provide the film industry with generous tax credits (Hagan 2015).[6] Thus, politicians have an incentive to inflate the offer prices, especially when they believe that they have no chance to win the investment based on the locality's own merits. This situation tends to bias all offers upward, even in localities that actually have a good chance of winning.

Following Vlaicu and Whalley (2016), we argue that electoral incentives in mayor-council systems are more salient than in council-manager systems.[7] The link between political accountability and local electoral institutions is well documented in the literature.[8] In fact, the council-manager system, often termed the "reform" choice of government, emerged during the Progressive Era due to perceived problems posed by electoral institutions. By the 1920s, it had spread to over 500 cities (Rice 1977). This form of government was designed specifically as a means of changing leaders' time horizons and limiting the corruption rampant in mayoral systems (Feiock et al. 2003).[9] City managers are still appointed

---

[6] Hagan is far from the only official or pundit to use this terminology. See, for example, Miller (2011, p. 288), the *Orlando Sentinel* (2009), and Talton (2014).
[7] For work that also examines the relationship between government form and local economic development, see Mason and Thomas (2010) and Sharp and Mullinix (2012).
[8] See Feiock et al. (2003) for a thoughtful discussion of this literature. See Schiesl (1977) for a rich description of municipal reform from 1880 to 1920.
[9] Rauch (1995) shows that these forms of government do have an impact on economic growth and infrastructure investment.

5.2 Adapting Our Theory and Main Hypotheses to US Cities

by elected city councils, but the literature has stressed that these institutions are more insulated from electoral pressures than directly elected mayors.

Building on this literature, we argue that strong mayors in mayor-council systems aim to identify more clearly with voters' preferences and consequently have an interest in pushing for more generous incentive programs, which voters view as an effective policy for attracting investment. Although political leaders in council-manager systems still have reasons to pander to the public, the very creation of these council-manager systems in the Progressive Era represented an attempt to constrain local politicians' pandering and malfeasance. Therefore, rather than portraying council-manager systems as immune from pandering, we simply note the direct link between elected mayors and constituencies that highlights the mayor's responsibility for economic policy. This leads to our first testable hypothesis of this chapter.

Hypothesis 5.1: Cities with mayor-council systems will offer more generous incentives than other forms of municipal government.

It is important to note that our theory does not preclude other electoral mechanisms shaping the use of incentives. Instead, our main contribution in this piece is empirical, as we test if municipal electoral institutions affect the use of incentives. Finding support for Hypothesis 5.1 would be consistent with our theory; however, other alternative and complementary mechanisms linking elections to incentives may exist.

It is necessary to add that although Hypothesis 5.1 predicts an overall correlation between mayor-council systems and more generous incentives, it does not address *how* mayors are able to offer more generous incentives than other executives. One interpretation of this behavior could be that generous incentives are actually the correct policy choice and that council-manager systems fail to enact these policies because they lack electoral pressures.

However, we argue that by looking at the oversight of incentives, we find evidence that mayors tend to overpay for incentives compared to executives in council-manager systems. In addition, we contend that the problem with many incentives is that they are simply rewarding firms for what those firms would have done anyway or that they are too generous compared to the firms' impact on economic development. In this sense, monitoring incentives requires oversight of their costs and benefits along with constraints on their use ex ante in order to avoid adopting overly generous incentives (Weingast and Moran 1983).

Thus, we theorize that principals' ability to monitor and constrain their agents varies by institutional form. Specifically, executives in mayor-council systems have diffuse principals (i.e., voters) with limited information on the effectiveness of incentives. Therefore, these mayors will be subject to incentive oversight that is less formal, allowing for overly generous incentives. Conversely, executives in council-manager systems report to a smaller, more informed group of principals (i.e., city council members). Such councils can become more informed on economic development matters and are more motivated to build formal mechanisms of oversight for these incentives, including cost-benefit analyses (Sharp and Mullinix 2012). Thus, leaders will face very different types of oversight based on the form of local government. Overall, mayors are more prone to use incentives for electoral gain, and this tactic is enabled by weaker oversight of their provision of incentives. Although politicians may be constrained by the formal limits of their power, we argue that the type of local government institution affects the municipality's choice of how to oversee the use of incentives.

Consequently, we hypothesize that mayor-council systems are less likely to require elected mayors to perform a cost-benefit analysis of incentives beforehand and are less likely to require firms to meet stringent performance requirements afterward. In short, city councils can use their power to require rigorous oversight of incentive programs, which in turn can mitigate these programs' inefficiencies.

Interestingly, the information asymmetry between voters and politicians does not arise solely from the technical nature of offering incentives. Politicians with the most direct links to voters (i.e., mayors) will be more likely to limit information concerning the costs of incentives to voters. By contrast, city council members have every motivation to rein in the use of incentives by city managers, and they have the political ability to pass related legislation before hiring a manager. This leads to our second hypothesis.

Hypothesis 5.2: Mayor-council systems are less likely to have rigorous oversight of incentives; specifically, they are less likely to mandate performance requirements and cost-benefit analyses.

The two hypotheses highlight how electoral concerns – which vary, based on the type of local political institution – can influence both the specific policy instruments used and the levels of program oversight.

5.3 Research Design

We begin our empirical contribution to this book by observing potential patterns of incentive allocations that are consistent with electoral pandering. Thus, our focus is on linking the actual allocation of economic development funds and the oversight of these programs. We follow this

5.3 Research Design

chapter with a test of a main alternative theory – that elected officials need to attract campaign contributions for their reelection campaigns. We find no evidence for this theory. In Chapter 7, we directly test our pandering theory through the use of survey experiments in the United States and the United Kingdom.

This chapter should therefore be viewed as the first piece of the puzzle of incentive use: do we observe the use of incentives to be consistent with our pandering theory? Thus, rather than showing electoral gains from offering incentives, we focus on political elites' behavior in the allocation of incentives. We examine specifically how the form of government shapes both the allocation of incentives and the extent of their governmental oversight. In doing so, we focus on the US municipal level.

The complete universe of US municipalities consists of thousands of cities, towns, counties, and other forms of local government. Systematic data on cities with very small populations is difficult to obtain, and we therefore tend to observe only data on the small cities that are active in the attraction of competition rather than on small towns on the sidelines.[10] To avoid systematic bias in our analysis, we restrict our population to cities larger than 10,000 residents, which allows us to observe both municipalities that actively provide generous incentives and those that do not. Municipalities of over 10,000 residents represent 3,839 localities in the International City/County Management Association (ICMA) database.

Our institutions data is measured at the municipal level, using three waves of online economic development surveys conducted by the ICMA and the National League of Cities (NLC) in 1999, 2004, and 2009. These surveys include large samples of municipalities, which are drawn from the ICMA database. Individually, they have sample sizes of 406, 378, and 691 localities, providing a total of 1,475 cities with data on electoral institutions. In addition, roughly 437 localities are included in two of the three surveys, and 124 localities are included in all three. The survey data provides one of the most complete pictures of economic development activities and electoral institutions at the local level because of the high degree of representation (about one-third of the sample frame).

Note that our data only captures incentives that are both offered by municipalities and accepted by firms. This implies that localities that are not attractive investment locations for more traditional reasons (e.g., infrastructure, human capital, proximity) should have fewer observations. More importantly, if one believes that incentives have some impact on investment

---

[10] Our ICMA survey data includes very few municipalities having less than 10,000 people, which raises the reasonable question of why those cities appear in the database and others do not.

decisions, then cities that offer uncompetitive, small incentives should have fewer observations in this data because firms will reject such offers.

This point is important because our main hypothesis (Hypothesis 5.1) suggests that council-manager systems will offer smaller incentives than mayor-council systems. This would create a form of selection bias whereby "small" offers by council-manager systems would not appear in the data. We would only observe the large offers made by council-manager systems. In short, this potential selection bias is against our main hypothesis because council-manager systems will appear to give a more valuable package than they actually do, diminishing the average difference from mayor-council systems. Thus, this research design is an extremely conservative one that likely underestimates the true effects of direct elections on incentive allocations. We return to this point when we discuss our results.

The Independent Variable: Elected Mayors

The most useful feature of the ICMA/NLC surveys is a clear coding of local political institutions. Our independent variable is the type of local political system, contrasting elected mayors in mayor-council systems with executives in council-manager systems. Although a number of hybrid systems could potentially complicate this simple comparison (Frederickson et al. 2004), Nelson (2011) argues that these hybrid forms are still relatively rare. Therefore, we code the variable *Elected Mayors* as 1 for cities with mayor-council systems and 0 otherwise. In our sample, 370 cities (25% of the 1,475 cities in the ICMA/NLC survey) have mayor-council institutions.

The Dependent Variable: The Frequency and Size of Incentives

Our dependent variable for Hypothesis 5.1 is based on the characteristics of incentives offered from January 2010 through December 2012, as recorded by IncentivesMonitor, which is a for-profit incentive tracking database.[11] The entire database sample for this time period consists of 3,894 incentives worth approximately $30 billion. From these incentives, we removed forty-three federal incentives (worth approximately $13 billion) as well as 418 incentives that were not associated with a specific municipality (worth $1.6 billion).[12]

---

[11] www.IncentivesMonitor.com

[12] In some cases, it was difficult to separate whether the incentive was provided by the municipality directly or by the state government after consultation with the municipality. We treat these two situations as equivalent in the empirical analysis. Fortunately,

5.3 Research Design

The next step was to match incentives to local government institutions using the ICMA/NLC data. Of the incentives allocated to municipalities, we were able to match 1,284 to the ICMA/NLC data. The remaining incentives either were given for investment in cities too small to be included in the ICMA data or were in cities that did not respond to the ICMA survey. Thus, our total sample consists of 1,284 incentives allocated to 1,475 municipalities between January 2010 and December 2012. Our drop in observations from 3,894 to 1,475 incentives is largely due to matching with the ICMA data. More specifically, the ICMA survey response rate, which was roughly 30% of municipalities, leads us to capture only 37% of the possible incentives. Lobao and Kraybill (2005), however, have not found any systematic response bias in this data. Thus, our dropped observations are the result of missing data at the city level that should have no impact on our empirical analysis other than decreasing our estimation's efficiency.

Using this database, we build two datasets. One is a *project-based* dataset that contains 1,284 observations of individual incentives, which are each associated with a particular project. We have data on every project's size of investment, labor, and equity ownership along with other features of the project itself. The second dataset is the *municipality-based* dataset, which aggregates the incentive project data at the municipal level. The data in this set ranges from municipalities providing no incentives to one municipality offering $405 million in incentives (which was spread across ninety-five different projects and totaled up to $405 million). In this dataset, we cannot control for the specific features of the project.

Balance Between the Electoral Treatment and Control Groups

A naïve analysis would find that the raw difference-in-means of the dependent variables demonstrates tentative evidence for our core hypotheses. Mayor-council systems tend to offer more money for incentives and have fewer constraints on their ability to provide them (e.g., required performance criteria or cost-benefit analyses). Nevertheless, our treatment is far from an ideal experiment.

For instance, the statistical difference in population size between these groups is large. Municipalities with mayor-council systems tend to have smaller populations than council-manager systems (despite some metropolises, such as New York and Chicago, having mayor-council systems). Figure 5.1 displays the population distribution graphically; clearly, a disproportionate share of mayor-council systems (57% versus 48%) is in the

including state incentives biases against the possibility of identifying differences between mayors and managers.

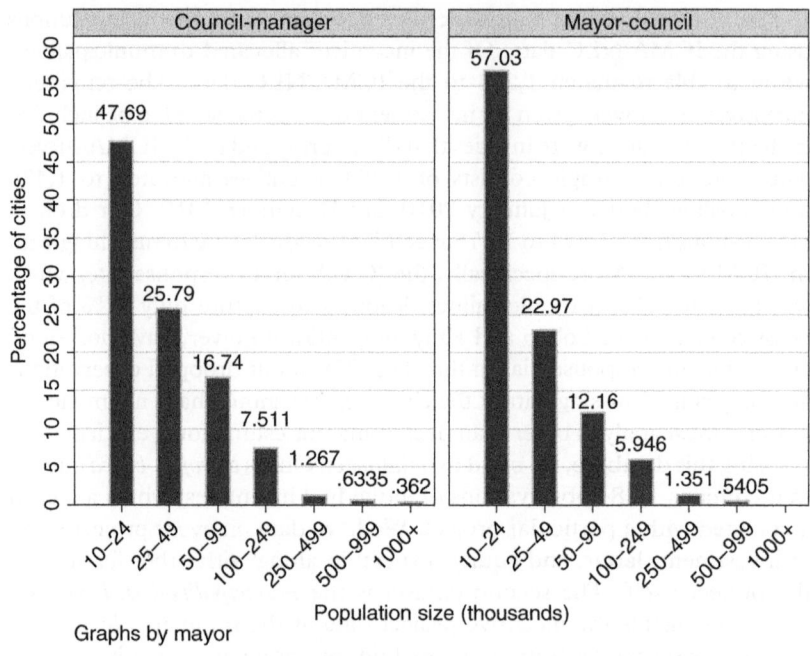

Figure 5.1 Population statistics by type of city government.

10,000 to 24,000-person category. Since there are reasons to suspect that population size drives incentive decisions, there is potential for omitted variable bias. We address this problem through entropy balancing.[13]

Entropy Balancing

In Table 5.1, we test how the variable *Elected Mayors* influences the use of incentives offered by cities. To assess our theory, we construct two dependent variables: (1) whether a project incentive was offered by a city at all, and (2) if offered, the value of the investment in US dollars measured at the project level, of which we take the natural log to ease interpretation. Measuring our dependent variable at the project level poses some empirical challenges, which are discussed below, but this measurement is essential in determining whether mayor-council systems are overpaying for incentives.

[13] However, the results are substantively similar if we control for population in a standard regression specification or drop very small municipalities.

Table 5.1 *Entropy balancing with elected mayor as the treatment*

Treatment = City has a mayor-council system

Before:	A. Before entropy balancing						B. After entropy balancing					
	Treatment=Elected mayor			Control=Council			Treatment=Elected mayor			Control=Council		
	Mean	Variance	Skewness	Mean	Variance	Skewness	Mean	Variance	Skewness	Mean	Variance	Skewness
Jobs created (ln)	3.79	2.19	−0.57	3.95	2.43	−0.58	3.79	2.19	−0.57	3.79	2.59	−0.51
Capital value (ln, US)	10.5	53.93	−0.66	10.7	56.07	−0.64	10.5	53.93	−0.66	10.5	55.07	−0.62
Population (1 to 7)	3.68	3.08	−0.31	2.85	2.48	0.59	3.68	3.08	−0.31	3.68	2.79	0.09
Unemployment Rate (%)	6.11	5.50	1.13	6.98	42.97	10.53	6.11	5.50	1.13	6.11	6.82	0.85
Other taxes	2.06	1.99	0.21	2.52	4.99	1.82	2.06	1.99	0.21	2.06	3.00	1.31
Foreign Competition=1	0.19	0.16	1.56	0.27	0.20	1.06	0.19	0.16	1.56	0.19	0.16	1.56
Brand new Investment=1	0.36	0.23	0.59	0.42	0.24	0.34	0.36	0.23	0.59	0.36	0.23	0.59
Economic Development plan=1	0.73	0.20	−1.05	0.74	0.19	−1.09	0.73	0.20	−1.05	0.73	0.20	−1.05
Location												
Northeast=1	0.11	0.10	2.42	0.10	0.09	2.75	0.11	0.10	2.42	0.11	0.10	2.42
Northcentral=1	0.40	0.24	0.40	0.38	0.23	0.52	0.40	0.24	0.40	0.40	0.24	0.40
South=1	0.46	0.25	0.17	0.43	0.25	0.28	0.46	0.25	0.17	0.46	0.25	0.17

Table 5.1 (cont.)

Treatment = City has a mayor-council system

	A. Before entropy balancing						B. After entropy balancing					
	Treatment=Elected mayor			Control=Council			Treatment=Elected mayor			Control=Council		
Before:	Mean	Variance	Skewness	Mean	Variance	Skewness	Mean	Variance	Skewness	Mean	Variance	Skewness
Metro area=1	0.71	0.21	−0.94	0.53	0.25	−0.13	0.71	0.21	−0.94	0.71	0.20	−0.94
Suburb=1	0.17	0.14	1.77	0.32	0.22	0.75	0.17	0.14	1.77	0.17	0.14	1.77
Sector												
Automotive =1	0.08	0.07	3.19	0.08	0.07	3.07	0.08	0.07	3.19	0.08	0.07	3.19
Basic materials=1	0.08	0.07	3.19	0.10	0.09	2.75	0.08	0.07	3.19	0.08	0.07	3.19
Consumer goods=1	0.10	0.09	2.65	0.11	0.10	2.52	0.10	0.09	2.65	0.10	0.09	2.65
Creative industries=1	0.01	0.01	8.45	0.01	0.01	8.57	0.01	0.01	8.45	0.01	0.01	8.45
Electronics=1	0.03	0.03	5.17	0.03	0.03	5.26	0.03	0.03	5.17	0.03	0.03	5.17
Food and drinks=1	0.10	0.09	2.65	0.09	0.08	2.89	0.10	0.09	2.65	0.10	0.09	2.65
Industrial goods=1	0.16	0.14	1.84	0.14	0.12	2.11	0.16	0.14	1.84	0.16	0.14	1.84
Information tech.=1	0.06	0.06	3.61	0.09	0.08	2.92	0.06	0.06	3.61	0.06	0.06	3.61
Tourism=1	0.03	0.03	5.38	0.02	0.02	7.19	0.03	0.03	5.38	0.03	0.03	5.38
Life sciences=1	0.10	0.09	2.61	0.10	0.09	2.63	0.10	0.09	2.61	0.10	0.09	2.61
Non-renewable Energy=1	0.02	0.02	6.45	0.02	0.02	7.19	0.02	0.02	6.45	0.02	0.02	6.45
Energy=1	0.00	0.00	14.83	0.03	0.03	5.94	0.00	0.00	14.83	0.00	0.00	14.83
Services=1	0.17	0.14	1.77	0.14	0.12	2.08	0.17	0.14	1.77	0.17	0.14	1.77
Survey year												
2004 =1	0.22	0.17	1.39	0.24	0.18	1.25	0.22	0.17	1.39	0.22	0.17	1.39
2009 =1	0.49	0.25	0.03	0.50	0.25	−0.01	0.49	0.25	0.03	0.49	0.25	0.03

5.3 Research Design

In fact, a simple count of incentives in mayor-council versus council-manager systems shows that much of the variance in the dollar amounts between the two types could be attributed to the number of incentives offered. Municipalities with mayor-council systems offered on average 1.24 incentives in our two-year sample, whereas municipalities with council-manager institutions offered on average 0.58 incentives. If we simply calculated the total dollars spent on incentives at the city level, we would be unable to distinguish the difference between higher frequency and greater scale of incentives.

Our theory, however, is more nuanced than simply speculating whether mayor-council systems offered more incentives than council-manager systems. We hypothesized that mayor-council systems would provide more generous incentives to firms in their attempts to attract investment despite the obvious financial costs. This argument helps shed light on the studies we reviewed in Chapter 4 that found some municipalities actually offered greater financial incentives than they could hope to recover through higher revenue or job creation. In some cases, these inefficiencies are generated by offering incentives to firms that would locate in municipalities even without these benefits; in other cases, the inefficiencies may stem from politicians offering incentives to firms that are too large relative to the size of the firms' local investments (i.e., the particular benefits to the municipality from the firms' investments).

With this in mind, two potential issues pose inferential threats to our analysis. First, mayor-council and council-manager systems differ on a number of observable characteristics. In a study like ours, there is always a fear that observable or unobservable features drive both the selection of the dependent and independent variables. For example, in addition to population, we are concerned about the primary competitors for investment. Although the majority of managers indicated that their primary competitors in attracting firms were cities within their own state or in neighboring states, the response "foreign locations" increased dramatically after 1999. In 1999, 12% of managers indicated that foreign locations were their primary competitors; this figure jumped to just over 20% in both 2004 and 2009. Thus, in our analysis, we include the variable *Foreign*, coded 1 for cities identifying foreign locations as their main competitors and 0 otherwise.

Regional patterns are also important. Previous research has identified regional patterns in the types of local government (Montjoy and Watson 1993), including variation in local government institutions based on whether a municipality is in a metropolitan area (*Metro*) or the suburbs of a metropolitan area (*Suburb*). We also include a control variable representing whether a municipality has a written economic development plan (*Development Plan*) as a control for the municipality's professionalism. Finally, two additional confounders affect a municipality's likelihood of offering incentives: the local unemployment rate (*Unemployment Rate*) and the existence of other tax policies (*Other Taxes*). *Other Taxes* is an important variable because, for example, cities that have a personal property tax may offer an exemption to firms on this tax, whereas cities that do not have this tax cannot offer an exemption on it.

Although far from the experimental ideal, matching techniques have been proposed as one possible remedy to this problem. In this section, we employ a variant of matching, called entropy balancing (*ebalance*), suggested by Hainmueller (2012). Ebalance reweights the observations to statistically generate a region of common support where mayor-council and council-manager systems are comparable on structural covariates. Ebalance achieves reweighting directly by incorporating covariate balance into the weight function that is applied to the sample units.

To apply this technique, we impose a set of balance constraints – which imply that the covariate distributions of the treatment and control groups in the preprocessed data match exactly on all pre-specified observations – taking care to use only pre-treatment variables in the balancing equation. The entropy balancing algorithm then searches for the set of weights that satisfies the balance constraints but remains as close as possible to a set of uniform base weights to retain information. This recalibration technique assures maximum balance between the treatment and control groups (Hainmueller 2012). After reweighting, mayor-council and council-manager systems are matched directly in terms of average value, variation, and skew (see Table 5.1).

Taking advantage of this statistically generated region of common support, we estimate the following sets of analyses. First, we examine the probability of a city offering an incentive in Model 1, using the municipality-based dataset. Then, using the project-based dataset, we examine whether mayor-council systems offer larger incentives, conditional on firms accepting these incentives. The results are presented in the top panel of Table 5.2 in Models 1 and 2. They are similar to the naïve specifications.[14] Taking survey effects into account, the results show that the mayors do not offer incentives more frequently, but when they do offer an incentive, it is 33.2% larger at the project level.

One concern with our matching is that although we are comparing cities of the same population, region, and municipality professionalism, the underlying size of municipal budgets can substantially shape local

---

[14] We replicate all results using ordinary least squares in Jensen et al. (2015, appendix, table A5.5) and include a number of additional robustness tests.

Table 5.2 *The effect of electoral institutions on tax incentives (after entropy balancing)*

1) Results after entropy balancing on whether city has a mayor-council system

Dependent variable	Offered incentive=1 (1)	Value of incentive in millions USD (ln) (2)	Value of incentive as % of budget (3)	Performance criteria (=1) (4)	Cost-benefit-analysis (=1) (5)	Performance criteria (0 to 6) (6)
Elected mayors	−0.004 (0.033)	0.332** (0.146)	1.657*** (0.333)	−0.096** (0.046)	−0.071 (0.046)	−0.338*** (0.125)
Constant/Pbar	0.771	13.178*** (0.189)	−0.894** (0.367)	0.558	0.675	1.418*** (0.107)
Observations	1,399	1,116	430	1,083	1,083	1,083
(Pseudo) R-squared	1.72e-05	0.010	0.089	0.00681	0.00460	0.011
Chi-squared	0.0119			4.289	2.366	
Log likelihood	−753.1	−2154	−1014	−738.4	−679.4	−2033

2) Results after entropy balancing on whether state has default mayor policy

Dependent variable	Offered incentive=1 (1)	Value of incentive in millions USD (ln) (2)	Value of incentive as % of budget (3)	Performance criteria (=1) (4)	Cost-benefit-analysis (=1) (5)	Performance criteria (0 to 6) (6)
Default mayor clause	−0.070 (0.050)	0.329 (0.212)	0.722* (0.373)	−0.110** (0.052)	−0.020 (0.054)	−0.483*** (0.161)
Constant/Pbar	0.828	12.959*** (0.185)	−0.449 (0.273)	0.635	0.713	1.644*** (0.120)
Observations	1,399	1,116	430	1,083	1,083	1,083
(Pseudo) R-squared	0.09941	0.009	0.024	0.00988	0.000388	
Chi-squared	1.923			4.216	0.135	
Log likelihood	−636.5	−2187	−966.3	−703.7	−649.4	−2118

Notes: All models implement STATA's ebalance procedure (Hainmueller 2012) to address observed differences between (1) mayoral and council-manager systems, and (2) states with default clauses and those without on pre-treatment covariates. Robust standard errors are clustered at the state level. *** p<0.01, ** p<0.05, * p<0.1

leaders' ability to offer incentives. Using survey data on the size of the annual economic development budget, we include a third model that scales the size of the incentives as a percentage of the local economic development budget. Although this variable is the most theoretically appropriate measure, it has a large number of missing values, and we thus present it primarily as a robustness test of our original estimates. As presented in Model 3, mayor-council institutions are associated with a larger percentage of their economic development budget going to incentives.

Although these results alone are compelling, our theory offers an additional observable implication, which is that mayor-council systems tend to have less rigorous oversight of their incentives. In this section, we test Hypothesis 5.2 by focusing on three questions in these surveys. First, do these incentive programs have written performance criteria requiring specific elements from firms (e.g., job creation) in order for them to be eligible for the incentive programs? Second, do municipalities perform a cost-benefit analysis before offering location incentives? Third, if performance criteria are used, how many different items are considered in assessing the project's effectiveness?

The ICMA survey presents respondents with a list of six performance criteria, asking them to check off each one that they currently use. The list includes jobs created, capital invested in construction and labor, capital invested in land, existing company sales, and the number of new businesses attracted. These policies directly limit the discretionary use of incentives for political gain. Thus, we expect to find greater incentive use in municipalities governed by council-manager rather than mayor-council systems. To maximize our explanatory power, we combine the data from the 1999, 2004, and 2009 surveys.[15]

We present our results in Models 4 through 6, using the municipality-based dataset. We find that mayor-council systems are 9.6% less subject to performance requirements and 7.1% less subject to cost-benefit analyses, and they require 0.34% fewer performance criteria per project. However, note that our standard errors are considerably larger for these models than the ordinary least squares (OLS) results.[16] Thus, our cost-benefit-analysis dependent variables in these models do not achieve conventional statistical significance. Nevertheless, these results are consistent with the previous findings because they show that even after we address the nonrandom assignment of elected mayors, we still find that electoral motivations have perverse effects on the use of generous incentives.

---

[15] The coefficient sizes remain similar when the models are run separately by survey year, but they are estimated less efficiently because of the reduced statistical power.
[16] We present these results in Jensen et al. (2015, online appendix A6).

5.3 Research Design

Exogeneity in Institutional Selection

It is critical to note that matching techniques, including advanced ones like entropy balancing, do not address unobserved heterogeneity, which is a severe threat to our analysis. Although municipal institutions tend to be clustered regionally and few cities change their institutions, there is the possibility that cities (or citizens) select their municipal institutions in order to mitigate the abuse of incentives. As we noted above, council-manager systems were labeled "reform" institutions during the Progressive Era, specifically because cities changed their forms of government in an attempt to root out corruption. If this is the case, we might be attributing causality when what we are observing is merely a correlation between two variables that are both capturing concerns for governmental malfeasance.

Fortunately, we have a theoretically informed causal identification strategy. Many US states have formal laws concerning the "default" municipal political institution (Nelson 2011). Although the laws vary across states, for these default states, a status quo bias favors selecting mayor-council municipal institutions. Nelson (2011) documents that twenty-one US states have laws requiring that newly chartered cities have mayor-council institutions as the default form of government.[17] In our data of 1,475 cities, 526 (36%) of these cities are in states that have this requirement.

Default clauses provide an exogenous obstacle to switching forms of government. As Figure 5.2 shows, the status quo bias has an important influence on the share of cities in a state with mayor-council systems. Although the sample distribution changes slightly by year, mayor-council systems govern about 37% of the cities in states with default clauses but only 18% of the cities in states without these clauses.

To test the effect of default clauses, we re-run the entropy balance analysis, balancing this time on whether the state has a default clause, thereby treating mayors as a post-treatment variable (Panel 2 of Table 5.2).[18] In other words, we explore how much of the variance in incentive behavior we can explain simply by studying the impact of these state default clauses on incentives before municipalities have the opportunity to alter their exogenously imposed default institutions.[19] The

---

[17] Nelson (2011) creates an index of institutions that shape municipal government. We focus on this single instrument. We provide more details on this instrument in Jensen et al. (2015, appendix 2). We thank Kimberly Nelson for sharing this data.

[18] See Jensen et al. (2015, online appendix, table A4) for entropy-balancing descriptive statistics for these variables.

[19] In Jensen et al. (2015, appendix, table A2), we note that states with and without default clauses already differ very little on a range of reasonable covariates, including demographics, wealth, economic structure, government spending, and political leanings.

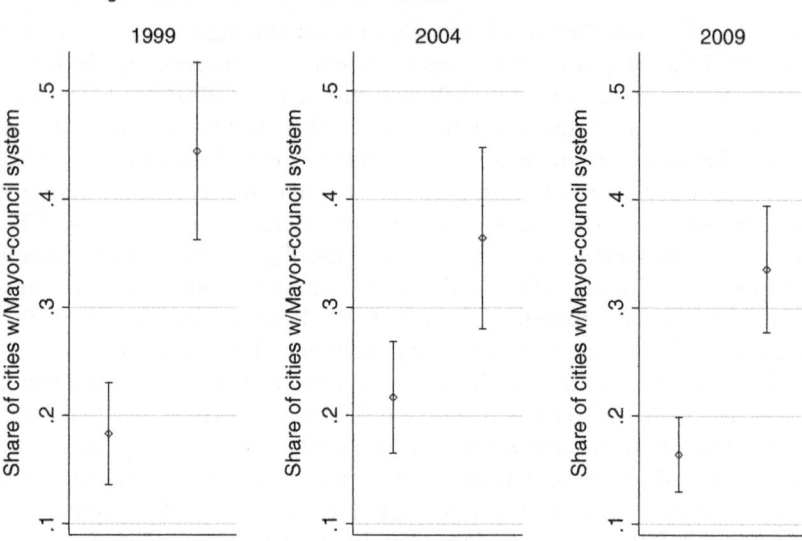

Figure 5.2 Default mayor clauses and the share of mayors.

results show that even after addressing the threat of endogenous selection, the results are very similar. Cities in states with default mayor requirements face significantly fewer constraints on using incentives and offer significantly more generous incentives to new projects.

The Electoral Mechanisms Thus far, we have shown that municipalities with council-manager systems provide less generous incentives, coupled with more extensive oversight of these programs. We have demonstrated that the large size of this effect is consistent across different empirical specifications and with control variables. We also have addressed the nonrandom assignment of municipal institutions by using state laws governing local institutions.

However, we need to address alternative hypotheses that might explain the association between local institutions and incentive allocations. For example, council-manager systems may have more veto players involved in policy making, limiting governments' ability to allocate incentives in the first place.[20] A similar argument could be made in terms of how municipal

[20] However, we find no evidence of this in our empirical analysis.

5.3 Research Design

institutions affect the time horizons of leaders. Council-manager executives, by design, not only are elected indirectly but also tend to have longer time horizons than mayors serving two- or four-year terms (Clingermayer and Feiock 2001). These longer time horizons have been linked to greater risk aversion in economic policy (Feiock et al. 2009).

Therefore, we designed our final test to differentiate the electoral mechanism from these plausible alternative mechanisms by taking advantage of the variation in election timing across municipalities. We created a database of 439 municipal election dates based on election timing data from the US Conference of Mayors as well as our own original data collection. Using these data, we coded a dummy variable representing municipalities that planned to have local elections in 2012.[21] Our expectation is that although municipalities will not alter oversight programs generally from year to year, executives in mayor-council systems are more likely to offer generous incentives than council-manager systems, and this effect will be amplified during election years.

In Table 5.3, we present the OLS results that replicate our fully specified model of the size of incentives with an additional interaction between our independent variable *Elected Mayors* and having an *Election in 2012*.[22] The statistical insignificance of this interaction term is likely due to this model's limited power; specifically, only seventeen mayoral systems had elections in 2012. Nevertheless, the signs on all three coefficients are in the expected directions, and the coefficients are sizable, despite being estimated imprecisely. Thus, for illustrative purposes, we explore the predicted effects from the estimation in Table 5.4.

In the first panel, we show the predicted effects for the four main groups generated by the interaction. Although none of the cells are statistically significantly different from one another, the substantive differences in the average sizes of the incentives are quite large. To illustrate, we undo the log transformation in the second panel. Here, we can see clearly that election years do not appear to generate additional incentive allocations in council-manager systems. In fact, cities with council-managers facing elections actually marginally reduced their incentive usage from $406,000 to $371,000 per project. On the other hand, elected mayors increased their usage of incentives in election years, shifting their offers from $668,000 to $731,000 per project.

These final results are suggestive but are not a silver bullet. Our sample size is less than half of our fully specified model, and measurement error in

---

[21] Given the lack of comprehensive, historical municipal election data, we coded all municipalities with elections in 2014 as also having expected elections in 2012. Although this coding could introduce some measurement error, it is unlikely to bias our results.

[22] See Jensen et al. (2015, model 7, table A5.5).

Table 5.3 *Conditional effect of elections in 2012*

	Value of incentive in millions USD (ln)		
Independent/dependent variables	OLS (1)	OLS (2)	OLS (3)
Elected mayors	0.372*	0.526**	0.490*
	(0.198)	(0.246)	(0.284)
Election in 2012		−0.044	−0.098
		(0.204)	(0.242)
Mayor * election			0.189
			(0.455)
Development plan	0.120	0.052	0.060
	(0.198)	(0.180)	(0.181)
Population	0.054	0.071	0.069
	(0.055)	(0.053)	(0.053)
Foreign competition	0.242	0.153	0.146
	(0.183)	(0.198)	(0.200)
Metro area	0.400	0.295	0.302
	(0.264)	(0.295)	(0.293)
Suburb	0.618**	0.385	0.393
	(0.242)	(0.261)	(0.260)
Jobs created (ln)	0.552***	0.542***	0.543***
	(0.070)	(0.070)	(0.070)
Capital value (ln, US)	0.035***	0.038***	0.038***
	(0.011)	(0.010)	(0.010)
Brand new investment	0.151	−0.038	−0.036
	(0.178)	(0.185)	(0.185)
Unemployment rate (%)	−0.009	−0.005	−0.005
	(0.006)	(0.006)	(0.006)
Other taxes	0.005	0.002	0.003
	(0.034)	(0.031)	(0.032)
Constant	10.551***	10.698***	10.667***
	(0.758)	(0.735)	(0.774)
Survey year FE	Yes	Yes	Yes
State FE	Yes	Yes	Yes
Sector FE	Yes	Yes	Yes
Observations	520	427	427
City	252	209	209
States	38	38	38
R-squared	0.401	0.381	0.379
RMSE	1.355	1.302	1.304

Note: For Models 1–3, the unit of analysis is the dependent variable is the natural log (ln) millions of USD. Data on incentives is from the individual project. And of size of the incentive in 2011 and 2012, but basic city information was captured in different ICMA/ NLC surveys. Fixed effects address confounding based on survey year.
*** $p<0.01$, ** $p<0.05$, * $p<0.1$

Table 5.4 *Predicted effects of city government & elections in 2012*

	1. Local government system		2. Predicted incentive size in USD	
Scheduled election in 2012	Council-manager	Mayor-council	Council-manager	Mayor-council
No	12.92 (12.8 13.1) n=640	13.41 (13.0 13.8) n=74	406,801	668,191
Yes	12.82 (12.4 13.2) n=117	13.50 (13.1 14.0) n=17	371,164	731,974

Panel 1 shows predicted effects of Table 5.3 (Model 3). Natural Log of incentives in millions of USD. Parentheses display 90% Confidence Interval.
Panel 2 presents the same predictions in USD.

the timing of previous elections works against finding clear results. However, we believe that these results, coupled with the existing evidence concerning incentives, provide a relatively comprehensive picture of how electoral institutions shape the use of incentives.

5.4 Conclusion

In this chapter, we directly examined the use of incentives to attract investment to US municipalities using observational data. We argue that politicians can exploit their information advantage over citizens to offer generous incentives for political gain – by providing both too many and too generous incentives to firms. Although all types of municipalities offer incentives to firms, we contend that the form of government shapes these economic development policies. Specifically, firms considering investments in municipalities with mayor-council systems are offered more generous incentives. In addition, mayor-council systems are less likely to impose conditions on firms in order that they qualify for these incentives, and they often fail to require even a simple cost-benefit analysis of incentives. Further, the impact of mayor-council institutions on incentives is heightened during election years.

In Chapter 6, we examine an alternative mechanism linking elections and incentives that is consistent with the overuse of incentives. It is entirely plausible that elected politicians, attempting to build up war chests for reelection, are trading taxpayer-funded incentives for legal campaign contributions. As compelling as this story seems, we find no evidence for this quid pro quo exchange.

Thus, our theory on electoral motivations provides the key mechanism that leads to the over-allocation of incentives. But understanding the political benefits of location incentives requires a test of how voters respond to incentive programs. In Chapter 7, we present data from a number of original survey experiments. Complementing this chapter, we show that major rewards await incumbent politicians overusing incentive programs.

Chapters 5, 6, and 7 form the core of our empirical contribution. We follow these chapters with more speculative work on how our general theory of pandering can help explain the overuse of incentives in non-democratic contexts.

6 Money for Money
Campaign Contributions in Exchange for Incentives?

If everything is bigger in Texas, then the Texas Enterprise Fund (TEF) is no exception. This $295 million "deal-closing" fund – which is dramatically larger than the competitor programs in other states – is the Texas governor's tool for offering additional, targeted incentives to Texas firms.[1] This fund has generated major controversy. Public watchdogs like Texans for Public Justice have documented that recipients of TEF funds gave over $7 million in campaign contributions to then Governor Rich Perry and the Republican Governors Association (Texans for Public Justice 2011).

This example illustrates an alternative relationship between electoral motivations and investment incentives: money in politics could be driving incentive use. Incumbent politicians can harness campaign contributions to increase the probability of winning office (Snyder 1990), and firms can harness incentives as a form of economic rent to increase profitability (Thomas 2007). Consequently, individual politicians can tailor their activities to attract contributions, which includes offering incentives to individual firms. In the next section, we survey the existing literature on campaign contributions and provide an empirical test using data from the TEF.

This alternative theory has a clean logic and makes sense. Moreover, it shares an observable implication with our theory of electoral pandering – that incentives should be tied to an electoral calendar. In this chapter, we give as fair a test as possible to this alternative hypothesis using the TEF as a critical case. We find very weak evidence for this patronage pattern, leaving us dubious that these mechanisms explain the puzzlingly inefficient use of incentives. While campaign contributions have some explanatory power for the use of these policy levers, they are dwarfed by electoral motivations. Also telling is our finding that politicians do not hide their allocation of incentives to firms. They parade these incentives on their websites and issue press releases touting the support that their

---

[1] Although the initial allocation was for $295 million, size of the fund has varied over time.

government gave to firms. This behavior is far from what we would expect from under-the-table exchanges of campaign contributions for financial support.

6.1 Campaign Contributions and Incentive Programs

Although some political economy models, such as Grossman and Helpmann's (2001), assume that campaign contributors can purchase policy goals – anticipating a simple quid pro quo of politicians' incentive packages for firms' campaign contributions – this form of exchange has been harshly criticized in the political science literature (Ansolabehere et al. 2003). Firms may use money to influence politics, but the use of campaign contributions to buy specific policies is problematic for a number of empirical and theoretical reasons.

Beginning with Tullock (1972), political scientists have mused as to why private businesses do not funnel more money into politics, given the tremendous stakes. With most companies spending more money on charitable contributions and bad corporate art than formal lobbying and campaign contributions, the allocation of money to swing policy does not pass the sniff test. Among industries such as defense, where multiple firms are bidding for contracts, companies should escalate their spending on campaign contributions in an effort to buy politicians' favor. Yet, as pointed out by Ansolabehere et al. (2003), most firms spend just a few thousand on campaign contributions and the majority of them do not even spend up to the legal limit.

Second, these exchanges are essentially unenforceable contracts, and legislators can renege on these contracts after receiving business support (Baron 1989). In 2010, when British Petroleum (BP) was in the spotlight after the Deepwater Horizon oil spill in the Gulf of Mexico, few legislators exerted effort to protect the firm despite it being one of the biggest campaign contributors in US elections. Politicians will take money from companies, but what assurances does a company have that a politician, when forced to choose between casting an unpopular vote and supporting a company, will be in the company's corner? This uncertainty severely limits the ability of firms to influence policy.

Third, as pointed out by Morton and Cameron (1992), trading votes for policy can lead to electoral backlash from disenchanted voters. This point is obvious, but worth noting. Politicians may actually feel pressure to distance themselves from campaign contributors to avoid appearing biased or corrupt. Again, this hesitancy limits firms' ability to influence politics through contributions.

6.1 Campaign Contributions and Incentive Programs 85

While this scholarship has pointed out the limits of campaign contributions, the restrictions do not indicate a lack of relationship between money and policy. Focusing on lobbying rather than campaign contributions, Richter et al. (2009) find that firms spending more on lobbying in a given year pay lower effective tax rates in the next year. Increasing registered lobbying expenditures by 1% appears to lower effective tax rates by the range of 0.5 to 1.6 percentage points on average. In an indirect test of campaign contributions, Gordon et al. (2007) examine how the structure of CEO compensation packages affect political giving. In companies where CEOs' pay is more closely linked with firm performance, these executives provide more in campaign contributions, suggesting that individuals' contributions are political investments, not personal expressions of political preferences.

Other studies have highlighted ways in which campaign contributions can affect government policy on the margins. For example, contributions may be used to help fund the reelection campaigns of already sympathetic politicians (Poole and Romer 1985) or the enforcement of regulatory activities (Gordon and Hafer 2005, 2007).

Given this heated debate, our analysis empirically tests the impact of campaign contributions on the provision of location incentives. These tests complement our theory that was outlined in Chapter 2, allowing us to parse out the use of incentives for electoral pandering from patronage or rent allocation to political supporters.

We specifically focus this second part of our analysis on one of the largest location incentive programs in the United States, the TEF. We also highlight the program's discretionary nature and the role of Texas Governor Perry in allocating the incentives, although we do not that oversight of this program allows for the "clawing back" of incentives for investments that fail to fulfill their obligations.

By focusing on this single program, we can construct a clear hypothesis for the relationship between campaign contributions and tax incentives; we look at contributors to the governor's campaign, the firms that received TEF grants along with those that were rejected, and the grant's dollar amount. Because the governor remains the same over time, we do not need to concern ourselves with the unobserved heterogeneity in the political acumen or the incumbent politician's policy views – two factors that have bedeviled other studies. This leads to the following hypothesis:

Hypothesis 6.1: Firms providing campaign contributions to a governor's election campaign are more likely to receive incentives.

As in Chapter 5, our next hypothesis explores the intensive margin of campaign contributions. Rather than affecting the probability of receiving incentives, we empirically test how contributions affect the size of the incentives. Politicians may be loath to provide incentives to underserving firms or to cut off funds from deserving firms, which could be political fodder for opponents. A less transparent mechanism for rewarding supporters is to provide them with larger incentives. This leads to the following hypothesis:

Hypothesis 6.2: Firms providing campaign contributions to a governor's election campaign receive larger grants relative to similar firms not providing campaign contributions.

6.2 Analysis of Campaign Contributions and State Incentive Programs

In the previous chapter, we examined how local electoral institutions shape the use of investment incentives, demonstrating a lack of oversight and an emphasis on discretion in cities that are headed by elected mayors. These compelling results are consistent with both the pandering and the contributions hypotheses. Elected officials may prefer discretion in providing financial benefits as exchange for campaign contributions or to pander voters. To differentiate between the pandering hypothesis and the campaign-contribution hypothesis, we draw on a novel dataset.

While every US state has some form of incentives that are essentially automatic, many governors have access to discretionary "deal-closing" funds. These funds can supplement existing tax credits to clinch investment deals when executives appear to be wavering. According to a study by Kansas Inc. (see Caplan and Associates 2009), thirty states have these deal-closing funds, with the median program in the $7–$10 million range. The biggest of these funds at the time of the study, by quite a margin, is the $250 million TEF.

This program was initiated by then Texas Governor Rick Perry in 2003 and has now provided financial incentives to over one hundred investments in Texas. Ultimately, funding a project requires the approval of the governor, the lieutenant governor, and the speaker of the Texas House of Representatives.

While this program's flexibility is often seen as one of its greatest benefits because it allows the Texas government to nimbly respond to investors' concerns and to structure firm-specific incentive packages, the approach has serious costs. Governors can selectively use deal-closing funds to price discriminate and to offer larger incentives to close deals with investors.

The TEF provides the details of each funded project online. Of course, evaluating only funded projects would amount to selecting on the dependent variable (Geddes 1990; King et al. 1994). To really understand the

6.2 Analysis of Campaign Contributions

selection process, we also need to know which projects did not get funded. It may be that the governor's selections included the investments that would have the greatest impact on employment and economic prospects in Texas. If these projects would have been selected anyway, whether a few of them had political connections to Governor Perry is irrelevant. The only way to know if politics played a role is to see if political factors outweighed the projects' economic benefits, meaning that bad projects were selected while good investors were left at the altar.

Using public information requests to Governor Perry's office, we obtained data on the unfunded projects. Thus, we can compare the ninety-nine funded projects (plus others that have been accepted, but the funds have yet to be distributed) with the eighteen rejected projects. We also have data on firms that were offered funding but decided not to invest in Texas (sixteen projects) and firms that withdrew their applications prior to a final decision (six projects).

One interesting figure is total campaign contributions to Governor Perry by firms and employees of these firms.[2] For the funded projects, the average total campaign contribution (corporate contributions and individual contributions directly to Perry's campaign in 2002, 2006, and 2010) was $5,070. The rejected applications averaged $508.

While this suggests a role of politics in the allocation of grants, there are two concerns with this simple interpretation. First, the aggregation of all campaign contributions across the entire time period may miss the importance of contribution timing. Thus, we take detailed data on the timing of both the TEF grants received and campaign contributions into account.

Second, the heterogeneity across firms is considerable, with larger firms more likely to provide campaign contributions. To achieve a simple, descriptive presentation, we create a measure of the log of jobs proposed by the firm divided by the total dollar amount of the grant. In Figure 6.1, we present descriptive data on the log dollars of grants received on the x-axis and the log of jobs proposed in the TEF application on the y-axis.

This simple description of the data reveals two noteworthy patterns. First, as noted earlier, a large number of companies provide no campaign contributions. Second, there is no clear relationship between contributions and TEF grants; these discretionary grants are largely determined by the jobs that are proposed by the investment.

This descriptive data of the bivariate relationship between grant and contributions should be taken with a grain of salt for one very important reason: the jobs proposed by the firms could be manipulated. In fact, at least one report suggests that Governor Perry inflated job numbers for

---

[2] Thanks to Adam Bonica for data suggestions.

88 Money for Money

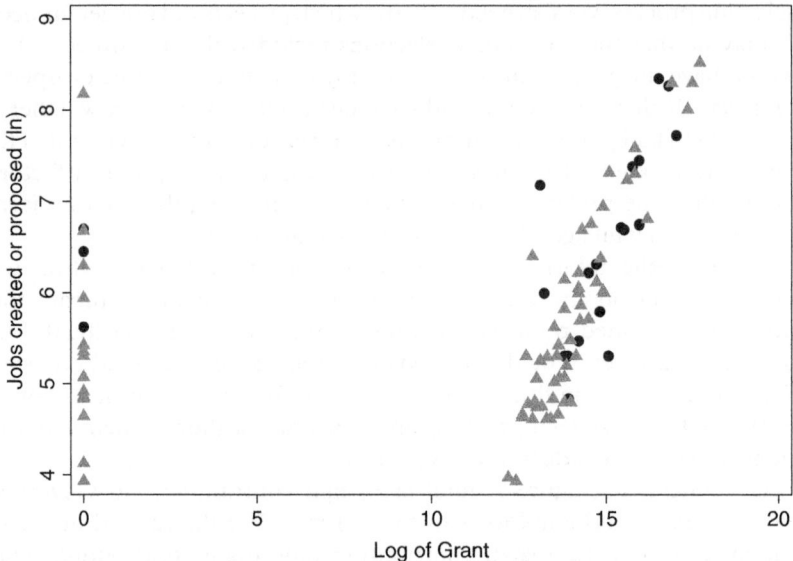

Figure 6.1 Jobs proposed and grant size for the Texas Enterprise Fund. Note: Triangle represent campaign non-contributors. Circles represent campaign contributors.

firms contributing to his campaign (Texans for Public Justice 2010). Thus, our data may create a semblance of fairness in the allocation of grants when, in reality, manipulating job numbers is the mechanism by which the governor provides extra incentives. Consequently, associating projected job growth on future projects with incentives can be seen as a form of pandering; after all, the governor can stake a claim to having funded multiple job-producing businesses prior to an election.

In this section, we use multiple regression analysis to test the relationship between campaign contributions and TEF grants. We employ a probit specification with robust standard errors, where the dependent variable is coded 1 for accepted TEF proposals and 0 for rejected proposals from 2004 to 2011. We also include a small number of control variables, including the natural log of jobs proposed for both accepted and rejected applications. Unfortunately, as we noted above, these job proposal numbers may be inaccurate, and some have accused Governor Perry of inflating them – specifically, for politically connected firms (Terbush 2011). As an alternative measure, we conduct secondary data

6.2 Analysis of Campaign Contributions

Table 6.1 *Determinants of rejected TEF projects*

	Model 1	Model 2	Model 3
Campaign contributions	−0.014	0.002	0.008
	(0.013)	(0.009)	(0.012)
Jobs proposed	−0.043		−0.063*
	(0.042)		(0.036)
Company size		−0.022*	−0.023
		(0.012)	(0.015)
Observations	92	114	88
Pseudo R-sq	0.0415	0.0536	0.0787

Note: All models are probit models presented as marginal probabilities with robust standard errors in parentheses. The dependent variable is coded 1 for rejected projects and 0 otherwise. *** $p<0.01$, ** $p<0.05$, * $p<0.1$

collection on the parent company and include a variable for the log of parent company employment as a proxy for firm size.

While we have campaign contribution data during the whole period, some care is required in the aggregation of contribution data, and tough choices need to be made in identifying the timing of contributions. First, we aggregate corporate contributions and individual contributions of employees. Second, we examine the timing of contributions, generating three new variables: contributions made prior to the governor's reelection campaign (*Pre-Election*), after the election (*Post-Election*), and immediately before or after the election (*Political Contributions*).

We present our results in Table 6.1. In Model 1, we test how the jobs proposed and the total amount of campaign contributions affect the probability of rejection. In Model 2, we include a measure of the log of the parent company employment as a proxy for company size. Model 3 includes both measures.

The bottom line is that campaign contributions provide little leverage in explaining the pattern of rejected applications. Contributions are not statistically significant in any of these regressions, and the coefficient is substantively small.

This first test examines the determinants of receiving a TEF grant, although we note that outright rejections are rare – only eighteen cases of rejected applications are in our dataset. In the next set of OLS regressions on the relationship between campaign contributions and the size of TEF grants, we use two alternative samples. First, we included both accepted and rejected applications (companies that did not receive grants were coded 0) and used the log of grant size for companies that received TEF

Table 6.2 *TEF grant size (Rejected and Accepted Projects)*

	Model 1	Model 2	Model 3
Campaign contributions	0.18	0.10	0.21
	(0.15)	(0.14)	(0.21)
Jobs proposed	1.377**		1.543**
	(0.59)		(0.69)
Company size		0.446*	
		(0.25)	
Constant	3.08	8.526***	1.45
	(3.32)	(1.83)	(3.93)
Observations	92	94	92
R-squared	0.12	0.09	

Note: Models 1 and 2 are OLS regressions with robust standard errors in parentheses. Model 3 is a Tobit regression with values left censored at zero. The dependent variable is coded as zero for rejected projects and is coded as the log of TEF grants in dollars for accepted projects.
*** $p<0.01$, ** $p<0.05$, * $p<0.1$

grants in Table 6.2. In Table 6.3, we only include the first companies that received grants. We present the results of an OLS analysis of the relationship between contributions and grants in Models 1 and 2, and a Tobit analysis of grant size in Model 3 that allows for censoring at zero.

This outcome paints a similar picture as Figure 6.1: the size of the grant is largely driven by the project's proposed number of jobs (or by the parent company size). Campaign contributions have no clear impact on the size of grants. This finding provides tentative evidence for pandering (Hypothesis 6.2) over the contributions hypothesis (Hypothesis 6.1).

One concern with the above analysis is that the relationship between contributions and incentives may run in two different directions. We have hypothesized that firms provide contributions to receive incentives, meaning contributions precede the incentives. An alternative story is that firms may receive incentives initially, and then choose to return the favor with subsequent campaign contributions. Unfortunately, we do not have information on the timing of the rejected applications. For the accepted projects, however, we not only know the timing of the grant, and we can also use campaign contribution data to code whether campaign contributions were made before or after the TEF grant was awarded. We generate three new variables using this data. First, we create a variable, *Election Contributions*, which is the log of all campaign contributions made in the year prior to the investment or in the year following the investment. We also break this variable into its component parts,

6.2 Analysis of Campaign Contributions

Table 6.3 *TEF grant size (Accepted projects only)*

	Model 1	Model 2	Model 3	Model 4
Log campaign contributions	0.022	0.110**		
	(0.03)	(0.05)		
Log jobs	0.983***		1.004***	0.988***
	(0.07)		(0.07)	(0.07)
Log company size		0.076		
		(0.05)		
Log election contributions			0.009	
			(0.02)	
Log pre-election contributions				−0.039
				(0.04)
Log post-election contributions				0.069**
				(0.03)
Constant	8.468***	13.481***	8.381***	8.480***
	(0.37)	(0.37)	(0.36)	(0.37)
Observations	74	79	74	74
R-squared	0.785	0.216	0.782	0.802

Note: All models are OLS regressions with robust standard errors in parentheses. The dependent variable is coded as the log of TEF grants in dollars for accepted projects.
*** $p<0.01$, ** $p<0.05$

coding contributions made to the Perry campaign before the TEF grant (*Pre-Election Contributions*) and contributions made after the award was given (*Post-Election Contributions*).

In general, the results on campaign contributions are statistically insignificant. We find some evidence that contributions increase after the award is given but only by a small amount. For example, increasing contributions to the maximum in the dataset ($135,000) has less than a 0.10 standard deviation increase in TEF money. In dollar terms, the sum amounts to $3.66 (Model 2), which is almost nothing. In contrast, a two standard deviation increase in proposed jobs leads to a 1.7 standard deviation increase in TEF money. By any measure, campaign contributions have a modest impact on grants that are allocated to companies.

This campaign contribution data does come with limits. First, we only analyze direct contributions to the Perry campaign. Donors can use other means of funneling money to the governor, including contributions to the Republican Governors Association. Second, although we have data on the precise timing of TEF funds, we do not have data for the timing of rejected applications. While these two concerns could affect our analysis, the descriptive data on the large number of accepted grants and the limited variation in grant size relative to jobs created makes us skeptical that measurement error is generating these non-results. The majority of firms accept TEF grants, and the sizes of these grants correspond to the size of the investments. Evidence is scant that these discretionary programs are used to reject worthwhile applications or to overfund unworthy projects.

We do not mean to say that politics is not at play in these programs. The TEF analysis allows us to conclude only that the political game being played is not one of providing rents to powerful supports. More likely, the key mechanism is pandering to the public by crediting incentive programs with job growth.

6.3 More on the Kansas City Border War

Our main test in this chapter focuses on the largest incentive program in the United States. By focusing on Texas, we not only identify the firms that received incentives but also, through the use of public data requests, identify the firms that did not receive incentives.

A second illustrative case is the aforementioned border war between Kansas City, Kansas, and Kansas City, Missouri (Chapter 1). Unfortunately, we do not have the rejected applications for incentives to make a parallel analysis to our Texas example. What we do have is information on all sixty-seven investments that received incentives, including details about campaign contributions to the Kansas and Missouri governors, and to other state and local officials.

The states of Missouri and Kansas, along with cities in the Kansas City metro area, competed fiercely over just two years (2010–2012) for sixty-seven firm investments. These sixty-seven incentives have cost the two states $312 million, with an average cost of over $4 million per investment.[3] The incentives were exceptionally generous, averaging over 50% of the firms' capital expenditures and $37,000 per job created. What is driving this border war?

We were astounded that these firms rarely provided direct contributions to either the Missouri or the Kansas governor's election campaigns; only four of the sixty-seven firms contributed directly to these campaigns in 2010 or 2012.[4] The biggest player by far was the engineering firm Burns & McDonnell. Further data work identified $137,000 in direct contributions by employees to the Jay Nixon (Missouri-D) campaign.

---

[3] www.incentivesmonitor.com (Accessed August 2, 2017).
[4] All data for state-level contributions is from www.FollowTheMoney.org (Accessed August 2, 2017).

6.3 More on the Kansas City Border War

Documentation by OpenSecrets, a website that tracks online campaign contributions, provides a more complete picture of their contributions, including those from political action committees.[5] This company has a political action committee that mostly funds incumbent members of the federal and state senates and houses of representatives across the country. The key point is that although this company is politically active in the state of Missouri and beyond, it is by far the exception. The other three contributors to the Nixon campaign provided $3,500, $2,000, and $1,000.

We also examined the contributions of employees of these sixty-seven companies beyond governor elections and coded any campaign contributions by employees to state politicians. Only six more companies (bringing the total to ten) provided contributions. Burns & McDonnell and insurance broker Lockton Companies both gave roughly $22,000. The remaining companies gave an average of just over $1,000 each. In summary, the sixty-seven incentive recipients gave an average of $3,000 across all state and local elections in Missouri and Kansas in 2010–2012.

The use of campaign contributions – at least the direct ones that we can track – does not seem to be the deciding factor in shaping incentive decisions. Similar to Texas, the correlation between the number of jobs created and the size of the incentives is strong (correlation of 0.30).

If campaign contributions are not responsible for this incentive war, perhaps the tough competition for capital is driving it. In most cases, we could not find evidence of competing incentive bids, nor even concrete evidence that the firms were considering an alternative location. Thirty-one of the sixty-seven firms were expanding existing operations in their existing locations. Others were jumping to the other side of the border; "new" investments can receive incentives, whereas existing plants, unless they expand, often cannot. We could only find evidence of competition with other locations in twenty cases, with many companies citing "other Midwestern locations" or making similar vague claims. In six of the twenty cases, the competition was from across the state line in either Kansas or Missouri. In only two of the cases, could we find direct evidence of competing offers, where two firms locating in the Kansas City, Kansas, suburb of Overland Park received competing incentive bids from Missouri. Thus, in the majority of cases, there is little evidence that direct competitive forces, such as bids from alternative locations, were driving these incentives.

While we cannot conclusively identify what is driving this border war, our data collection efforts document that most of these firms do not provide any campaign contributions, nor were these incentives an obvious outcome of a bidding war. In many cases, firms received only

---

[5] This data comes from www.opensecrets.org/influence/. (Accessed August 2, 2017).

one offer, often to jump across the border to Kansas or Missouri. While not a smoking gun, such offers suggest that the political logic of credit claiming is driving these decisions.

6.4 Conclusion

Money's influence on public policy remains an evasive topic of study. First, the factors that initially lead a firm to give money, such as its size, could be causally related to its ability to receive handouts from government. Our results show that firms that have absolutely no chance of getting incentives might not contribute to political campaigns, whereas firms that have a reasonable chance of receiving incentives may do so. The obvious ensuing biases lead researchers to overstate the impact of campaign contributions on favorable policy. Even with the bias in this direction, the data in this chapter reveals very little relationship between political giving and the allocation of incentives.

A second concern, which is much more problematic, is that firms can give money in a number of ways that are difficult for researchers to detect. Not only do firms have many opportunities to give soft money to political candidates; companies can funnel money into politics in many ways that go undetected in our analysis. In short, firms can be creative about how they avoid public scrutiny.

In this book, our main motivation is not to strike down the idea that money influences politics. Rather, our goal is to show how our theory of pandering influences the allocation of scarce financial resources relative to alternative explanations. While observational data on contributions, elections, and incentives will often be plagued by these potential problems, we believe that this chapter provides empirical evidence suggesting that campaign contributions are not the main factor driving incentive decisions.

We note that the programs analyzed in Texas, Missouri, and Kansas all have some degree of oversight of incentive use. These states have the ability to claw back incentive awards for firms that fail to meet the obligations. In Chapter 10, we directly address the issue of clawbacks and how this form of oversight only has a limited effectiveness in improving incentive programs. Throughout this book we maintain that the problem with these incentive programs actually rests in public perceptions of incentives and a politician's ability to use these incentives to pander to voters.

In the next chapter, we set up an experimental test of how allocations of incentive programs affect voters, showing that voters reward incumbent politicians for the use of incentives. Even if money can influence policy, we show that vote-maximizing politicians gain direct electoral benefits by allocating incentives to firms.

7 Political Pandering in the United States
A Survey Experiment on Incentives and Investment[1]

The massive sports entertainment company ESPN sent shockwaves through the state of Connecticut in 2013 when it threatened to relocate "the mother station," it's international headquarters, to another state. For many in the state and the city of Bristol, the very idea was apostasy. After all, ESPN had had its start in the town over thirty years before, and the company and Bristol had grown up together in a symbiotic relationship that enriched the company's founder and investors, and which had also sparked a media industry revolution in Bristol, employing thousands both directly and indirectly through upstream service providers. Despite the mutual dependence, ESPN made it clear to its longtime benefactor that the company's plans were contingent on the city and state supplementing its already extraordinary incentive package. Despite Bristol's proximity to New York, excellent infrastructure, and specialized labor force, which were all ideal for the company, ESPN was confident that the state could dig deeper into its pockets. After all, it was an election year, and Daniel P. Malloy, the incumbent governor, did not want to be the one who let ESPN get away. As the *New York Times* described it, "Mr. Malloy brought a hard hat, a shovel, and an incentive package worth $25 million" (Eder 2013). This giveaway was on top of $260 million in documented incentives over the previous twelve years.

Threats to leave the state were clearly part of the rhetoric by both the company and the elected politicians. Disney, ESPN's parent company, had operations in many states, and the company president was keen to point this out during the incentive negotiations. The governor, up for reelection, had no choice but tout the state's undying support for ESPN.[2]

The story of ESPN is all too common. Sports teams, movie companies, and iconic manufacturing firms have employed such threats to convince politicians to provide them with tax incentives to stay put or jump ship to

---

[1] This chapter presents statistical analyses from Jensen et al. (2014).
[2] The governor's official website has numerous press releases about the incentives offered to ESPN (www.portal.ct.gov/governor/press-releases; accessed August 2, 2017).

another city, taking lucrative jobs and the hearts of diehard sports fans with them. Moreover, similar arguments regarding the necessity of incentives have been offered by politicians all around the world, despite the lack of evidence for these policies' effectiveness. But, as we note, politicians have very little reason to evaluate the effectiveness of incentives. Thus far in the book, we outlined our theory of how politicians use investment incentives to "pander" to voters. Our simple logic is that firms choose to locate in cities, states, and countries for a variety of reasons, many of them purely economic. Concurrently, politicians are often tasked with attracting investment to help generate jobs in their districts.

Conventional wisdom asserts that investment incentives are just one among a variety of tools used to attract these investments; politicians sweeten the deal for firms, attracting new businesses or retaining existing ones by offering enough extra incentives to sway a location decision. But as we noted in Chapters 1 and 2, both the ability of politicians to evaluate the exact price at which companies will move and the ultimate importance of incentive programs in swaying investment decisions are seriously suspect. There is simply no convincing evidence that these policies are effective tools for developing local economies.

In this book, we have focused our attention on the information asymmetry between voters, politicians, and firms, and how this asymmetry can lead politicians to use incentives not to necessarily swing investment decisions but to take credit or reduce the blame for economic outcomes. In other words, if voters believe that these policies are effective, politicians will implement these policies regardless of their real influence over investors.

In Chapter 5, we tested our theory, finding that incumbent politicians facing electoral pressure were more likely to use incentives than city managers, who were shielded from such pressures. In Chapter 6, we showed that patronage and campaign finance do not appear to influence the allocation of incentives, lending greater support to our pandering theory. While these findings are helpful for documenting politicians' actions, we have yet to explore whether these strategies actually generate more votes. As the saying goes, it takes two to tango; politicians would not find pandering to be an effective strategy if it did not yield votes. In this chapter, we test whether voters might actually be convinced by the political use of incentives. Can promising incentives help swing an election for an incumbent? Our theory predicts that it should.

In testing this hypothesis, we highlight that the competition for investment across US states can help us understand other within- and across-country fiscal wars for investment. While our theory applies to democratic regimes in general, several features of the United States – in particular, governors' provision of "deal-closing" incentives – provide a clean causal test for our model.

7.1 The United States as a Laboratory

To test the theory that we put forward in Chapter 2, in this chapter we examine how attracting investment affects the political fortunes of incumbent US governors. Why focus on US states? Our theory generalizes across countries, yet we believe American states are an excellent laboratory for examining how investment affects politicians' electoral fortunes. States vary greatly in their incentive policies and their performance in attracting investment while holding constant political institutions, culture, and other non-observed factors that can lead to unobserved heterogeneity and bias results.

We focus on governors rather than members of the state and federal legislatures for four reasons. First, while members of Congress certainly engage in activities to increase investment, their efforts predominantly take the form of informal persuasion. They do not have control over formal state-level policy levers that voters see and associate with investment projects. Second, voters have limited ability to assign credit when multiple politicians operate within the same state. Large investment projects create revenue, employment opportunities, and business spillovers that reach beyond an individual congressman's electoral district, and policies to attract these activities are often the result of legislation requiring the support of many legislators. By contrast, governors' activities to attract investment are clearly attributable to a single actor, allowing voters to assign responsibility to the governor for his or her performance.[3]

Third, governors are often both active and visible when creating new programs or re-tailoring existing ones to attract or retain specific investments. For example, much like the ESPN story, in January 2008, New Jersey Governor Jon Corzine created the Urban Transit Hub Tax Credit "largely to stop financial services giant, *BlackRock Private Equity Partners*, from moving more than 1,000 jobs from Plainsboro to Pennsylvania" (Morley 2011). Governors across the country travel abroad on commercial visits and use the powers of their office to offset investor start-up costs, such as tax holidays, property tax reductions, and other incentives. Indeed, governors are perceived to be the actors most responsible for attracting investment, and voters have the ability to reward them for their performance. Finally, in thirty US states, "contingency funds" or "deal-closing

---

[3] See Hellwig and Samuels (2008) for a cross-national analysis of how institutions affect the attribution of responsibility.

funds" average between $7 and $10 million in additional incentives that can be added to existing incentive packages. The largest of these funds is the behemoth $250 million TEF, which we studied in detail in Chapter 6.

How do voters evaluate the performance of US governors? First, scholars have argued that voters reward governors for economic outcomes that reflect the governors' actions, but filter from their assessment the influence of economic events outside the politicians' locus of control (Wolfers 2002, p.1). Cohen and King (2004) make a similar point in looking at voters' focus on a government's ability to generate jobs, arguing that voters recognize state governments' limitations to affect the economy. For Cohen and King (2004) the level of unemployment *relative* to other states has the largest effect on voting. More broadly, Arceneaux (2006) finds that in federal systems, such as the United States, citizens sanction politicians for policy decisions over which their level of government has responsibility.

These studies all identify the importance of state economic conditions for governors' reelection prospects and indicate that voters use a level of sophistication in assigning credit and blame to specific politicians. As we have shown, both these factors are generalizable outside of the United States, where models of economic voting at the state level share commonalities with those across countries. Existing theoretical work has not fully explored the relationship between elected officials' policies and how they map onto voting intentions.

7.2   A Survey Experiment of US Residents

Our empirical analysis builds on the existing observational studies on incentives, yet our research design offers a number of advantages over existing work. First, given the increasing trend of offering incentives to attract investment, it is difficult to harness observational studies. Other theoretical and empirical issues – such as endogeneity – complicate statistical identification. Especially germane is the issue of unobserved heterogeneity among governors. In particular, entrepreneurial governors may be the most popular and the most likely to offer investment incentives, leading to a correlation without a direct causal relationship.

Second, we directly examine if these policies are relevant for voters. In a study of trade, Guisinger (2009) finds that voters have little knowledge of individual trade policy and that trade has very little impact on vote choice. We address this issue in the context of attracting investment by focusing on how offering incentives affects individual voters' *voting intentions*.

Limitations to causal inference can be mitigated through an experimental approach. Specifically, we utilize a survey experiment to randomize

7.2 A Survey Experiment of US Residents

treatment across individuals, which allows us to test the causal mechanism linking policy to individual voters' perceptions. Rather than focusing on vote choice, we utilize a question that directly asks how a policy (on tax incentives) *changes* the probability of voting for the incumbent. Consequently, we can isolate the differential effects of incentives from the underlying flow of investment. This test of our hypotheses is especially rigorous.

Our analysis utilizes a survey experiment placed in a nationally representative survey of Americans. This survey was part of the Cooperative Congressional Election Survey (CCES), an Internet-based survey administered by YouGovPolimetrix in October 2009 to 13,800 respondents. Respondents answered questions on demographics, voting, and partisanship, and they were tested on their ability to identify how their elected officials voted on specific legislation. We added questions to a nationwide CCES subsample of 1,974 respondents.

Our main question was a survey experiment on how attracting an investment project and offering tax incentives affected the respondent's intention to vote for the governor. We provided only very limited information on the investment project – specifically, the number of jobs created so that the respondent recognized the event as influential on the state's economy. Small investment projects would likely not be considered important enough to alter voting behavior. We offered no other information on the investment, including no negative information, for three reasons. First, our ultimate research question is whether incentives help politicians claim credit for positive economic outcomes. Second, the slight framing effect is dictated by our theoretical model, where voters are assumed to associate investment with increases in income for constituents. Priming voters to associate investment with employment serves this objective with minimal contamination. Third, and most critical for our design, the relatively positive depiction of the investment has no impact on voters' ability to separate their approval of the investment from their approval of the incentive policy (also randomly assigned), which is the ultimate goal of our research design. Thus, our survey experiment is a realistic test of how politicians claim credit for economic performance.

The survey experiment divides the sample into four treatment groups, with respondents being randomly assigned to one of the four groups. Each treatment consisted of two dimensions – investment attraction and tax incentives. Our question reads as follows, with the value of each treatment dimension brackets:

Your state competed with a number of other states over a new manufacturing plant that will create 1,000 jobs.

With the support of the governor, your state offered a tax incentive (break/ reduction) package *that was [greater/equal or less]* than that of the other states. If your state [*receives/does not receive*] this investment, how would this affect your evaluation of your governor's performance in office?
(1) I would be much more likely to vote for the governor in the next election.
(2) I would be slightly more likely to vote for the governor in the next election.
(3) My vote choice would not be altered.
(4) I would be slightly less likely to vote for the governor in the next election.
(5) I would be much less likely to vote for the governor in the next election.

In selecting our question wording, we first felt obligated to use the nonconventional, hypothetical construction "how would this ... " because investment projects of the scale we reference in our survey are rare and well documented in reality. Reasonably knowledgeable respondents would be aware if such large investments opened in their states. We did not want these respondents to perceive that they were being overtly misled. As a result, we chose a prospective construction that speculated about new investment in the future. Public opinion researchers have long debated about whether hypothetical questions are problematic and lead to inaccurate responses.[4] Other scholars disagree, however, particularly those who use anchoring vignettes, experiments, and especially contingent valuation designs in the economics literature. These scholars have shown empirically that respondents can give meaningful answers to hypothetical questions if a neutral or "don't know" option is provided for uninformed respondents and the question allows respondents to draw upon relevant previous experiences to place the hypothetical in context (Mitchell and Carson 1989, p.173). We took precautions to make sure both of these conditions were met in our question.

This choice had two downstream effects. First, the answer options needed to be prospective as well, referencing a vote choice that had not yet taken place. Second, the prospective construction made it difficult to devise a realistic control group as recommended by Gaines et al. (2007) because respondents could not be asked to evaluate how their vote would change when their state *did not* compete for investment and their governor took *no* actions.

For this design, the natural baseline is the state that offered less tax incentives and did not receive the project. From that cell, which receives a zero on both dichotomous options (Group 1: 0,0), we can calculate the impact of winning the project with incentives less than or equal to a competitor's (Group 2: 1,0), offering an incentive that is greater than a competitor's but losing the project (Group 3: 0,1), and offering an

---

[4] Converse (1964, 1974) and Cummings et al. (1995).

7.2 A Survey Experiment of US Residents

incentive that is greater than a competitor's and winning the project (Group 4: 1,1). In short, we derive all marginal effects calculated in the empirical analysis by comparing shifts in incentives and investment to the baseline category (0,0). A final consideration was whether to use vote choice in the option or the standard job-approval scale. We opted for vote choice because we wanted to simulate, as closely as possible, the political logic of our formal model. Moreover, we were concerned that using approval ratings would overstate the impact of the investment, which might play only a small role in voters' ultimate calculations (Guisinger 2009). We also offered a neutral category of "My vote choice would not be altered" to allow respondents, for whom economic issues are less important than others, an opt-out opportunity. Both the opt-out and vote choices are conservative and were intended to bias against our hypotheses. As a robustness check, we control for the respondents' previous governor approval rating in the analysis to approximate the level of change in a respondent's vote choice.

We note that although this question was designed for our survey in the United States, we believe that it is generalizable to other countries as well. As we noted in Chapter 2, many EU incentives are directly tied to the number of jobs created. Middle income and developing countries also often build their incentives based on job creation; Rodríguez-Pose and Arbix (2001) note that Brazilian incentive programs even have the word "employment" as part of their formal name. Serbian incentive programs are often denominated per job. Indeed, incentives in the IncentivesMonitor database (www.incentivesmonitor.com) are formally calculated per job, ranging from €,5000 to €10,000 per job created.

Thus, our survey experiment – which provides information on the jobs created, on whether the investment materialized, and on the incentives offered by the government – is generalizable across countries.

Our survey was designed to test the two main hypotheses of this book. We restate these two hypotheses:

Hypothesis 7.1 (Credit claiming): Voters are more likely to vote for incumbent politicians when firms were attracted with incentives than for incumbent politicians who attracted the same firms without incentives.

Hypothesis 7.2 (Blame avoidance): Voters are more likely to reelect incumbent politicians who failed to attract firms despite offering incentives than incumbent politicians who failed to attract the same firms without incentives.

In our survey experiment, our randomization process was successful, bar a few very small exceptions; the four treatment samples do not differ dramatically from one another across factors (see Table 7.A1 in the appendix). This result indicates that the treatments were uncorrelated with voters' characteristics and can therefore be assessed directly. Mutz and Pemantle (2015) argue that the display of balance tables is not necessary for survey experiments since randomization can occasionally lead to unbalanced covariates on some factors. In fact, when controlling for these factors, scholars themselves can actually bias results more so than a sampling error. In our case, however, the relatively high non-completion rate (about 30%) of the web-based Polimetrix survey does create concerns about differential attrition rates in some demographics that could be correlated with the treatments. Fortunately, this concern is not serious enough to damage our results.

As a first-cut, we provide a comparison of means of these four groups based on collapsing our dependent variable from a five-point Likert scale. We invert this scale with scores of 5 ("much more likely to vote for the governor") and 1 ("much less likely"). We can now construct Table 7.1 based on the two different treatment dimensions for the entire sample of 1,974 respondents.

As is to be expected, respondents who learned that their state won the investment project were more likely to reward their governor than those whose state had not. Winning the investment increases the likelihood of voting for the governor (checking 4 or 5 on our scale) by about 20% (2.85 to 3.37). This result was statistically significant at the 95% level of confidence, providing evidence for the positive impact on investment for politicians. Offering an investment incentive also has a statistically significant but substantively small impact in isolation. Confirming Hypothesis 7.1, 2.4% more voters say that they are likely to vote for the governor after hearing an incentive was offered (3.05 to 3.15).

The First Panel of Table 7.1, however, reveals that the impact of incentives is conditional on whether the project was won. For states that attracted investment, the difference in the likelihood of voting for the governors barely exceeds zero, which is inconsistent with Hypothesis 7.2. For states that lost the project, however, 3.5% of voters would shift their vote in favor of a governor who offered an investment incentive, raising the average score from 2.76 to 2.95, lending tentative support for Hypothesis 7.2. This result is significant at the 0.05 level and appears to indicate that voters, as a whole, are supportive of greater investment but may not be responsive to credit claiming on the part of elected officials. Rather, they respond more positively to visible effort in losing causes, tentatively confirming Hypothesis 2.

Looking for credit claiming across the entire electorate, however, may be too ambitious. Party affiliation is strong among American voters, and depending on the state, a significant portion of the electorate may not be motivated to alter their vote choice at all, much less because of a single incident of investment attraction, as indicated by the thresholds in

Table 7.1 *Likelihood of vote for governor (by party affiliation)*

		Tax incentive greater than competitors							
		Yes	No		Yes	No		Yes	No
		All (N=1974)			**Independents (N=453)**				
Received investment	Yes	3.38	3.37	Yes	3.51	3.38	Yes	3.41	3.35
		(3.284, 3.469)	(3.279, 3.458)		(3.323, 3.706)	(3.211, 3.558)		(3.295, 3.620)	(3.262, 3.564)
	No	2.95	2.76	No	3.09	2.72	No	2.92	2.78
		(2.856, 3.037)	(2.664, 2.848)		(2.923, 3.253)	(2.526, 2.919)		(2.807, 3.123)	(2.618, 2.937)
		Democrats (N=580)			**Republicans (N=505)**				
		Yes	No		Yes	No			
	Yes	3.41	3.35	Yes	3.19	3.33			
		(3.295, 3.620)	(3.262, 3.564)		(3.067, 3.396)	(3.157, 3.520)			
	No	2.92	2.78	No	2.91	2.78			
		(2.807, 3.123)	(2.618, 2.937)		(2.726, 3.083)	(2.550, 2.938)			

Note: Comparison of mean responses to the question "How would this affect your evaluation of your governor's performance in office?" Responses: (1) Much less likely, (2) Slightly less likely, (3) Vote choice would not be altered, (4) Slightly more likely, (5) Much more likely. The vertical axis displays the investment treatment. The horizontal axis displays the incentive treatment. 90% confidence intervals are in parentheses.

Figure 7.1. According to our data, about 62% (35% Democrat versus 27% Republican) self-identify as strong or as weak members of a particular party. Party identification has been among the strongest determinants of vote choices in repeated analyses at national and local levels (Bartels 2000; Hetherington 2001). As every political consultant worth his paycheck knows, the battle for election lies in the middle of the distribution among voters who are likely to change their mind based on policy choices. Although true independents are a relatively small portion of the electorate (about 12.5%), if we include those who self-identify as independent but lean towards a particular party (8% Democrat versus 15% Republican), we are able to carve out a reasonable subsample of 453 observations for analysis.[5]

Panels 2, 3, and 4 analyze the impact of the treatments individually on Democrats, Republicans, and independents, respectively. While all three groups reward the attraction of investment (Republicans more weakly than the others), the impact of investment incentives is only significant among independent voters.

Among investment recipients, 44% of independents whose state offered bigger incentive packages claimed that they were more likely to vote for the governor, as opposed to 39% whose state offered an equal or smaller incentive. This leads to a 0.13 difference in mean scores on our Likert scale, which is just shy of traditional standards of statistical significance. Incentives offered in losing efforts also pay a higher dividend as regards independents. While they have a marginal impact on favorable votes (about 2.2%), their most important impact is shifting 19% of the negative voters to the neutral category, thereby significantly increasing the overall vote scale by 0.37 points. Substantively, this result is important, and it lends further credibility to our experimental treatment. All voters were given information about the investment project, providing details on employment creation, with no negative information about the project; yet, only independent voters significantly responded to tax incentives.

Ordered Probit Analysis

While an illustrative first-cut, the use of a mean score across the Likert scale assumes that one-point shifts across each level of the scale are

---

[5] Petrocik (2009) distinguishes between true independents and leaners, who are just as partisan and unlikely to be persuaded as those who self-identify as weak members of a particular party. Unfortunately, we can do little to resolve this problem. Self-identified independents represent a very small group (179 observations), providing less than fifty observations per cell. Randomized treatments on such small groups offer insufficient statistical power. As a second-best alternative, we use only independents who registered to vote. This choice should bias against finding differences between independent and partisan voters.

equivalent. This assumption may be cavalier, as a shift from a score of 2 ("slightly less likely to vote") to 3 (no difference), may be very different from a shift from 4 ("slightly more likely") to 5 ("much more likely"). To address this problem, many social science scholars have adopted the use of the ordered probit (*oprobit*) specification for regression analysis (McKelvey and Zavoina 1975).[6]

Table 7.2 displays an ordered probit analysis of the two treatment dimensions on voter choice. Model 1 presents the results for the entire sample. Both investment attraction and tax incentives are significant at the 95% level. Receiving an investment project increases the probability of a vote for the governor by 18.2% (option 4: 6.7%; option 5: 11.5%), whereas offering an incentive increases the likelihood of a vote for the governor by 3.4% (option 4: 2.1%; option 5: 1.3%).

While these results are strong, one concern is that responses to the treatments may be correlated with characteristics of the respondent, leading to omitted variable bias. By design, randomized survey experiments are meant to sidestep this problem by ensuring that voter characteristics are orthogonal to the treatments, and the descriptive statistics in Table 7A show a clear balance across covariates. Nevertheless, while the treatments are randomly assigned, governors are not. The treatments may therefore have differential effects depending on the interaction between voters and governors.

To address this problem, Model 2 adds two state-level additional control variables that are critical in the electoral performance of incumbent governors – the previous year's state-level approval ratings and unemployment. In states with highly unpopular governors, the treatment may be too weak to sway vote choices. The opposite may be true in states with very popular governors or with excellent economic performances over the past year. How much more certain can a voter be that he or she would vote for the incumbent? State-level approval rating proves statistically significant but substantively small. Each 1% increase in prior approval ratings increases the likelihood of a vote increase by 0.02%. The effect of unemployment, however, is not statistically different from zero. Most importantly, our treatment variables are not affected.

The two controls above are insufficient to rule out state-level effects. There is a possibility that our results are driven by unobservable factors among a small group of states where changes in voter choice are most likely. State fixed effects in Model 3 allow us to address unobserved state-

---

[6] Use of this specification also addresses problems of heteroskedasticity in multiple regressions and eliminates the possibility of a predicted probability for a particular unit on the scale that is larger than 1.

Table 7.2 Ordered probit model of likelihood of voting for governor

Dependent variable: likelihood of voting for governor in next election	Full sample				Independents				Democrats				Republicans			
	(1)	(2)	(3)	(4)	(5)	(6)	(7)	(8)	(9)	(10)	(11)	(12)	(13)	(14)	(15)	(16)
Incentive> Competitor	0.11**	0.13**	0.13**	0.15***	0.27***	0.195*	0.31***	0.333***	0.112	0.194*	0.119	0.140	−0.00520	−0.0278	−0.00793	−0.0124
	(0.0493)	(0.0550)	(0.0497)	(0.0516)	(0.103)	(0.117)	(0.110)	(0.112)	(0.0916)	(0.103)	(0.0948)	(0.0984)	(0.0985)	(0.109)	(0.107)	(0.110)
Received investment	0.576***	0.570***	0.570***	0.582***	0.622***	0.629***	0.688***	0.728***	0.588***	0.585***	0.599***	0.611***	0.445***	0.461***	0.491***	0.541***
	(0.0516)	(0.0575)	(0.0520)	(0.0545)	(0.108)	(0.123)	(0.113)	(0.114)	(0.0958)	(0.107)	(0.102)	(0.106)	(0.102)	(0.114)	(0.111)	(0.115)
Governor approval 2010 (State-level)		0.00538***				0.000669				0.000539				0.0121***		
		(0.00219)				(0.00410)				(0.00433)				(0.00463)		
State unemployment 2009–2010 (State-level)		0.0121				0.0411				−0.0418				0.0846**		
		(0.0189)				(0.0402)				(0.0341)				(0.0393)		
Pre-test governor approval (Individual-level)				0.463***				0.465***				0.440***				0.418***
				(0.0322)				(0.0750)				(0.0676)				(0.0856)
State fixed effects	NO	NO	YES	YES	NO	NO	YES	YES	NO	NO	YES	YES	NO	NO	YES	YES
Cut point 1	−0.961***	−0.586**	−0.830***	0.216	−1.044***	−0.622	−1.461***	−0.398	−0.960***	−1.105**	−0.986***	−0.163	−0.939***	0.420	−0.592*	0.645
	(0.0480)	(0.250)	(0.172)	(0.220)	(0.107)	(0.504)	(0.315)	(0.415)	(0.0885)	(0.466)	(0.142)	(0.175)	(0.0962)	(0.525)	(0.353)	(0.458)
Cut point 2	−0.641***	−0.286	−0.507***	0.570***	−0.588***	−0.236	−0.970***	0.132	−0.645***	−0.793	−0.637***	0.204	−0.724***	0.634	−0.354	0.905*
	(0.0459)	(0.249)	(0.173)	(0.220)	(0.0986)	(0.506)	(0.317)	(0.414)	(0.0842)	(0.467)	(0.136)	(0.170)	(0.0959)	(0.523)	(0.359)	(0.464)
Cut point 3	1.010***	1.375***	1.175***	2.375***	1.005***	1.390***	0.761***	1.975***	1.040***	0.931***	1.196***	2.150***	0.976***	2.316***	1.540***	2.896***
	(0.0500)	(0.251)	(0.174)	(0.224)	(0.107)	(0.514)	(0.317)	(0.419)	(0.0932)	(0.470)	(0.145)	(0.195)	(0.103)	(0.533)	(0.363)	(0.477)
Cut point 4	1.521***	1.906***	1.698***	2.942***	1.678***	2.111***	1.512***	2.813***	1.492***	1.383***	1.686***	2.640***	1.370***	2.702***	1.988***	3.363***
	(0.0572)	(0.253)	(0.175)	(0.226)	(0.125)	(0.526)	(0.321)	(0.427)	(0.106)	(0.474)	(0.157)	(0.206)	(0.112)	(0.539)	(0.369)	(0.482)
Observations	1,974	1,595	1,974	1,874	453	356	453	441	580	468	580	552	505	411	505	491
States	50	50	50	50	50	50	50	50	50	50	50	50	50	50	50	50
Pseudo R-squared	0.0270	0.0283	0.0389	0.0890	0.0353	0.0347	0.0981	0.145	0.0281	0.0340	0.0844	0.118	0.0161	0.0238	0.0929	0.125
Log likelihood	−2523	−2029	−2523	−2400	−593.2	−459.0	−593.2	−579.0	−732.6	−584.7	−732.6	−692.4	−618.3	−508.8	−618.3	−601.3
Chi-squared	127.6	107.5	208.5		36.71	28.27	1328		38.23	37.35			19.07	21.67		

Note: Robust standard errors in parentheses. Standard errors clustered at state level. The dependent variable is measured on a 5-point scale from 1 ("much less likely") to 5 ("much more likely"). Observations drop in Models 2, 6, 10, and 14 since approval ratings were not available for all states. Chi-squared test statistic of overall model fit could not be calculated in the presence of state fixed effects in some models. *** $p<0.01$, ** $p<0.05$, * $p<0.1$

	Marginal probability of voting for governor from ordered probit								
Sample (Value selected)	Full sample		Independents		Democrats		Republicans	
	(4)	(5)	(4)	(5)	(4)	(5)	(4)	(5)
Received investment	0.0672***	0.115***	0.0930***	0.117***	0.0608***	0.122***	0.0410***	0.0918***
	(0.0074)	(0.0105)	(0.0194)	(0.020)	(0.0125)	(0.020)	(0.0112)	(0.0207)
Incentive> Competitor	0.0131**	0.0215**	0.0416***	0.0501**	0.0120	0.0229	−0.000488	−0.00108
	(0.0059)	(0.0097)	(0.0161)	(0.0195)	(0.00995)	(0.0187)	(0.00924)	(0.0204)

Note: From Models 1, 5, 9, and 13. Change in probability of selecting values 4 ("more likely") and 5 ("much more likely") from a one-unit change in the treatment variables.

level heterogeneity, ensuring that our results are not an artifact of large swings in only a handful of states. Our results are robust to this change in specification, but it is worth noting that the inclusion of state effects increases the substantive effect of investment attraction.[7]

Model 3 illustrates that our findings are robust to the inclusion of state fixed effects. Out of caution, however, we interpret the substantive effects from the unadjusted Model 1.

Finally, Model 4 controls for a respondent's governor approval rating, which is determined in the CCES preceding our experimental question. Controlling for pre-treatment governor approval does not offer a perfect baseline comparison or diff-in-diff analysis, but it does allow us to differentiate a respondent's change in views about the governor occurring as a result of the experimental treatment from the pre-treatment assessment. The control variable, which is substantively large and statistically significant, indicates that many respondents held to their opinions of the governor despite the new information. Nevertheless, the additional control strengthens the marginal effects of both the incentives and investment attraction.

For the next three panels of Table 7.2, we re-run all four models but restrict the analysis to independents, Democrats, and Republicans, respectively. All three groups are positively affected by the attraction of new investment, but the effect for independents is greater than the other two groups. Investment attraction has less impact on Republican voting than the national average. When it comes to incentives, differences become even starker. Offering incentives greater than the next competitor has a positive impact on voting for the governor only among independent voters. In Model 5, the marginal effect of incentives on the probability of independents voting for a governor is 9.2%. The impact for Democrats and Republicans is not significantly different from zero.

Conditional Effects of Incentives

Hypothesis 2 stated that voters respond more favorably to investment incentives if the state loses the project rather than gaining it. Drawing on the economics literature, voters may be unwilling to pay incentives for investments that they believe the state would have won anyway. Tentative support for this conclusion was found in the comparison of means in Table 7.1. To test the conditional effect of investment incentives more rigorously, we interact the two treatment dimensions in Table 7.3. Model

---

[7] A substantial econometric literature has expressed concerns about fixed effects leading to bias in probit and logit estimates (Abrevaya 1997; Katz 2001; Greene 2004; and Coupe 2005). This bias, however, is thought to be most pronounced when the number of dummy variables is less than twenty. As we have fifty states, the bias should be limited.

1 performs the analysis for the full sample, whereas Model 2 limits the observations to independents. Models 3 and 4 demonstrate that the results survive state fixed effects, while Models 5 and 6 add the pretreatment, respondent-level governor approval rating.

Caution should be taken in interpreting the interaction effects in Table 7.3. Norton et al. (2004) have shown that the calculation of interaction effects in non-linear models is not analogous to linear models; therefore, coefficients cannot be read directly off regression tables, and signs of the effects may differ across levels of the component variables in the interaction. Thus we take care to appropriately calculate the predicted effects for all four treatment possibilities.[8] The marginal effects of incentives under different conditions are displayed in Table 7.4.

Beginning with the baseline treatment in the full sample (no project, no extra incentive), we find that the predicted probability of options 4 and 5 (higher likelihood of voting for the governor) is 14.5%. Respondents who learned that their state won the investment without offering a greater incentive had a predicted probability of voting for the governor of 35%; this 20% marginal effect of investment attraction is statistically significant at the 0.05 level. For states that offered a greater incentive but did not attract investment, the predicted probability of voting for the governor was 19.6%. Investment in the presence of greater incentives increased the predicted probability of voting for the governor to 42.7%, thus the marginal effect of investment attraction in the presence of incentives (shifting from Group 3 to Group 4) is 23.1%.

The marginal effect of investment attraction is less interesting than the marginal effects of tax incentives, and far more interesting from the perspective of our pandering model is the marginal effect of greater tax incentives on voter behavior. We depict these effects in Table 7.4. The results clearly indicate that incentives are less effective in generating votes when the state has successfully attracted the project. When the project is won, incentives only provide the incumbent governor 0.032% of the vote among all respondents, which is not significantly different from zero. Incentives offered in a losing effort, however, are far more beneficial, providing the governor with a statistically significant vote bonus of 5.2%, consistent with Hypothesis 2. For independents, incentives offer even greater opportunities for credit claiming, increasing votes for the governor by 5.6% in a winning effort, which is about half their impact on votes garnered in the losing effort (10.6%) – a statistically significant difference.

---

[8] Norton et al.'s (2004) prepackaged program *inteff* for analyzing non-linear interactions is only applicable to dichotomous variables; however, its intuition has been built into STATA's *prvalue*, which can be used with the *oprobit* model. Once again, we use Models 1 and 2 to calculate substantive effects to avoid any positive bias that may be caused by the presence of fixed effects.

Table 7.3 Conditional effects of experimental treatments on vote

		Ordered probit (5-point scale)					Probit (dichotomous)
Dependent variable: likelihood of voting for governor in next election	Full sample (1)	Independents (2)	Full sample (3)	Independents (4)	Full sample (5)	Independents (6)	Full sample (7)
Incentive> Competitor	0.204***	0.391***	0.222***	0.523***	0.278***	0.632***	0.170**
	(0.073)	(0.102)	(0.076)	(0.128)	(0.081)	(0.139)	(0.081)
Received investment	0.673***	0.740***	0.668***	0.906***	0.711***	1.031***	0.156
	(0.072)	(0.153)	(0.076)	(0.183)	(0.061)	(0.173)	(0.134)
Incentive* investment	−0.195**	−0.244	−0.197**	−0.448**	−0.258***	−0.616***	−0.082
	(0.099)	(0.180)	(0.099)	(0.220)	(0.090)	(0.230)	(0.102)
Pre-test governor approval (Individual-level)					0.465***	0.475***	
					(0.036)	(0.063)	
Governor approval 2010 (State level)							0.002
							(0.002)
Incentive* approval							−0.003*
							(0.002)
Investment approval							0.002
							(0.003)
Incentive* investment* approval							0.001
							(0.002)
Unemployment 2009–2010							0.002
							(0.009)
State fixed effects	NO	NO	YES	YES	YES	YES	NO
Cut point 1	−0.916***	−0.990***	−0.774***	−1.370***	0.289***	−0.270*	
	(0.057)	(0.099)	(0.053)	(0.087)	(0.109)	(0.160)	

Cut point 2	-0.596***	-0.531***	-0.450***	-0.872***	0.644***	0.272*
	(0.048)	(0.088)	(0.041)	(0.085)	(0.099)	(0.163)
Cut point 3	1.058***	1.066***	1.235***	0.871***	2.454***	2.140***
	(0.070)	(0.127)	(0.066)	(0.109)	(0.102)	(0.199)
Cut point 4	1.569***	1.737***	1.758***	1.621***	3.022***	2.978***
	(0.072)	(0.145)	(0.069)	(0.139)	(0.110)	(0.218)
Observations	1,974	453	1,974	453	1,874	441	1,595
States	50	50	50	50	50	50	50
Pseudo R-squared	0.0278	0.0365	0.0396	0.102	0.0903	0.152	0.0538
Log likelihood	-2523	-593.2	-2523	-593.2	-2400	-579.0	176.9

Note: Robust standard errors in parentheses. Standard errors clustered at state level. For Models 1—6, the dependent variable is measured on a 5-point scale from 1 ("much less likely") to 5 ("much more likely"). Model 5 uses a dichotomous variable if the ordinal scale is equal to 4 or 5. The table depicts marginal effects for Model 7. Observations drop in Model 7 since approval ratings were not available for all states. *** $p<0.01$, ** $p<0.05$, * $p<0.1$

Table 7.4 *Marginal effects of tax incentive greater than competing states (Change in probability of voting for governor in next election)*

All respondents			Independents		
State won investment project			State won investment project		
Much less likely	−0.001	(−0.0162, 0.0143)	Much less likely	−0.0115	(−0.0340, 0.0110)
Slightly less likely	−0.0006	(−0.0007, −0.0005)	Slightly less likely	−0.0122	(−0.0165, −0.0078)
No change	−0.0016	(−0.0017, −0.0016)	No change	−0.0328	(−0.0352, −0.0304)
Slightly more likely	0.0009	(0.0008, 0.0010)	Slightly more likely	0.0184	(0.0136, 0.0232)
Much more likely	0.0023	(−0.0342, 0.0388)	Much more likely	0.0381	(−0.0365, 0.1126)
State lost investment project			State lost investment project		
Much less likely	−0.0485	(−0.0811, −0.0159)	Much less likely	−0.0774	(−0.1364, −0.0183)
Slightly less likely	−0.0153	(−0.0176, −0.0130)	Slightly less likely	−0.042	(−0.0537, −0.0303)
No change	0.0122	(0.0083, 0.0161)	No change	0.0128	(−0.0025, 0.0282)
Slightly more likely	0.0237	(0.0214, 0.0261)	Slightly more likely	0.0586	(0.0487, 0.0686)
Much more likely	0.0278	(0.0088, 0.0468)	Much more likely	0.0479	(0.0112, 0.0845)

Note: 95% confidence intervals in parentheses. Results derived from Table 7.3 (Models 1 and 2). Marginal effects for interactions are calculated with STATA's prvalue function (Long and Freese 2005).

That incentives pay political dividends even in losing efforts is important because this strategy can be a dominant one for governors under certain conditions. An incumbent governor will receive a large vote bonus from investment relocation in his or her state and a slightly smaller, extra vote bonus from offering the incentive. If the governor loses the project, however, voters will still reward the governor for his or her effort, demonstrated by the incentive. Thus, both in our model and empirical analysis, an incumbent benefits from offering a tax incentive to a highly visible project.

A final empirical consideration is whether it is safe to generalize across states. The large substantive size of state fixed effects in these models leads to the hypothesis that credit claiming via incentives may be contingent on state-level economic and political factors. In Model 5, we explore this conditional hypothesis by interacting state governor approval numbers at the time of the survey with the two treatment dimensions.[9] The model demonstrates that governor approval negatively conditions investment incentives. In other words, highly popular governors benefit less from investment incentives than unpopular governors.

Figure 7.1 charts the interaction effect between incentives and approval. The chart shows persuasively that whether a state wins or

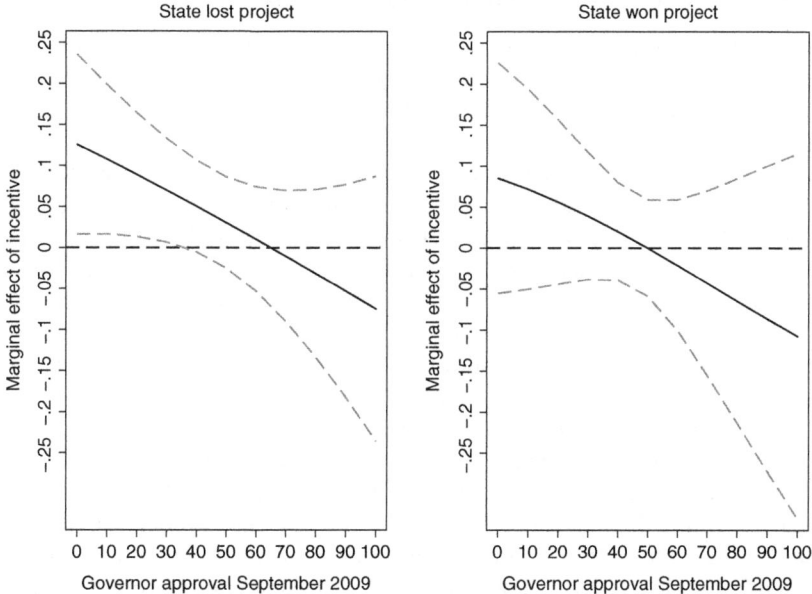

Figure 7.1 Marginal effect of offering a tax incentive greater than the competitor's conditioned by the governor approval rating (derived from Model 5, Table 7.4).

Note: On the y-axis we plot the marginal effect of incentives on changing one's vote for the governor, and on the x-axis, governor approval in 2009. The solid line charts predicted change in the probability of voting in favor of the governor when a greater incentive is offered. Dashed lines depict 95% confidence intervals. Panels are separated according to whether the state won or lost the investment. Marginal effects of triple interaction calculated using STATA's *prvalue* function (Long and Freese 2005).

---

[9] Interactions with state unemployment figures were substantively small and not statistically different from 0. Note that approval numbers are only available for thirty-three states.

loses the project, the vote bonus of offering the incentive declines with popularity. The positive effect of the incentives is only statistically significant for unpopular governors (below 50% approval) in losing efforts.[10]

The results indicate that offering incentives works best as part of a gambling-for-resurrection strategy, whereby unpopular governors have a higher incentive to engage in economically risky policy that might play well with voters.

7.3 What Do Voters Know About Incentives?

A potential concern when assessing the results of our core experiment is that it may artificially create knowledge of state-level investment incentives. If, in reality, voters do not know whether their states have offered investment incentives, the ability for politicians to use them as credit-claiming mechanisms would be severely impinged. Substantial debate exists in the empirical literature about the true policy knowledge of respondents. In a seminal paper, Aldrich et al. (1989) found that voters were more knowledgeable about foreign affairs than had been previously acknowledged, but specific incentive packages may be too nuanced even for informed voters. Furthermore, focal points – a common substitute for limited policy information – may not be available on such a narrow topic (Lupia and McCubbins 1998).

To analyze this issue, a separate item in the survey instrument asked voters to answer a simple yes/no query about whether they had knowledge of their states' investment incentives. On average, about 25% of respondents claimed they had such knowledge. To put this number in perspective, it is roughly equivalent to the proportion of Americans who say they attend church regularly. The percentage is sizable enough to offer sufficient rewards for credit claiming.

More importantly, significant differences are found across the political orientation of candidates, confirming Basinger and Lavine's (2005) results. As Figure 7.2 reveals, independents – the target audience for credit claiming, with a mean of 30.7% – are marginally more likely than partisan voters (23.8%) to claim knowledge of state incentives.[11] This mean ranking is robust to multiple regression analyses, controlling for candidate-level characteristics. Extrapolating to the electorate as whole,

---

[10] Unfortunately, this same effect cannot be estimated efficiently for independents since too few observations have been generated by the two treatments and interactions in each of the cells.

[11] Republicans and Democrats have almost identical levels of self-reported knowledge (23.8%).

7.3 What Do Voters Know About Incentives?

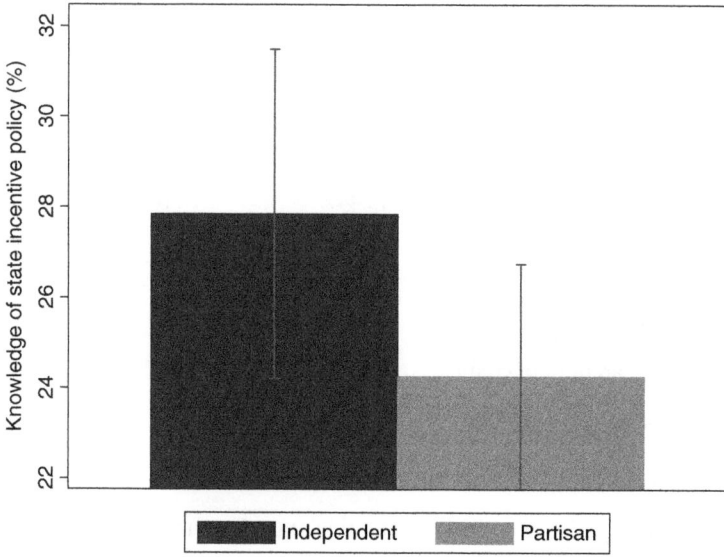

Figure 7.2 Respondent knowledge of investment incentives. Note: 95% confidence intervals.

25% of constituents and 30% of registered independent voters are certainly sizable enough groups to influence election results.

Beyond the survey results, in which voters may inflate true knowledge to avoid embarrassment, a simple LexisNexis search of US newspapers reveals 507 stories in the past two years about tax or other incentives offered by individual states. Many states also have investment promotion bureaus online that publicize incentive policies offered to particular investors.[12] It is clear that there are significant political benefits to informing voters about these activities.

A 2012 follow-up survey to our original survey experiment, where we repeated the analysis (see Chapter 10), includes another aspect worth noting. In that survey, we included an additional follow-up question to all respondents. Respondents who were told that their state won an investment were provided the following question:

How much credit do you think the Governor deserves for attracting this investment?

---

[12] See, for example, Nevada Governor's Office of Economic Development. 2016. www.expand2nevada.com/globaltrade.html.

Table 7.5 *Assigning credit or blame to the governor*

	Credit	Blame
Great deal	6.64%	13.14%
Fair amount	26.76%	18.02%
Some	39.32%	36.11%
Very little	13.84%	16.80%
None	3.31%	4.89%
Don't know	10.13%	11.05%

(1) A great deal of credit.
(2) A fair amount of credit.
(3) Some credit.
(4) Very little credit.
(5) No credit.
(6) Don't know.

Individuals who were told that their state lost an investment were provided this question:

How much blame do you think the Governor deserves for not attracting this investment?

(1) A great deal of blame.
(2) A fair amount of blame.
(3) Some blame.
(4) Very little blame.
(5) No blame.
(6) Don't know.

The results are striking (Table 7.5). Over 30% of respondents think their governor either deserves a great deal or a fair amount of the credit or blame.[13]

7.4 Credit Claiming in the United Kingdom

Thus far in this chapter we have focused on US subnational competition for investment, showing systematic evidence for the use of tax incentives for credit claiming and blame avoidance. US governors can offer lucrative financial incentives to firms, and if a firm comes to a governor's state, the governor reaps additional credit; if the investor chooses another state, the governor receives less blame.

As part of a survey experiment fielded in the United Kingdom in 2012, we had the opportunity to field an additional two questions to compare

---

[13] We do not find any clear pattern on how incentives affect this credit or blame attribution.

7.4 Credit Claiming in the United Kingdom

our results in the United States with the United Kingdom. The United States shares some commonalities and some important differences with the United Kingdom that are worth noting. The most important of these is that the majority of incentives provided in the United States are largely unregulated by the US federal government, while UK incentives are tightly regulated by the European Union (see Chapter 2). The ability to offer incentives in wealthier parts of the country is severely limited in the United Kingdom, and regional aid rules for incentives must be met, even in its poorest regions. Our experiment in the United Kingdom focuses on *international* competition for investment.

With these major differences aside, we fielded the following question, which is similar to our question in the United States, as part of a nationally representative Internet survey of 1,500 respondents through YouGov UK. The survey is thus extremely comparable to the US survey. Our question wording is as follows:

We now present you with a hypothetical scenario on government tax incentives.
 Britain competed with a number of other countries over a new manufacturing plant with 200 employees. With the support of the Prime Minister's party, Britain offered a tax incentive (break/reduction) package that was greater than that of competitor countries. If Britain receives this investment, how would this affect your evaluation of the government's performance in office?

(1) I would be much more likely to vote for the Prime Minister's party in the next election.
(2) I would be slightly more likely to vote for the Prime Minister's party in the next election.
(3) My vote choice would not be altered.
(4) I would be slightly less likely to vote for the Prime Minister's party in the next election.
(5) I would be much less likely to vote for the Prime Minister's party in the next election.

We present our results in Table 7.5, where we collapse 1 and 2 ("much more likely" and "slightly more likely") into a single variable coded 1 if respondents indicate they are more likely to vote for the prime minister and 0 otherwise. In sharp contrast to our results for US governors, we find very little difference in how individuals assign credit or blame based on the incentives offered. Prime ministers who attract investment receive an additional 22–23% of voters, indicating that they are more likely to vote for the prime minister, which is in line with the US experiment. What differs, however, is that the effect does not vary by whether the respondent was treated with incentives greater than those in other countries or less than/equal to those in other countries.

118   Political Pandering in the United States

Table 7.6 *Support for the UK prime minister*

	Incentive	No incentive
Investment	0.2233	0.23
	(.1893,.2614)	(.1959,.268)
No investment	0.1032	0.0806
	(.08,.1321)	(.0599,.1075)

Note: 95% confidence intervals in parentheses.

We find similar results for the "blame avoidance" hypothesis. Table 7.5 shows that there is little difference between individuals likely to support the prime minister in the next election if larger incentives are given. As an additional test, we also created a variable coded 1 if the respondent was less likely to vote for the prime minister (combining "much less likely" and "slightly less likely" into a single category). Again, we find very little difference if incentives are offered (not reported).

What explains the differences in the US and the UK results? One possibility is that while US governors are perceived as having much control over investment in their respective districts, prime ministers may be assigned less responsibility. Equally relevant is that while individuals in the United States may believe that their politicians have a lot of power, UK citizens may be more skeptical of the power wielded by their elected officials.[14]

Fortunately, we included a follow-up question, similar to the question that we presented in the previous section on credit and blame:

How much blame do you think the Prime Minister's party deserves for not attracting this investment?
(1) A great deal of blame.
(2) A fair amount of blame.
(3) Some blame.
(4) Very little blame.
(5) No blame.
(6) Don't know.

We present the survey-weighted responses in Table 7.7 and include the information from Table 7.5 to make a direct comparison to the United States. The responses are strikingly similar between the United States and the United Kingdom, with the exception of UK respondents being more

---

[14] For recent work on how the "clarity of responsibility" affects evaluations of political leaders, see Hellwig (2008) and Hellwig and Samuels (2008).

Table 7.7 *Credit and blame in the United States and the United Kingdom*

	Credit (US)	Credit (UK)	Blame (US)	Blame (UK)
Great deal	6.64%	4.86%	13.14%	12.22%
Fair amount	26.76%	18.16%	18.02%	17.83%
Some	39.32%	34.63%	36.11%	29.93%
Very little	13.84%	15.63%	16.80%	16.3%
None	3.31%	11.73%	4.89%	4.78%
Don't know	10.13%	14.87%	11.05%	18.65%

likely to indicate "don't know" to both the credit and blame questions than US respondents. Yet, overall, individuals in the United States and the United Kingdom hold their government officials accountable for attracting investment.

7.5 Conclusion

In this chapter, we address politicians' political motivations in offering generous incentives to attract investment projects despite the uncertainty of their economic benefits. Rather than focus on uninformed politicians or distributional considerations, we constructed a pandering theory in Chapter 2 in which politicians provide incentives even if they are well aware of their ineffectiveness. Politicians use incentives to take credit for new investment or to deflect blame for investment that locates in other states – and thus reap electoral rewards for an economically inefficient policy.

This chapter tests our theory from Chapter 2, using a survey experiment of a nationally representative sample of Americans and finding strong evidence that voters, especially independents, are more likely to vote for incumbent politicians who use incentives to attract investment. Politicians are rewarded more strongly if they offer incentives in a losing effort, making this strategy a dominant one under certain economic conditions. In fact, regardless of a state's chances of winning a project, the governor should demonstrate some public effort by offering an incentive package better than those offered by other states. Finally, we show that the motivation for governors to offer investment is mediated by their approval rating. Popular governors have less need to gamble for resurrection by pursuing economically damaging but politically advantageous policies. In addition, we highlight a number of other provocative findings on the relationship between incentives, voters, and credit.

Our findings have broader implications for the relationship between globalization and the state. While numerous scholars have examined how trade and investment can constrain state behavior, few have focused on how globalization affects political accountability. We find evidence that movement of capital can provide politicians with opportunities to pander to the public and take credit for new investment naturally flowing into their districts. Thus, rather than making domestic politics irrelevant, globalization can lead to increased political activity, in the midst of which politicians take credit or mitigate blame for globalization's economic outcomes. As politicians become more constrained in their ability to make policy choices, such as monetary policy, we may see an increased incentive for highly visible politicians to take credit for global market forces.

Our results from the United Kingdom are less clear. While we find that politicians do receive credit for the attraction of investment, there is less clear-cut evidence that politicians can use incentives to claim credit or avoid blame. We suggest that this could be due to the complicated nature of UK incentives, largely constrained by EU rules at the time of the survey.

Despite no direct evidence for the positive benefits of incentives use in the United Kingdom, there are no obvious costs to their use. If an incentive *might* help relocate a firm, politicians are free to use money from the public coffers without fear of any blowback.

Appendix Table 7.A1   *Sample characteristics by treatment group*

Sample characteristics	No FDI. No incentive		FDI. No incentive		No FDI. Incentive		FDI. Incentive	
(Number of observations)			522		489		509	477
Likelihood vote for governor	Mean	SE	Mean	SE	Mean	SE	Mean	SE
Five-point scale	2.76	0.05	3.37	0.05	2.95	0.05	3.38	0.05
Dichotomous	14.3%	1.5%	36.0%	2.2%	17.9%	1.7%	37.2%	2.2%
Demographics	Mean	SE	Mean	SE	Mean	SE	Mean	SE
Age	46.7	0.7	46.8	0.7	46.3	0.7	45.0	0.7
Male	43.5%	2.2%	46.2%	2.3%	46.6%	2.2%	44.0%	2.3%
White	71.3%	2.0%	72.1%	2.0%	71.9%	2.0%	73.4%	2.0%

7.5 Conclusion

(*cont.*)

Sample characteristics	No FDI. No incentive		FDI. No incentive		No FDI. Incentive		FDI. Incentive	
Black or Hispanic	22.0%	1.8%	22.6%	1.9%	22.8%	1.9%	21.2%	1.9%
Church attendance[a]	3.85	0.08	3.83	0.08	3.81	0.08	3.88	0.08
Protestant	41.4%	2.2%	40.9%	2.2%	42.4%	2.2%	41.3%	2.3%
Rural resident	15.9%	1.6%	15.6%	1.6%	13.8%	1.5%	13.4%	1.6%
Urban resident	36.0%	2.1%	36.3%	2.2%	39.7%	2.2%	36.3%	2.2%
Party affiliation	*Mean*	*SE*	*Mean*	*SE*	*Mean*	*SE*	*Mean*	*SE*
Democrat	36.8%	2.1%	35.7%	2.2%	34.6%	2.1%	34.8%	2.2%
Republican	24.7%	1.9%	26.7%	2.0%	26.7%	2.0%	32.1%	2.1%
Independent	28.4%	2.0%	27.7%	2.0%	26.5%	2.0%	26.4%	2.0%
Pre-test governor approval	2.24	0.04	2.32	0.04	2.22	0.04	2.29	0.04
Partisan distance from gov.	2.26	0.08	2.25	0.08	2.39	0.08	2.17	0.08
Economics	*Mean*	*SE*	*Mean*	*SE*	*Mean*	*SE*	*Mean*	*SE*
Employed full-time	38.3%	2.1%	39.4%	2.2%	41.3%	2.2%	37.1%	2.2%
Unemployed or part-time	17.0%	1.6%	16.6%	1.7%	18.3%	1.7%	22.0%	1.9%
Union member	30.8%	2.0%	31.2%	2.1%	30.3%	2.0%	30.3%	2.0%
Home owner	67.8%	2.0%	69.4%	2.1%	67.0%	2.1%	62.3%	2.2%
Stock owner	46.1%	2.2%	49.5%	2.3%	48.7%	2.2%	45.9%	2.3%
Taken economics class	53.8%	2.2%	51.2%	2.3%	53.6%	2.2%	48.6%	2.3%
Economic performance[b]	1.99	0.05	2.05	0.05	1.99	0.05	2.03	0.05

[a] Six-point scale ranging from 1 ("more than once a week") to 6 ("never").
[b] Retrospective assessment of economic performance, ranging from 1 ("much worse") to 5 ("much better").

8 Pandering Upward
Tax Incentives and Credit Claiming in Authoritarian Countries

In July 2005, Vietnam's Ministry of Finance cited thirty-three provinces which had provided super incentives – tax incentives beyond those permitted under central law (Burke and Nguyen 2005; Vu Long 2005). Such incentives include tax holidays as long as twenty years, free land rental for foreign-invested projects, and lower profits taxes (Thai Press Reports 2006). These policies tended to be one-off gifts to new investors. As an official from the province of Binh Duong's Department of Planning and Investment noted, "Incentives are merely cosmetic and are thus unsustainable," – a bit like putting lipstick on a pig (Mekong Private Sector Development Facility 2004). Eventually, these incentives were declared invalid by the General Department of Taxation, and the Vietnamese government moved to terminate all of the fence-breaking incentives.[1]

The official further contrasted the experience with the super incentives to that of Binh Duong. The province is a hotbed of foreign investment activity that accounts for over a quarter of Vietnam's FDI attraction and output. It did not offer targeted incentives. "What's most important," the official commented, "is to create a transparent and enabling business environment" (Mekong Private Sector Development Facility 2004, p. 2). His anecdotal analysis of the incentives is consistent with a more rigorous empirical analysis, which found that the use of these fence-breaking incentives was uncorrelated with investment attraction and implementation. In short, investors did not appear to consider super incentives in their long-term decisions (Vu Thanh et al. 2007; Malesky 2008a). More surprisingly, super incentives did not even appear to lead to higher profitability among foreign firms, which are the disproportionate recipients of most incentives in Vietnam. Despite the significant discounts on taxes and land fees that were registered to investors over the

---

[1] Although they maintained national incentives and continued to allow provinces a great deal of discretion in offering a range of fiscal incentives for investors locating in industrial zones or areas designated as underdeveloped areas. We exploit the variation in these targeted policies in our tests below.

time period, the average foreign investor was over four times more profitable in provinces without super incentives (VND 23.8 billion per year) than in provinces with them (VND 5.5 billion per year) (Malesky 2008a).

The story of the thirty-three fence-breakers presents an important puzzle for the larger theoretical argument that we have made thus far in the book. In almost every way, the story mirrors the general pattern that we observed in our detailed empirical analyses of the United States. As in Chapter 3, we find that intense competition between subnational governments to lure investment contributed to the allocation of various targeted incentives to investors. And as in Chapter 4, these incentives appear to be highly ineffective. They were not correlated with actual investment attraction or performance, which was instead predominantly explained by infrastructure, human capital, proximity to markets, and the general regulatory environment (Vu Thanh et al. 2007).

The key difference, however, is that Vietnam is an authoritarian single-party regime with the top leadership selected internally by elite party members in the Central Committee. The highly manipulated elections to the Vietnamese legislature are contrary to the democratic elections we observed in our analysis of gubernatorial and city elections in the United States (Malesky and Schuler 2011). In this sense, the presence of incentives offers a sharp challenge to the electoral competition story articulated thus far in the book.

To see the conundrum, it might be helpful to briefly review the logic of our argument. In Chapter 2, we argued that incentives were a form of political pandering; in other words, politicians use the incentives to identify themselves in voters' minds with large and important investment projects. Even though politicians are aware that the direct effects of incentives are highly uncertain and can even be costly, they can rely on rationally ignorant voters (Tullock 2005; Downs 1957) who deem incentives to be effective. Politicians take advantage of this information asymmetry to take credit for attracting investments or to escape blame if investors ultimately chose different localities. In survey experiments, we showed that voters do indeed reward politicians who offer incentives, whether or not companies actually came to the locality. In Chapter 5, we demonstrated that US mayors, who were subject to direct elections, offered more lucrative incentives to firms than city managers, who were connected to voters only indirectly through the oversight of the elected city council. Thus, we concluded that electoral competition is a key driver of the proliferation of fiscal incentives in the United States and throughout the world.

If electoral pandering is the answer, then what explains the widespread use of incentives in Vietnam? As we reviewed throughout the book, incentives are seldom effective in attracting investment and are excessively costly. In our own original data collection in this chapter, we find that roughly two-thirds of foreign firms that received incentives and invested in Vietnam indicated that the incentives did not affect their investment decisions. This ratio is strikingly similar to Chapter 4's review of the cross-national findings on the redundancy of incentives and to our own survey of firms accessing the Kansas PEAK program. The majority of incentives have no impact on the locational decisions of firms.

Vietnam's story is actually reflective of a larger, global pattern. Incentives are allocated to firms by governments around the world with little evidence that these are effective economic development policies. Yet this finding on the use of incentives in an authoritarian context is seemingly at odds with our theory and evidence on the role of political pandering in the use of incentives. Scholars who have looked closely at incentives have actually concluded that authoritarian countries offer greater tax incentives to foreign investors than their democratic counterparts, both in terms of the variety and size of the reductions (Li 2006, 2016; Klemm and Van Parys 2012).

If economically inefficient policies are generated by political pandering, why do we observe the use of these policies in systems with few motivations for *electoral* pandering? In this chapter, we explore the reasons for this puzzle. Using cross-national data, we demonstrate that the authoritarian anomaly is conditioned by whether the authoritarian country has strong mechanisms of meritocratic promotion for subnational leaders. In these countries, the *upward* accountability generated by the promotion mechanism substitutes for the downward accountability to voters. In other words, the higher incentives observed in authoritarian countries results from the pandering of subnational leaders *to their central benefactors*. By contrast, regimes characterized by personalism – where promotion is based more on loyalty performance – are less likely to harness incentives as an economic development strategy. To explore these insights more deeply, we employ rigorous causal inference designs and precise micro-level data to test the logic of our pandering-upward argument in Vietnam – an archetype of the single-party system – and Putin's Russia, a prime example of growing personalism.

The importance of this chapter for our larger contribution cannot be understated. Our theoretical model explains that the use of incentives can be explained by patterns of accountability at the national and subnational levels. Elected officials attempting to retain their positions must show to their constituency that they are delivering benefits, including investment, to their districts. While the accountability links between citizens and elites is more tenuous in authoritarian regimes, politicians are far from unaccountable. As we have noted, accountability in many authoritarian contexts is upward since local and regional officials are dependent on the central government for political survival and advancement. We argue that variation in electoral accountability within these regimes is key to understanding the use of incentives in nondemocratic contexts.

8.1 Pandering Upward in Single-Party Regimes

To begin to answer the puzzle of authoritarian incentives, it is helpful to engage in a bit of brush clearing. A dynamic and growing literature has begun to demonstrate that the residual category of "non-democracy" obscures more than clarifies. In this section, we explore the wide variety of authoritarian regime types and the very different relationships they imply between state and citizens. Next, we drill down deeper into arguably the most successful form of authoritarianism, measured by political stability, regime duration, and economic performance – the single-party system, which includes both single-party states and hegemonic regimes.

After exploring a variety of reasons for single-party success, we highlight a less prominent feature of many of these regimes – within-party promotion of leadership positions based on concrete indicators of performance, including, in many countries, FDI attraction targets.[2] While scholars have provided evidence that promotion in some single-party regimes is based on economic performance, serious concerns have been raised about the quality of the data used in promotions and the distortionary activity that is often employed to meet targets. We suggest that this imperfect meritocracy creates an analogous asymmetric information problem to the one we observed in democracies. In this case, however, the principals are central elites and the agents are subnational officials who want to claim credit for meeting FDI attraction targets but who, like their counterparts in democratic systems, recognize that incentives may be superfluous and inefficient. In other words, single-party systems generate opportunities for pandering upward, which is why they overuse incentives. What is more, upward pandering solely accounts for the anomalous relationship between authoritarianism and fiscal incentives that has been pointed out by other scholars.

Varieties of Authoritarianism

Included in the catchall grouping of non-democracies are constitutional monarchies ruled by kings or sultans where succession is determined by

---

[2] Bell (2015) has called this feature "political meritocracy" in his analysis of Singapore and China.

family lineage (e.g., Brunei, Jordan); military juntas, where rule is monopolized by a small collective of military leaders (e.g., Thailand, Egypt); single-party states where opposition parties are outlawed and a vanguard party rules in the name of the citizens (e.g., Vietnam, China); and hegemonic/dominant parties where multiparty elections are allowed but manipulation, patronage, and fear conspire to keep the opposition from taking office (e.g., Malaysia, Singapore) (Geddes 1999a, Geddes 1999b; Brooker 2014).

Within each of these categories, we also see variation in the level of personalism, defined as power consolidation by a single individual (Svolik 2012). Where the level of personalism is high, political decisions are dominated by a small group around the top leader, and loyalty to him or her determines ascent to the top ranks (Weeks 2014; Geddes et al. 2014). Although the elite leader could have a military background or may have formed a party as a tool of power (Slater 2003), military and party institutions do not have independent decision-making authority. The top leader's discretion is the paramount decision-making mechanism (Bratton and Van de Walle 1994; Geddes 1999b; Hadenius and Teorell 2007). North Korea is an excellent example of a personalist single-party system, while Russia under Putin today provides an excellent example of a hegemonic party system with strong personalist tendencies (Isaacs and Whitmore 2014). We return to the role that personalism plays in the use of incentives below.

The Success of Single-Party States

Among various forms of autocracies, single-party regimes stand out for their performance across a number of key metrics. Single-party states are more durable than juntas and personalist regimes, and have lower failure rates and longer terms in office (Geddes 1999a; Magaloni and Kricheli 2010; Geddes et al. 2014). They are more resilient in the face of destabilizing threats, such economic crises and the rise of popular opposition (Smith 2005; Brownlee 2007; Magaloni and Kricheli 2010). They generate higher levels of economic growth (Gandhi 2008; Keefer 2009) and private investment attraction (Wright 2008; Gehlbach and Keefer 2012), and even score better in quality of governance (Charron and Lapuente 2010). Political leaders in one-party regimes are less likely to experience coups (Boix and Svolik 2013; Svolik 2012) and consequently stay longer in office (Gandhi and Przeworski 2007; Geddes 2008; Magaloni and Kricheli 2010).

Two competing theories have been offered to explain the relative success of single-party systems (Magaloni and Kricheli 2010). First, scholars argue that authoritarian ruling parties serve as a co-optation or distributive device; the rulers are able to co-opt opposition elites, distribute shares of spoils to key constituents, reward supporters, or arguably, provide for a collective action by other elites to hold their top leaders accountable (Diaz-Cayeros 2006; Lazarev 2005; Brownlee 2007; Magaloni 2008; Blaydes 2010; Gandhi 2008; Gehlbach and Keefer 2012). A second branch of the literature focuses on the benefits of party organization, including the hierarchical committee system, manipulability of cadres (i.e., the party controls groups of deployable personnel with largely interchangeable skills), and top-bottom control over agents (Schurmann 1968; Selznick 1952). Svolik's (2012) work is especially important on this point by illustrating how successful regime parties selectively recruit ideologically close elements at grassroots level and repress ideologically distant ones. Because authoritarian parties control political appointments and maintain hierarchies of services and benefits, they are able to attract the ideologically proximate segments of the population as long as old cadres retire at a sufficiently high rate. Retirement is obligated through mandatory retirement ages, which opens up space at the top and thereby convinces new recruits that their loyalty will be rewarded.[3] Authoritarian parties deter defection by encouraging sunk investment among grassroots members.

Meritocratic Promotion and Local Incentives in Single-Party Regimes

A key feature of the party organization system is how officials are promoted and advanced in single-party systems. Low-level members are forced to invest in party service and meet party goals. These credentials pay off in terms of party promotion but have little value elsewhere. Party goals are outlined, and complicated systems are put in place to decide whether officials have achieved these goals. This interjurisdictional yardstick competition promotes party objectives and breeds loyalty to the party as long as sufficient space is opened up for advancement (Maskin et al. 2000; Lazarev 2005). While performance is rewarded in many regimes, the critical difference between single-party states and other authoritarian systems is that published standards, formal review institutions like the Chinese Party Organization Committee, and clear promotional ladders from functionary to elite levels make these performance criteria more credible (Magoloni 2008; Reuter and Turovsky 2014; Reuter, forthcoming, pp. 13, 79).

Recently, Bell (2015) has been a vocal advocate for the benefits of such political meritocracy in Singapore and China, arguing that this way of

---

[3] This insight plays a critical role in our analysis of Vietnam.

selecting elite officials is better than that found in democratic polities. Evans and Rauch (1999) have also observed that developing countries with more Weberian bureaucracies (particularly characterized by meritocratic promotion) had higher levels of economic growth and investment attraction than competitors with more patrimonial and personalist-based systems. Testing this theory in China, scholars have documented correlations between economic performance and promotion to higher office (Li and Zhou 2005; Chen et al. 2005; Landry 2008; Lü and Landry 2014). On average, officials who have exceeded performance targets for growth in GDP and for revenue attraction have been the most likely to be promoted. Critically for us, Yu Zheng (2012, 2014) highlights the widespread use of FDI attraction targets for many provincial leaders in China.

Of course, dispute rages about whether meritocracy is an appropriate way to describe these systems of cadre promotion. Scholars have offered concerns about the validity of the criteria used, the problem of weighting performance on multiple (Jia et al. 2015) and often contradictory indicators (economic growth and environmental protection), and the strength of the relationship between performance on these indicators and promotion, particularly at elite levels (Shih et al. 2012). More damningly, scholars have shown that these indicators are often fabricated (Wallace 2016) or lead to distorted efforts of local officials (Gang 2009; Ghanem and Zhang 2014; Png 2013). Most relevant to our work, Chen and Kung (2016) show that local officials in China disproportionately direct public resources towards ostentatious, white elephant projects that signal their local development achievements at strategic times so that they might be rewarded for promotion. Ultimately, these gratuitous public-works projects pay little dividends and actually detract from economic growth.

It is precisely the uncertainty regarding the promotion criteria that drives the analogy with pandering in competitive regimes. In democracies, as we described in Chapter 2, the voters are the principle and the politician is the agent. In the case of single-party regimes with internal promotion criteria, the orientation of subnational officials is inverted. Their main principles are high-ranking party officials who can promote them to new positions in other provinces or central government, or nominate them for higher party offices. As with voters, however, central politicians who set the promotion criteria do not have the accurate information that subnational politicians have about the relationship between policy choices and the outcomes that the central politicians desire. In fact, Chenggang Xu (2011) argues that this information imbalance is the secret to Chinese economic success, which he terms regional decentralized authoritarianism (RDA). Central elites lay forth criteria – such as GDP growth, revenue growth, FDI attraction, and blue sky days – but

8.1 Pandering Upward in Single-Party Regimes

they remain agnostic about how subnational officials achieve these objectives (Huang 2013). On the one hand, this space allows for a great deal of local experimentation that can identify solutions to critical national issues (Xu 2011; Coase and Wang 2012). On the other hand, RDA can generate distortions when local officials attempt to use state investment and manipulation to generate spikes in growth directly prior to key promotional periods (Guo 2009; Wallace 2016; Chen and Kung 2016).

In many single-party states, there is documented evidence that attraction for foreign investment is directly or indirectly part of the promotion criteria for local officials.[4] All of these statements incentivize attraction but do not offer details on how best to achieve it in the limited time that officials are in office. Local officials can choose whether to prioritize infrastructure, land clearance, governance reforms, or education and human capital improvements. The standard policies to lure investment may be expensive and time consuming (e.g., infrastructure), may not pay in dividends before the local politician leaves office (e.g., human capital), or may antagonize rivals and subordinates in the province by depriving them of rents (e.g., governance reforms). Even more importantly, local officials may have trouble claiming credit for investment attracted by infrastructure and human capital developed by their predecessors.

As we established in Chapter 4, the use of economic development incentives has largely been identified as costly and ineffective. If we simply found that countries with single-party systems provide more pro-growth economic development policies, our work would be similar to the existing literature on the topic. Where we part ways from current thinking about single-party regimes is at the point of analyzing what drives their use of incentives; this practice is consistent with a pandering logic, wherein credit claiming generates *inefficient* economic policies. As we show below, the motivations for credit claiming can lead to the overuse of incentives even in an authoritarian context.

Thus, our line of reasoning concerning the use of incentives in authoritarian regimes is that, as in democracies, subnational officials in single-party regimes are motivated to offer incentives that tie them directly to the locational choice of a foreign company. Because central party elites have prioritized incentive attraction in promotion and because officials possess asymmetric information over central officials on the relationship between policies and outcomes (Chibber 2002), offering fiscal incentives means that officials can claim credit for attracting investment regardless of the

---

[4] On authoritarian Taiwan and Korea, see Cheng et al. (1998); for a comparison of authoritarian development states, see Doner et al. (2005); on China, see Zheng (2012, p. 12, fn13); on Singapore, see Krause (1987, p. 55) and Mauzy and Milne (2002, p. 193); on Vietnam, see Jandl (2014).

incentives' actual influence on foreign companies' choices. This leads to our first and most general hypothesis for authoritarian countries:

Hypothesis 8.1: Countries with single-party systems are more likely than other authoritarian regimes to offer incentives to foreign companies.

When this motivation is removed due to term limits or retirement age and officials are no longer eligible for promotion, they are more likely to choose policies that are closer to their private preferences (Li and Zhou 2005, p. 1747; Liang 2015, p. 291; Smart and Sturm 2013). In other words, we believe that subnational officials know that incentives are ineffective and distortionary and that they are likely to reduce the use of incentives and favor other policy options. Thus, we expect:

Hypothesis 8.2: When officials are no longer eligible for promotion, they will reduce their use of incentives compared to peers who remain eligible.

Personalism and Incentives In sharp contrast to authoritarian systems with quasi-meritocratic elements, personalist systems dampen the motivation for local officials to offer incentives to firms. A flurry of recent work has demonstrated that personalist leaders, because they have effectively silenced domestic opposition and consolidated power (Svolik 2012), behave dramatically differently in their interactions with other countries and international actors (Weeks 2008, 2014).[5]

Magaloni et al. (2013) emphasize that personalism is inherent in all authoritarian regimes and should be coded as a supplementary measure rather than a separate regime type. Thus, a country like China can vary in its level of personalism – from highly personalized under Mao to minimally personalized under Hu Jintao – while never changing its status as a single-party regime. Geddes et al. (2014) allow for personalism to be combined with other types of regimes by coding hybrids, so that a country such as Indonesia under Suharto could exemplify both personalistic and party-based traits. Similarly, Svolik's (2012) approach allows for the consolidation of leadership into an established dictator across all types of authoritarian regimes.

---

[5] Magaloni et al. (2013) offer two interrelated definitions of personalism. First, personalist regimes face fewer checks on executive power, allowing them more discretion over policy and personal choices. Second, these regimes are associated with particular individuals, although pinning down the depth of those associations is difficult. An autocratic regime overseen by a single ruler is highly personalist but could be viewed as less personalist over time as successful successions see various different individuals serving at the top. Alternatively, a group of elite decision-makers (rather than an individual) with either formal or informal powers reduces personalism; and as the single regime experiences regular leadership changes, personalism is further reduced. The less a particular regime is tied to specific individuals, the less personalist it becomes.

In personalist systems, loyalty to the top leader trumps the performance of officials (Geddes 1999b; Weeks 2014). Whereas competent leaders could potentially pose a challenge, less competent subnational officials owe their advancement to a single individual and are less likely to threaten or disobey the regime (Egorov and Sonin 2011), even when it may be in their voters' interests (Reuter and Robertson 2012). In a heavily personalist system, subnational officials will prioritize mobilizing public support for the top leadership, suppressing embarrassing displays of dissent, and promoting the leader's authority over economic growth. Reuter (forthcoming, pp. 79–85) offers a slightly different take, arguing that top personalist leaders may value competence but that promises of promotion and a share of regime spoils are not credible in the absence of clear standards and pathways forward. While explanations differ, scholars tend to agree that personalism undermines political motivations to exert effort to achieve strong economic performance. The resulting limited effort can clearly have negative consequences for economic performance, but it also restricts the benefits of upward pandering. Local government officials who see few rewards for their ability to attract investments will exert less effort. This lack of action could result in a poor provision of local public goods, a good supply of which would increase the attractiveness of the local business environment.

Our focus on incentives isolates a policy area that has been identified as inefficient, yet provides officials the opportunity to claim credit outsized for investment. Thus, our seemingly counterintuitive argument is that personalistic regimes are less likely to harness these inefficient economic development policies. This leads to our third hypothesis.

Hypothesis 8.3: In authoritarian regimes characterized by high degrees of personalism, subnational leaders will offer significantly less incentives than in other authoritarian states.

8.2 Comparing Incentives Between Democracies and Non-Democracies

In this section, we explore cross-national patterns to ask whether the observed patterns are consistent with our theoretical logic above. First, in general, do non-democracies actually provide more generous incentives than democracies? Second, do we observe greater incentive activity in single-party regimes? Third, is there an association between countries with quasi-meritocratic promotion and incentive usage? And finally, do personalist regimes demonstrate reduced incentive usage among subordinate officials?

As we pointed out in Chapter 2, it is not easy to compare incentive regimes across countries because most incentives are firm specific and reporting standards differ dramatically across countries. Two methods have been used by scholars studying comparative incentives. The first approach is to simply count up the variety of incentives that are legally allowable under the country's tax regime. Li (2006, 2016) uses US Country Commercial Guides on incentives to create a six-point scale measuring how many of the various forms of incentives are used, including value added tax, CIT, property tax, licensing fees, import duties, and sales tax (Li 2006, p. 69). Li refers to this measure as "generosity," but that is a bit of a misnomer because it does not capture specifically how generously each of these packages was applied. For example, a 20% CIT reduction is coded exactly the same as a 2% cut. Similarly, tax holidays ranging from six months to ten years are coded equally as an additional point on the six-point scale.

An alternative approach is to generate an effective tax rate based on publicly available incentives. The tax rate calculates how much firms that are entering the country could legally be given by politicians who are attempting to woo them. This estimate is still a noisy one because we do not know whether every new entrant was actually granted an incentive package and, as the Vietnamese fence-breaking indicates, government officials have been known to surpass official guidelines. Klemm et al. (2012) use this approach to calculate an effective tax rate for forty-five countries between 1996 and 2008. We present both the Klemm et al. (2012) and Li (2006) data in Table 8.1.

Table 8.1 divides the Klemm country-years into countries coded as democratic or authoritarian according to the Cheibub et al. (2010) scheme, which makes a simple distinction based on whether there has been a reversal of power in a free and fair election.[6] The first row shows that the official CIT is significantly higher for authoritarian country-years than democratic observations (30% versus 27%). The rest of the table, however, shows that the official CIT is illusory since foreign firms entering authoritarian countries pay significantly lower taxes when fiscal incentives are taken into account. Row 2, for instance, shows that authoritarian countries allow for higher depreciation allowances on invested capital. Row 3 illustrates that the effective CIT of the average firm, once tax incentives are accounted for, is also significantly lower (21% versus 23%). The same direction is true of the marginal rate paid by the newest entrants, although it is not statistically significant. Most importantly, however, the best effective tax rate, which simulates the best possible

---

[6] Most countries do not change in the Cheibub et al. schema, but a few have democratic and nondemocratic spells throughout the period: Pakistan (25% observations are democratic), Peru (58%), Senegal (60%), Mexico (67%), Nigeria (73%), Indonesia (75%), and Ecuador, Kenya, and Thailand (83%).

Table 8.1 *Average generosity of tax regime*

Variables	Authoritarian (n=193)		Democracy (n=332)		Difference	P-Value
	Mean	SD	Mean	SD		
Statutory corporate income tax	30.1%	7.0%	27.8%	8.1%	2.29%	0.00
Present discounted value of depreciation allowance	24.4%	8.3%	20.5%	8.1%	3.87%	0.00
Average effective corporate tax rate	21.4%	8.4%	23.0%	9.6%	−1.60%	0.05
Marginal effective corporate tax rate	12.3%	23.3%	14.1%	42.7%	−1.83%	0.58
Average tax rate under best regime	11.1%	12.7%	14.2%	13.4%	−3.09%	0.01
Number of possible incentives	3.78	2.03	2.00	0.00	1.78	0.00

Note: Source Klemm et al. (2012) and Li (2006).

CIT offered on the books (based on official incentive policies), is a full three percentage points lower for authoritarian countries than democracies and highly statistically significant (p<.01). Indeed, under the best effective tax regime, authoritarian countries pay only 11% CIT, which is consistent with the Li (2006) finding that authoritarian states offer a greater variety of incentive policies (3.78 policies) than democracies (2 policies).

Tax Policies by Type of Authoritarian Country

As we noted above, however, a compelling comparative politics literature has established that authoritarian countries vary significantly in their institutional designs, which has critical implications for their economic and foreign policies. In particular, we hypothesized (Hypothesis 8.1) that single-party regimes with well-developed mechanisms for advancement and promotion in the government hierarchy might be more likely to use fiscal incentives since lower-level officials take advantage of the asymmetric information that they possess compared to central leaders regarding the true relationship between incentive utilization and investment attractions. By contrast, we argued that personalist regimes (Hypothesis 8.3) where promotion was primarily based on loyalty to an established dictator and where advancement promises were less credible would be less likely to use fiscal incentives.

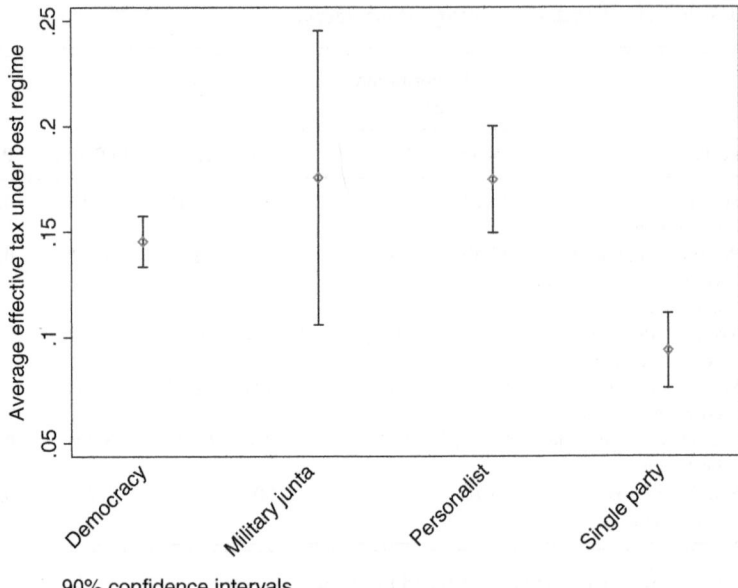

Figure 8.1 Best effective tax rates under different types of authoritarian regimes.
Note: Monarchies are dropped because the Klemm et al. (2012) data on best effective tax regime only includes one monarchy – Morocco. Classifications are based on the Geddes et al. (2014) coding system, but personalism is re-coded to include any hybrid that has a personalist element according to the authors.

Figure 8.1 provides an initial look into whether our theoretical expectations are upheld by further subdividing the Klemm et al. (2012) country-years into the classic types of authoritarian regimes first proposed by Geddes (1999a) and refined by Geddes et al. (2014).[7] The graph clearly shows that the democratic-authoritarian gap in the best effective tax rate was entirely driven by the countries classified as single-party systems, which offer a best CIT of 9.3% compared to 17% in military and personalist dictatorships/monarchies. Democratic countries offer best rates of about 14.5% on average. The plots hide a great deal of the underlying variation in best rates among regime types, so Figure 8.2 plots the full kernel densities of single-party regimes compared to all other authoritarian types. Again,

[7] Due to insufficient observations, we do not employ the hybrid categories of Geddes and simply aggregate countries by their dominant type. Similarly, personalist regimes include all countries coded as hybrids with a personalist element.

8.2 Comparing Incentives Between Democracies

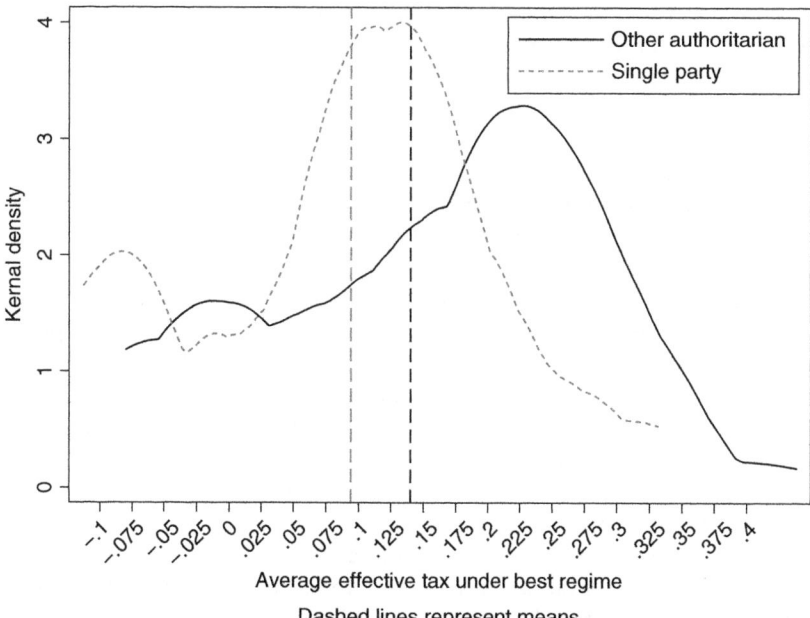

Figure 8.2 Full distribution of best effective tax rates (single party versus all authoritarian parties).
Note: Klemm et al. (2012) data on best effective tax regime. Classifications are based on the Geddes et al. (2014) coding system.

our expectations are upheld; authoritarian countries offer significantly better tax regimes for investors.

The simple difference-in-means analysis is potentially suspect due to omitted variable bias. Most importantly, we have not accounted for the global trends in greater incentives, which might be associated with changes in regime type. We have also not addressed important confounders, such as the size of the country's economy, population, and the presence of federal institutions (Li 2016). Table 8.2 uses multiple regression to test whether our main correlations hold once we address these reasonable concerns.

In Model 1, we present the same bivariate analysis from Table 8.1. Model 2 subjects the correlation to year fixed effects in order to address any trending over time, and the correlation appears robust. Model 3 adds reasonable controls for population, GDP per capita, and federalism. Once these controls are added, the democratic advantage disappears entirely. Model 4 then subdivides the authoritarian category by adding dummies for single-party and personalist dictatorships with military junta held as the reference category.[8] Even with a full set of controls, we again find that single-party regimes offer best CITs that are about nine percentage points lower than other authoritarian regimes. This relationship appears to be a function of institutional design and not underlying differences in democratic accountability. In Model 5, when we add a continuous measuring of democracy from Polity IV – which captures differences in participation, representation, and constraints on executive decision making – the coefficient hardly budges. Models 6 through 10 further test the strength of this relationship by throwing away all democracies and focusing solely on non-democracies. Here, we find that single-party states have effective CITs that are five percentage points lower than those offered by juntas. Models 8, 9, and 10 exchange the Geddes et al. (2014) coding of single-parties for the measures of single-party systems by Wright (2008), Hadenius and Teorell (2007), and Svolik (2012). These checks only strengthen the ultimate differences between single-party regimes and authoritarian alternatives.

We also find evidence consistent with Hypothesis 8.3 – that personalist regimes employ less tax incentives. In Model 8, the data demonstrates that personalist regimes have effective CITs about ten percentage points higher than juntas, on average. This figure jumps around considerably, however, since we use different operationalizations of personalism. As previously mentioned, authors have disagreed profoundly over which countries fall under this rubric (Geddes et al. 2014; Magaloni et al. 2013), although all agree on the personalism of Russia after 2006. More fine-grained approaches may be necessary to sort out the countervailing influence of personalist leaders.

Promotion and Upward Pandering

Single-party regimes and personalist regimes are somewhat blunt measures for the conceptual logic of our theory, which was really driven by the idea of imperfect, meritocratic promotion. Many single-party regimes allow the possibility for internal advancement based on an uncertain and shifting set of metrics. The incentive for promotion coupled with the uncertain relationship between the metrics used for promotion, on the one hand, and the true performance of subnational officials, on the other hand, creates similar motivations for pandering. If our theory is correct, we should observe, firstly, that single-party regimes are more likely to

---

[8] We are forced to drop the category "monarchy" since Klem only codes the tax regime for one monarchy, Morocco.

Table 8.2 *Multiple regression analysis of relationship between authoritarian type and best effective tax rate*

Dependent variable = Effective corporate income tax under best regime	All states					Only authoritarian					
	Bivariate (1)	Year FE (2)	Controls (3)	Party (4)	Polity (5)	Simple (6)	Year FE (7)	Controls (8)	Wright (9)	HT (10)	Svolik (11)
Democracy=1	0.031*** (0.012)	0.032*** (0.012)	0.001 (0.014)	−0.062*** (0.017)	−0.005 (0.021)						
Single party=1				−0.093*** (0.018)	−0.047** (0.021)	−0.052** (0.021)	−0.053** (0.021)	−0.053*** (0.018)	−0.109*** (0.028)	−0.257*** (0.029)	−0.243*** (0.029)
Personalist=1					0.094*** (0.022)	0.079*** (0.021)	0.078*** (0.022)	0.101*** (0.018)	0.049 (0.034)	0.062*** (0.018)	0.073*** (0.018)
GDP per capita (ln)			0.006 (0.008)	0.006 (0.008)	0.008 (0.008)			0.024*** (0.007)	0.018** (0.007)	0.024*** (0.006)	0.025*** (0.006)
Population (ln)			−0.011** (0.004)	−0.010** (0.004)	−0.011*** (0.004)			−0.022*** (0.005)	−0.023*** (0.006)	0.013** (0.005)	0.012** (0.005)
Federal system=1			0.079*** (0.014)	0.064*** (0.014)	0.066*** (0.013)			0.055*** (0.020)	0.061*** (0.021)	0.010 (0.017)	0.013 (0.018)
Polity IV									0.002 (0.002)	−0.001 (0.002)	0.000 (0.002)
Constant	0.111*** (0.009)	3.111*** (0.010)	0.227** (0.114)	0.300*** (0.110)	0.236** (0.109)	0.129*** (0.020)	0.131*** (0.021)	0.281** (0.115)	0.401*** (0.152)	−0.293*** (0.111)	−0.292** (0.114)
Year FE	No	Yes	Yes	Yes	Yes	No	Yes	Yes	Yes	Yes	Yes
Observations	525	525	445	433	433	181	181	178	178	178	178
R-squared	0.013	0.022	0.112	0.155	0.189	0.217	0.238	0.467	0.527	0.656	0.642
RMSE	0.132	0.132	0.128	0.123	0.120	0.108	0.110	0.0928	0.0878	0.0748	0.0764

Note: OLS regression standard errors in parentheses. The white panel includes all countries, while the shaded panel limits analysis to authoritarian countries. Regime type is coded from Geddes et al. (2014) except for models 10 and 11, which are replaced with Hadenius and Teorell (2007) coding and Svolik (2012) coding, respectively. *** $p<0.01$, ** $p<0.05$

138   Pandering Upward

offer more credible opportunities for internal advancement based on imperfect, meritocratic metrics. Secondly, we should find that these characteristics are associated with lower effective CITs.

Authoritarian countries are black boxes, and it can be difficult to know whether meritocratic promotion exists in practice. Evans and Rauch (1999) developed a nice measure of Weberian bureaucracies, but unfortunately, this data is only available for a handful of authoritarian countries. Fortunately, however, the Quality of Government Institute in Stockholm, Sweden, recently conducted an expert survey of political analysts around the world, which asked them to score their countries of interest on the exact same conditions (Teorell et al. 2011). These measures have perception bias, dependent as they are on local experts. Nevertheless, there is plenty of illustrative variation. In Figure 8.3, we

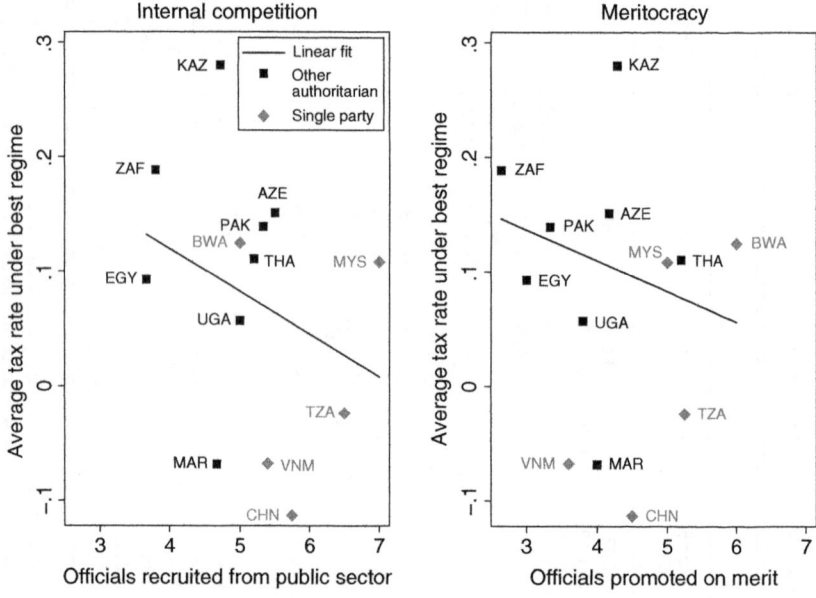

Figure 8.3 Political meritocracy and tax incentive usage.
Note: Klemm et al. (2012) data on best effective tax regime. Diamonds are single-party regimes and squares are all other regimes according to Geddes et al. (2014). The Teorell et al. (2011) expert survey is used. Left panel plots the relationship between the best CIT and experts' answers to the question, "Senior public officials are recruited from within the ranks of the public sector?" In the right panel, we plot answers the question, "When recruiting public sector employees, the skills and merits of the applicants decide who gets the job?"

8.2 Comparing Incentives Between Democracies

plot answers to two of the survey questions for the twelve countries on which the Klemm data and the Quality of Government Institute's expert survey overlap.

While only illustrative, due to the small sample size and nonrandom selection of countries, the relationships are consistent with our expectations. In the left panel, we plot the relationship between the best CIT and experts' answers to the question, "Senior public officials are recruited from within the ranks of the public sector?" In the right panel, we plot answers to the question, "When recruiting public sector employees, the skills and merits of the applicants decide who gets the job?" Both questions are coded on a seven-point scale, with 1 indicating strong disagreement and 7 indicating strong agreement. Two things are noticeable about the graph. First, single-party regimes are coded by experts as significantly more likely to recruit officials from the public sector (5.73>4.73, p=.007) and also to promote officials based on merit (5.73>4.73, p=.023). Second, an inverse correlation is evident in both graphs. Although it is not statistically significant due to the small sample size, it is clear that countries that score well on these mechanisms of meritocracy have lower effective tax rates.

By contrast, Figure 8.4 looks at personalist mechanisms drawn from the same survey. The left panel studies the relationship between the best CIT and expert answers to the question, "The top political leadership hires and fires senior public officials?" The right panel looks at answers to the question, "When recruiting public sector employees, the political connections of the applicants decide who gets the job?" Again, both questions are measured on a seven-point average scale. The first thing to notice about this picture is that while there is a negative relationship between single-party and personalist promotion practices, the top leader has much less influence over personnel decisions than in other types of authoritarian regimes (3.61<5.13, p=.006). By contrast, there is no relationship between single-parties and political connections. Especially in Vietnam, experts believe that connections are critical for advancing in the bureaucracy. Further, consistent with our theory, we see a positive relationship between personalism and the best CIT. When official promotional prospects are based on loyalty to the top leader, officials do not appear to compete by offering enormous tax incentives.

There is no relationship, however, between the importance of political connections and the size of tax incentives. Again, this result illustrates how different conceptualizations of personalism can radically change the answer to our vital question on upward pandering. When we define personalism as consolidated control of the elite leader, we see the expected relationship. When the definition is relaxed to include broader ideas of connections and loyalty, the relationship is obscured.

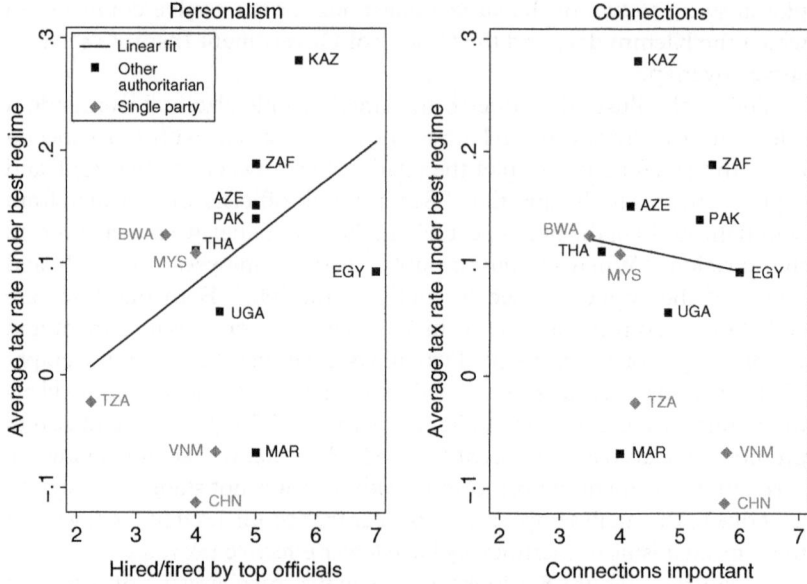

Figure 8.4 Personalist promotion and tax incentive usage.
Note: Klemm et al. (2012) data on best effective tax regime. Diamonds are single-party regimes and squares are all other regimes according to Geddes et al. (2014). The Teorell et al. (2011) expert survey is used. Left panel studies the relationship between the best CIT and expert answers to the question, "The top political leadership hires and fires senior public officials?" The right panel plots, "When recruiting public sector employees, the political connections of the applicants decide who gets the job?"

Discussion of Cross-National Results

Previous work has demonstrated a relationship between authoritarian countries and the use of fiscal incentives to lure investment (Li 2006, 2009; Klemm et al. 2012). The observed correlation, however, depends upon quite blunt measures of incentives and authoritarianism. The dependent variable accounts for the variety of the incentives but not the actual generosity in terms of the scale of the next tax reduction. And the independent measure of authoritarianism does not take into account the widely varying incentives that public officials have at their disposal to use in different types of authoritarian regimes.

Once we address these issues of conceptualization and operationalization, a very different pattern emerges. First, the difference between authoritarian and democratic countries is entirely accounted for by the subset of authoritarian countries with single-party regimes, which offer significantly more generous incentives than both their peers and democracies. Pushing the data a bit further, as we probe the mechanisms behind the effect of single-party regimes, we find that the association appears to be due to features of the promotional system. Single-party regimes are more likely to promote bureaucratic officials from within the party using meritocratic benchmarks. Moreover, the top leader's personal decisions are much less influential in the hiring and firing of lower-level subordinates. Thus, consistent with our theoretical discussion above, there appears to be evidence that meritocratic promotion combined with uncertainty about the true relationship between fiscal incentives and FDI attraction may result in pandering upward towards elite officials who are responsible for promotion decisions.

At this stage, the conclusion is highly speculative. First of all, institutions are not exogenously assigned and thus our analysis could be driven by unobserved features of the economy associated with both single-party regimes and the selection of incentives. Second, the test of mechanisms was based on a very limited sample of countries from an expert survey. Respondents to the survey may not have complete knowledge about promotional activities outside of their region of expertise, leading to anchoring bias and measurement error, which could be generating our correlations. In the next two sections of this chapter, we attempt to account for these methodological shortcomings by drilling more deeply into two quantitative case studies of Vietnam and Russia, which allow us to more directly test our theoretical mechanisms of meritocratic promotion and upward pandering.

8.3 Meritocratic Promotion and Pandering Upward: A Regression Discontinuity Approach in Vietnam

To test our pandering-upward theory more directly, we take advantage of a quasi-experiment in Vietnam. As the figures above illustrate, Vietnam is a useful case for our theory. The country's single-party, authoritarian regime scores highly on the expert analyses of meritocracy from the Quality of Governance Survey. Indeed, Bell (2015, p. 195), in his best-selling book on political meritocracy in China, singles out Vietnam as the most likely case of success outside of China because it is a "large and diverse country that is committed to a peaceful form of social and economic modernization under the guidance of meritocratically selected leaders." Moreover, Vietnam has a similar deep-rooted party system and a history of local experimentation across its sixty-three provinces (Bell 2015, pp. 195–196; Malesky 2008b; Jandl 2014). Vietnam therefore represents a critical case for our authoritarian pandering theory because it has the size, subnational authority, and institutional design where we are most likely to observe it.

Even better from a research perspective, Vietnam, like a lot of countries with regime parties, ensures healthy recruitment by maintaining frequent turnover of top party positions so that new recruits can move up through the party ranks and attain the higher benefits of office (Liang 2015). To accomplish this, many single-party regimes insist upon a retirement age and term limits for both senior and junior officials (Manion 1993; Svolik 2012). Vietnam has had an official retirement age of sixty years for public officials since its 1992 constitution, but for several years, its implementation was uneven, with some officials allowed to work beyond age sixty in unimportant positions (Vo 1994; Pham 2000). When it became clear that the ambiguity was being abused by some local officials, the Vietnamese Communist Party issued an unusually strong reprimand to those in noncompliance in 2000 (Pham 2002) and clarified the retirement rules in 2003. Accordingly, government officials in Vietnam are obligated to retire by the age of sixty. They may take an appointment if they are between two and five years away from retirement, but they cannot be reappointed after they hit the retirement age (Khai 2003). Because officials within one year of retirement age cannot be reappointed and terms are five years, officials aged fifty-nine years when their terms end are ineligible. Thus, only officials aged fifty-three and younger are eligible for promotion. Importantly for our research design, Provincial People's Committee chairmen (PCOMs) are subject to this law. PCOMs are the governor equivalents in Vietnamese provinces, having the same status as central government ministers. In addition, these subnational officials have legal authority over tax incentives. Prime Minister Nguyen Tan Dung (2010) reinforced the cutoff for promotion eligibility at age fifty-three.

Because terms are five years, PCOMs entering office above the age of fifty-three have no opportunity for promotion after they serve out their final term. Figure 8.5 demonstrates this situation plainly. It plots the share of PCOMs promoted for all 102 officials observed between 2006 and 2015. We define promotion as an appointment to a central-level government ministry or agency, to party secretary in the same province or elsewhere, or to a PCOM of one of the five national-level cities, which hold the same rank as a province but are considered to be more prestigious because of their larger wealth and population. Clearly, promotion probability declines precipitously with age, with zero officials on the far side of fifty-four being promoted beyond their current tenure.

8.3 A Regression Discontinuity Approach in Vietnam

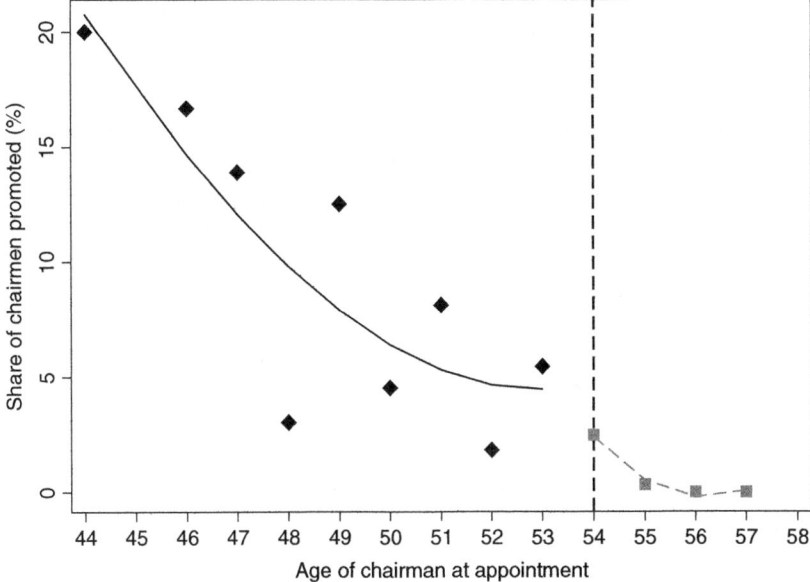

Figure 8.5 Promotion probabilities of People's Committee chairmen by start year.
Note: Coded by authors based on Vietnam's Administrative Handbook (2001–2015). The dashed line represents age 54 cutoff. The x-axis depicts the age of the officials when they started their most recent five-year term. Diamonds depict the promotion probability for officials below the threshold, while red squares show the promotion possibility for those fifty-four and above. Lines on either side are generated using lowess regression.

It is therefore safe to conclude that officials appointed to PCOM after age fifty-four have little motivation to try to enhance their promotion prospects by offering incentives. As we hypothesized above, if their true beliefs are that incentives are ineffective or distortionary, we should see a decline in incentive activity as a form of upward pandering once their opportunities for promotion are removed.

Sharp Regression Discontinuity Specification

The observation that officials appointed after age fifty-four face very different career incentives lends itself to a sharp discontinuity design, described formally in Equation 1 below. Our treatment variable is R, which equals 1 if the official was appointed after turning fifty-four (R=1 if Age>=54, R=0 if

Age<54). The forcing variable in the analysis is the age at start, which we re-center to zero by subtracting 54. One concern is strategic appointment or retirement around the threshold, which might violate the assumption of no sorting and thus indicate that the two groups are dissimilar on non-observables. Thankfully, a McCrary (2008) density test demonstrates continuity at the threshold between fifty-three and fifty-four.[9]

Our dataset is organized at the level of a firm's investment, such that we collect information on the individual investment and where the firm is located in Vietnam. This data allows us to examine how a politician's promotion opportunities (constrained by the politician's age) shape the allocation of incentives.

Individual PCOMs are indexed by i, each new firm entrant is indexed by f, and the entry year in our dataset is indexed by t, which ranges from 2006 to 2015. All firms entering before 2006 were dropped so that we could track the entire career of each PCOM. Entry year fixed effects (δ) account for potential trending in global incentives or in country allocation of incentives.

$$PR(incentive_{ift} = 1)$$
$$= \beta_0 + \beta_1 R_{it} + \beta_2 Age(-54)_{it} + \beta_3 R_{it} * Age(-54)_{it}$$
$$+ \gamma PCOM_{it} + \pi Firm_{ft} + \delta_t + u \quad (1)$$

The dependent variable for the analysis is *incentive*, which takes the value of 1 if the new foreign entrant received any incentive to help lure it to the province and 0 if it did not. Foreign firms in Vietnam are eligible for a wide range of incentives, ranging from CIT reductions, tax holidays, and reductions on land transaction fees to employment incentives that grant CIT reductions to firms employing females and minorities, and incentives for research and development. Key to our research design is that provincial officials have discretion over the targeted incentives that they can offer to new investors (PricewaterhouseCoopers 2016). As the story of the thirty-three fence-breakers illustrates, most incentives are set at the national level, with provincial leaders only formally allocated the ability to set land fee reductions. In practice, however, a large amount of discretion is provided to provincial leaders.[10] First, they have greater control over incentives when firms invest in industrial zones or districts classified

---

[9] Figure 8.A1 shows the graph for all People's Committee chairmen. The estimated difference in the number of appointments for ages 53 and 54 is very small, and the p-value indicates that we cannot not reject the hypothesis of no difference.

[10] Vietnam has had multiple investment laws, which have refined these choices over time. In the most recent investment law (Vietnam National Assembly 2014), Section 1, Clause 15 lays out the types of investment available, while Section 2, Clauses 33 and 38 describe the authority of the Provincial People's Committee and its chairman. These powers were also seen in the 2005 Investment Law (Vietnam National Assembly 2005).

8.3 A Regression Discontinuity Approach in Vietnam

as backward by the national government. Second, they can determine whether enterprises fit eligibility criteria in terms of size, targeted sectors, employment, sourcing from local vendors, and benefits to underprivileged groups such as women or minorities. Provincial leaders have interpreted and applied these criteria quite differently, meaning that the same firm can receive highly varying offers from neighboring provinces. Moreover, investors have learned that they can exploit the divergence to win themselves lucrative deals. The competition has created a tremendous collective action problem that has sapped Vietnam of critical revenue. As the International Monetary Fund (2014, pp. 11, 15) put it in a recent assessment:

Tax and tariff reductions and exemptions have contributed to a downward trend in revenues as a share of GDP, in contrast to regional experience, resulting in an expansionary revenue stance in cyclically adjusted terms ...

Staff recommended broadening the tax base by *eliminating exemptions, reducing incentives*, introducing a property tax, and including pensions under personal income tax.

To measure targeted incentives for particular foreign investors, we use the annual foreign investment survey of the Vietnamese Provincial Competitiveness Index (PCI), a US-AID funded project that is administered by the Vietnamese Chamber of Commerce and Industry. Each year (2010–2014), the PCI-FDI survey samples about 1,600 foreign firms to perform a comprehensive governance assessment of the country and province where they are located, allowing for a comparison of Vietnam's sixty-three provinces.[11] The PCI research team ensures that each year this survey is representative of the population of firms in Vietnam through stratified random sampling, returning a response rate of 25% (Malesky 2015, pp. 4–6). Foreign investment in Vietnam is largely dominated by firms from East Asia. The five largest investors, based on national data and the PCI sample, include Taiwan (18.41%), South Korea (15.56%), Japan (15.38%), China (4.83%), and Singapore (3.96%). The sample also includes 560 investors from the European Union, 176 investors from the United States, and 61 from Australia.

The main dependent variable (*incentive*) is taken from one of a battery of questions in Section B of the PCI-FDI survey regarding the firm's entry decision (p. 6), which probes the generosity of incentives in the location where the firm invested. These questions are detailed in Box 8.1. We code a firm as receiving an incentive if it answered yes to the first question, and

---

[11] For methodological details and background on the PCI-FDI survey, see Vietnam Chamber of Commerce and Industry (2015).

> **Box 8.1: Questions about tax incentives from the PCI-FDI survey (2014)**
>
> (6) Did the province you eventually selected offer you an investment incentive package?
> □ Yes *(If yes, please tell us a little more about the incentive package in question B6.1 to B6.5)*
> □ No *(Please skip to question B7)*
>
> | | | | | |
> |---|---|---|---|---|
> | 6.1. Was your firm provided with a corporate income tax? holiday? | □ | Yes | □ | No |
> | 6.2. Was your firm provided with a corporate income tax? reduction? | □ | Yes | □ | No |
> | 6.3. Were you provided with a reduction in land use right? purchase fees? | □ | Yes | □ | No |
> | 6.4. Were these the province's original offers or were they negotiated? | □ | Original offer | □ | Negotiated |
> | 6.5. Would you have invested in the province without the tax? incentive? | □ | Yes | □ | No |
>
> (7) If you considered investing in another province, how did the tax incentive (if any) of the other province compare to the one where you invested?
> a. Better
> b. About the same
> c. Worse
> d. Our business did not consider investing in another province.

0 if it did not. Between 2006 and 2014, 36% of firms received some sort of incentive. Of those receiving incentives, 75% received a tax holiday (median length=twenty-four months),[12] 42% received a tax reduction (median value=50%), and 24% received land fee reductions. Consistent with our theory that these incentives are often superfluous, 66% of respondents said that they would have invested in the province without the inducement, while 68% said that the package they were offered by a competing province was exactly the same as the province where they invested. Twenty-three percent of respondents acknowledged that the package from the competing province was actually better. In 42% of

---

[12] Details on the length and amount of packages were asked between 2010 and 2012 but were dropped in 2013 and 2014.

8.3 A Regression Discontinuity Approach in Vietnam

cases, the firm agreed to the province's initial incentive offer without negotiation, indicating that additional adjustment would make little difference in their decision. Finally, firms receiving incentives were not any more likely to purchase inputs from domestic providers but were significantly more likely to import inputs from their home country or a third-country supplier, demonstrating that the promise of domestic spillover benefits are unfounded.

These descriptive statistics are important for our research design. Similar to the academic studies on the economic impact of incentives reviewed through this book, most firms select locations for reasons unrelated to the incentive offers. These inducements have little impact on behavior, allowing us to test how political attributes shape incentive offers. If these offers were especially effective, we would observe most of the investment locating in districts where politicians have prospects for promotion (since these politicians exert more effort to attract investment). As we discuss later in our empirical section, politicians eligible for promotion and politicians facing retirement have no differences in their success in attracting investment. Thus, our empirical design captures how the inefficient allocation of incentives is shaped by pandering upward.

Figure 8.6 provides an initial graphical depiction of our analysis. Both graphs demonstrate that the share of entrants granted incentives increases up until the threshold. This is consistent with our career advancement story; officials try to gamble for resurrection, offering generous incentives to maximize their attractiveness in the last years before their ineligibility. Results are clearly not driven by the number of new entrants, which is steady prior to the threshold. After the threshold, the results are noisy since there is no clear theoretical relationship between being one year older and offering incentives. Thus, the use of incentives is lower on average but bounces up and down as age moves away from the threshold.

Although control variables are not necessary in a sharp regression discontinuity design (RDD) specification (Angrist and Pischke 2010, p. 256), the flexible specification does allow us to address possible confounders. In particular, there are three potential sources of heterogeneity that might affect our analysis.

First, particular characteristics of PCOMs might be associated with their career advancement. For instance, less well-educated PCOMs might advance more slowly through the bureaucratic ranks and thus have achieved a lower status when retirement calls. If that is the case, education might be correlated with our treatment variable. Alternatively, Vietnamese officials serving in their home province may be less ambitious than their peers who have parachuted in from outside. Remember that in contrast to China, a much smaller percentage of PCOMs are promoted, and most spend their entire careers in their home province (McCulloch and Malesky 2014). To the extent that the treatment variable captures career incentives, it might lead to a biased coefficient. To address these concerns, we control for whether the PCOM has an advanced degree (*MBA=1*) and whether they are serving in their home province (*hometown=1*) in a set of robustness tests.

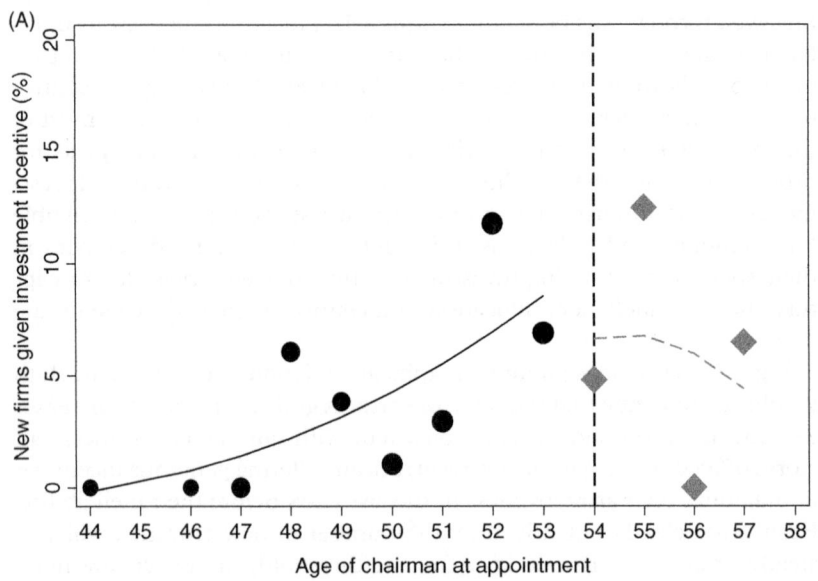

Bubble size = # of new entrants/chairmen

Figure 8.6 Tax incentive probabilities of People's Committee Chairmen by start year.
Panel A Firm-level lowess regressions
Panel B People's Committee Chairman-level averages quadratic fit
Note: *In Panel A*, the authors present lowess regressions at the firm level. On the x-axis, they plot the ages of the PCOMs when appointed to their most recent terms – the forcing variable in the RDD. The y-axis depicts the probability that the entering foreign-invested enterprise received an investment incentive (B8.1=1). The histogram depicts the share of total PCOMs for each age group. The dashed line in the graph provides the cutoff 54 years, when the PCOM becomes ineligible for promotion. Lowess regressions lines are plotted before and after the cutoff. In *Panel B*, the authors replicate the analysis at the provincial level, showing the share of firms at age group.

8.3 A Regression Discontinuity Approach in Vietnam   149

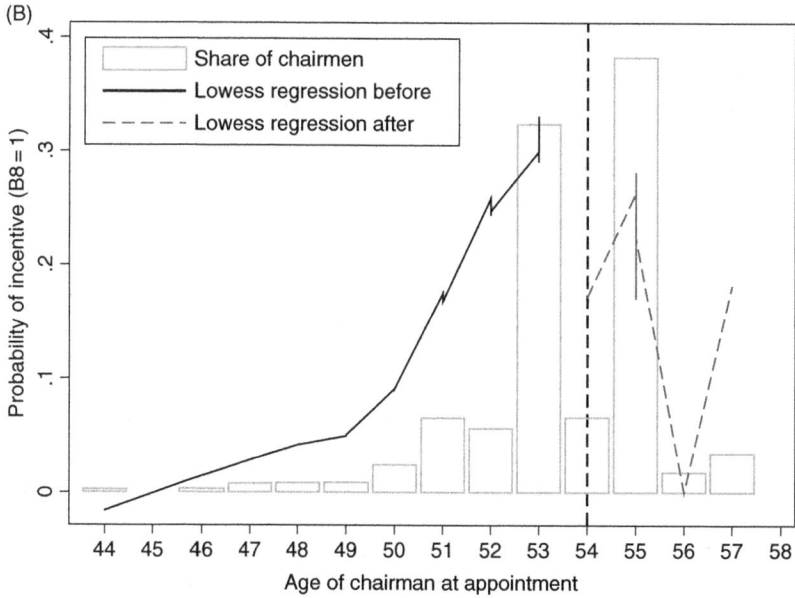

Figure 8.6 (Cont.)

Second, particular firms might strategically target officials who are below retirement age, knowing that they might be more likely to offer incentives. We address this set of confounders by adding a variable measuring the *employment size* of the firm[13] when it entered and two-digit *sector* fixed effects based on the International Standard Industrial Coding (ISIC) Revision 4 deciding system.

Third, strategic central officials might send soon-to-be retiring officials to particular provinces where growth is less important or less challenging, again causing the treatment variable to be correlated with features of the province. To address this concern, we control for *population* size (ln), provincial *GDP per capita* (millions of VND, ln), registered *FDI capital* (millions of USD, ln), and human capital proxied by the province's secondary school *graduation rate*.

The above variables are included in the regressions. More generally, however, we also tested for balance between our treatment group (must retire=1) and control group (eligible for promotion, but age at

---

[13] Firms' sizes range from 1 to 300,000 employees. The average firm in the sample has 160 employees with a standard deviation of 4,267, but this number conceals a sizable skew. Most foreign investment enterprises are on the small size. The median firm has four employees and 66% have under ten employees.

appointment >=50) on a range of potential confounders. In total, we looked at 106 potential confounders covering seven major categories: (1) personal characteristics of the PCOM; (2) quality of provincial infrastructure (i.e., roads, telecom, Internet, industrial zones); (3) development, covering economic development (GDP, industrial output, construction) and business development (number and performance of private and foreign companies); (4) human capital, measuring population, employment, and educational quality; (5) geography, covering distance from Hanoi and the location in Vietnam's seven different geographical regions, which vary widely in landscape, climate, and culture; (6) institutions and governance, including regulatory burdens, property rights, transparency, and corruption; and (7) change rates in economic development, human capital, and governance in the year before the PCOM took office. The latter category is particularly important because it accounts for whether provincial leaders were selected particularly to ride upon previous provincial glory or to help correct for performance.

The full set of 106 balance tests and sources for each variable are presented in Table 8.A1. Looking at a variety of different significance measures (Student's t-test, Wilcoxon sum-rank z-test, and Fischer's exact p-test) we do not find a single potential confounder that is significantly associated with the treatment variable. The approach is limited because our sample of PCOMS is small and the measures are too fine grained. For instance, we have thirty measures of governance alone. Like the proverbial blind men describing parts of the elephant, all of these individual tests might be too nuanced, capturing small perturbations but overlooking the larger movements in an underlying latent variable. Therefore, we run multivariate analysis of variance (MANOVA) estimations on the large baskets of indicators described above (Warne 2014). The p-values of these MANOVA estimations are plotted in Figure 8.7. Again, none of the potential baskets of confounders is close to statistical significance.

Critically, three measures have significant p-values. They are (1) the age at the start of term, which is our forcing variable; (2) the age at the time of the survey, which, of course, is related to the forcing variable mechanically; and (3) the share of PCOMs promoted at the end of their terms, which is the career incentive that drives our entire theoretical intuition. The significance of these three variables is important because they confirm the assumptions of our research design. Moreover, they indicate that the statistical insignificance of the other confounders does not result from lack of statistical power.

8.3 A Regression Discontinuity Approach in Vietnam

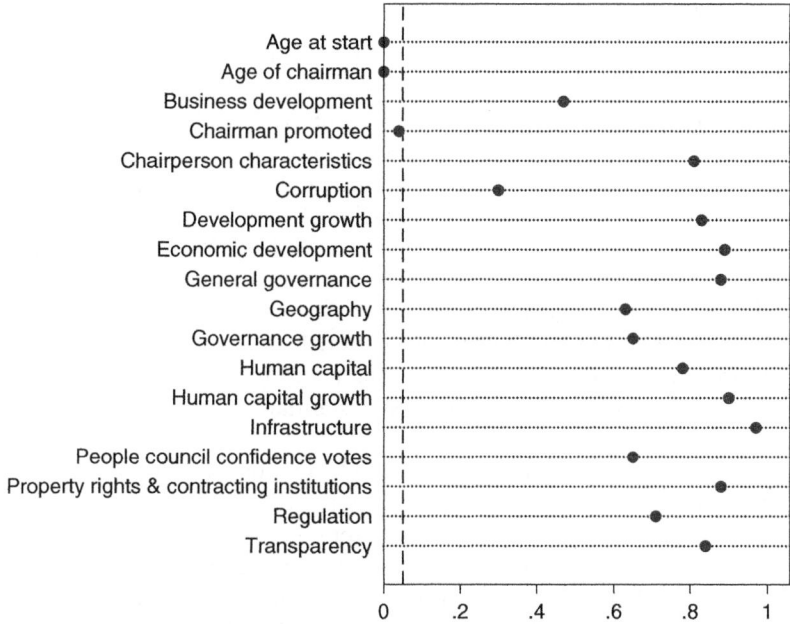

Figure 8.7 Balance tests of key confounders.
Note: Circles represent p-values from MANOVA analyses of grouped variables. The y-axis supplies the title of each grouping. A full list of indicators under each title can be found in Appendices 8E and 8F. The red dashed line represents p=.05 from the MANOVA analysis and separates confounders that vary significantly with the treatment from those that do not appear consequential. Thus, for dots below that number, the authors reject the null hypothesis that the treatment and control are different on that set of criteria.

The balance tests along with the McCrary density test provide confidence that the basic assumptions of the RDD are upheld. In less scientific jargon, it appears that we can treat retirement age as a reasonable natural experiment for assessing our pandering-upward theory. In almost every way, provincial leaders slightly above the cutoff year of fifty-four appear to be like the leaders slightly below. They have similar levels of education and career backgrounds, similar constellations of firms in their provinces, and work in similar provinces. While it is impossible to randomize career incentives and ambition across individuals, the artificial retirement gets us pretty close to a randomized experiment. All observable characteristics are essentially the same, and the only thing that obviously varies is the possibility of promotion.

Results of the Regression Discontinuity

Table 8.3 presents the main results of the RDD analysis. For this table, we calculate the optimal bandwidth of 3.63 using the Imbens and Kalyanaraman (2012) procedure. Since our provincial ages are measured as integers and our oldest PCOM was appointed at fifty-seven, in practice this implies a four-year bandwidth ranging from age fifty to age fifty-seven. All firms associated with provincial leaders younger than fifty were dropped from our analysis, leaving us with 1,829 firms that entered the country between 2006 and 2014. We employ a probit specification and calculate the marginal probabilities; all results, however, are substantively similar with a linear probability model. Because multiple firms are entering the province of the same leader and therefore cannot be considered independent draws, we cluster standard errors at the chairman level.

The table is divided into two panels. The first panel runs the traditional regression-based estimation approaches to RDD. In Model 1, we start with the standard difference-in-means approach, which includes only the treatment variable (retire) and the forcing variable (age at start) but does not include their interaction term. The jump at the intercept in this stripped-down approach is estimated to be a 14.8% lower probability of offering a tax incentive. As the intercept for officials younger than fifty-four is estimated rather than observed, it is advisable to interact the treatment and the forcing variable, so that the differences in the slopes on both sides are taken into account when estimating the discontinuity. Thus, Model 2 adds the interaction term. Focusing on the shift in intercept, we again see a 16.8% lower probability of incentives for those about to retire. To make sure that we do not confuse a discontinuity with nonlinearity (Angrist and Pischke 2010, p. 254), we follow Lee and Lemieux (2010) and test that our results are robust enough to include a quadratic transformation of the forcing variable (in Models 3–6). Model 4 adds entry year fixed effects to capture differences in the business environment faced by firms entering in different time frames. Finally, Model 5 adds the confounds highlighted above (leader characteristics, firm characteristics, and province characteristics), and Model 6 includes two-digit sector fixed effects. The shaded panel applies the more complex estimation approaches suggested by Imbens and Kalyanaraman (2012), Kaiser (2014), and Colinico et al. (2014).

Across all of the specifications, we observe the same pattern: retiring PCOMs are less generous in their allocation of incentives to incoming foreign-invested enterprises. In our preferred estimation – Model 5, which we believe is sufficiently parsimonious and conservative – we find

Table 8.3 *Regression discontinuity analysis of promotion probability and tax incentive usage*

Dependent Variable = Offered Any Incentive to Foreign Entrant	Diff-in-Means (1)	Regression specifications					Alternative approaches			
		Interactions (2)	Quadratic (3)	Entry Year FE (4)	Controls (5)	Sector FE (6)	Optimal BW (7)	CV-BW (8)	CTV (9)	CTV2 (10)
Must retire=1	-0.148** (0.058)	-0.168*** (0.036)	-0.131*** (0.043)	-0.157*** (0.053)	-0.193*** (0.049)	-0.256*** (0.040)	-.186* (.067)	-0.211*** (.079)	-0.154*** (0.142)	-0.197*** (0.142)
Age at start (-54)	0.044** (0.017)	0.105*** (0.019)	-0.002 (0.087)	0.110 (0.108)	-0.004 (0.114)	-0.036 (0.094)				
Must retire*age at start		-0.121*** (0.029)	0.069 (0.161)	-0.149 (0.201)	0.105 (0.215)	0.193 (0.189)				
Entry year fixed effects	No	No	No	Yes	Yes	Yes	No	No	No	No
Sector fixed effects	No	No	No	No	No	Yes	No	No	No	No
Controls	No	No	No	No	Yes	Yes	No	No	No	No
Observations	1,829	1,829	1,829	1,767	1,690	1,542	1,829	1,829	1,829	1,829
Chairmen clusters	81	81	81	68	53	24				
Pseudo R-squared	0.00680	0.0150	0.0164	0.0427	0.0434	0.0757				
Pbar	0.231	0.231	0.231	0.239	0.249	0.270				
Log likelihood									0.788***	0.788***
Kolmorgorov-Smirnov										
Rank Sum Z-test									26.005***	26.011***

Note: Models 1 to 6 use probit with marginal probabilities presented and robust standard errors, clustered at People's Committee Chairmen, in parentheses. Controls include whether the chairman is serving in his hometown, years of education, whether he possesses an MBA (=1), whether he is serving on a central committee (=1), firm size and sector, provincial GDP per capita, population, number of FDI projects, and high school graduation rate. Alternative approaches are employed in the shaded panel. Imbens-Kalyanaraman optimal bandwidth procedure (Model 7) and cross-validation bandwidth procedure (Model 8 implemented using STATA's rdcv package (Kaiser 2014). Calonico et al. (2015) implemented using STATA's rdrandinf procedure (Model 9). Model 10 runs rdrandinf with a quadratic transformation of the forcing variable. *** p<0.01, ** p<0.05, * p<0.1

that retiring leaders are 15.7% less likely to offer incentives than similarly situated peers in other provinces. This result is consistent with our theory that career incentives of provincial leaders are associated with upward pandering in single-party systems.

Robustness Tests

With RDD, two design choices can potentially influence results and pose a threat to causal inference – bandwidth and cutoff value. First, we might be concerned that choice of bandwidth could potentially eliminate observations at the high or low end and therefore influence results. To test whether this was a problem, we re-ran our preferred Model 5 multiple times, with bandwidth sizes ranging from two to eight years. We maintain the same cutoff of fifty-four years. The coefficients on the treatment variable for each estimation are plotted in Panel A of Figure 8.8. The figure demonstrates that our findings are quite robust. All coefficients are negatively signed and similarly sized. The exception is bandwidths of two, where the difference is effectively zero with a very large standard error.

Panel B addresses the cutoff value with a placebo test. To make sure our results are a function of the actual retirement age and not some other age-related factor, we again re-ran Model 3 but replaced the cutoff value with every year between fifty and fifty-six. Again, we assume the optimal bandwidth of 3.6 years. Only for the cutoff year of fifty-four do we observe the same significantly negative value, which provides strong confirmation for our theory. Years above fifty-four are not statistically different from zero. Years below fifty-four are positively signed and statistically insignificant. As we noted above, these results are also consistent with our theory, as officials attempt to bolster their retirement choices in their last years of eligibility.

A Closer Look at Incentives

In Table 8.4, we move away from the blunt measure of incentives and focus on more fine-grained measures of what firms actually received. The first column is derived from Question B2, which asks firms to compare the incentive that they received from the province where they located to the incentives offered by competing provinces. Respondents were less likely to state that the competition offered a worse incentive. In other words, retiring leaders rarely tried to match the offers of their competition. Digging deeper, respondents in provinces with retiring PCOMS were 29% less likely to receive a tax holiday, 69% less likely to receive a CIT

8.3 A Regression Discontinuity Approach in Vietnam

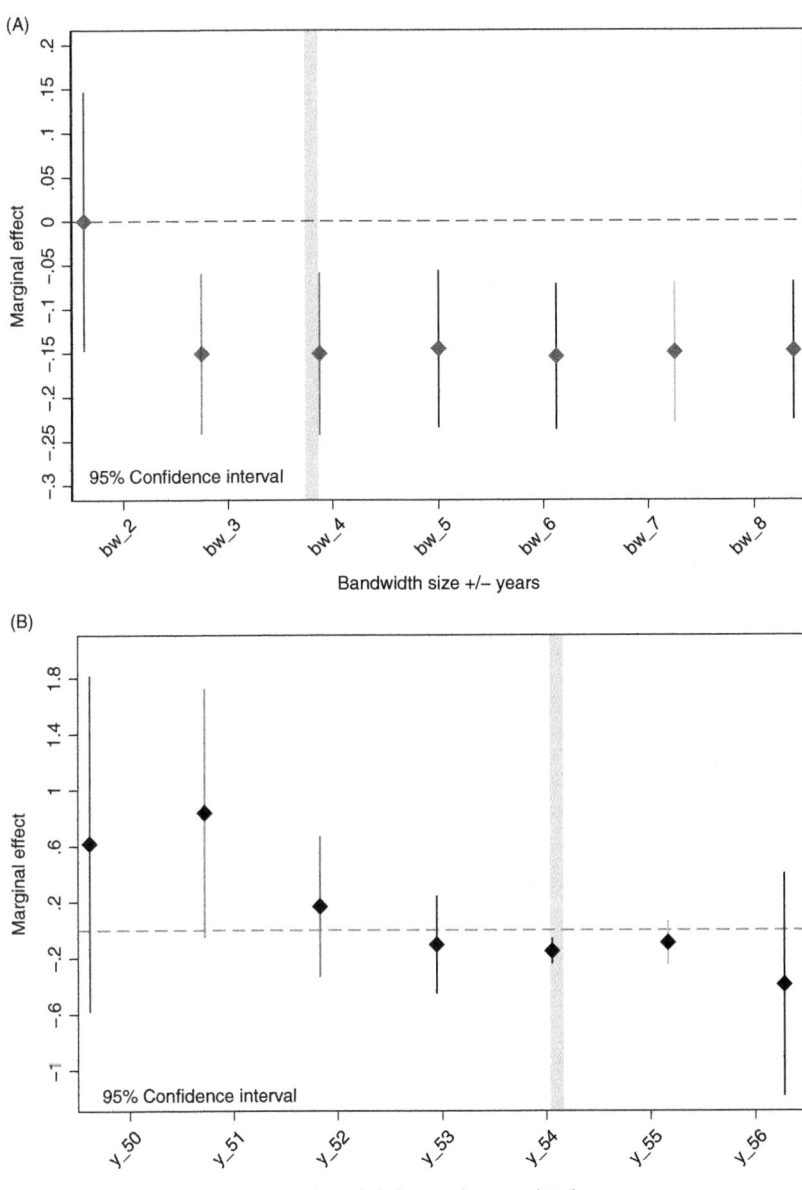

Figure 8.8 Sensitivity of main results. *Panel A* replicates Table 8.3 (Model 5) but alternates the number of years around the cutoff data of 54 used in the sample. *Panel B* replicates the same model but alternates the cutoff year. Diamonds represent coefficient estimates, and range bars represent 90% confidence intervals.

Table 8.4 *Alternative measures of incentives*

	Competition	Tax holiday	Holiday length	Tax reduction
Dependent variable	How did offer from competing province compare to this one ?	Did you receive a tax holiday?	Length of holiday	Did you receive a tax reduction?
Coding	1. Better; 2) The Same; 3) Worse	Yes=1/No=0	Months (In)	Yes=1/No=0
	(1)	(2)	(3)	(4)
Must retire=1	−0.220	−0.290***	−1.244*	−0.692**
	(0.129)	(0.111)	(0.638)	(0.285)
Age at start (-54)	0.124**	0.181**	1.016**	0.263
	(0.052)	(0.074)	(0.447)	(0.287)
Must retire*age at start	−0.013	−0.209**	−1.247	−0.057
	(0.058)	(0.098)	(1.223)	(0.309)
Entry year fixed effects	Yes	Yes	Yes	Yes
Observations	543	613	131	356
Pbar/mean DV	1.85	0.514	3.59	0.418
	Reduction size	Reduction length	Land fees	Offered /negotiated
Dependent variable	Size of reduction	Length of reduction	Reduction in land use fees	Was this the province's first offer or negotiated?
Coding	Percentage points	Months	Yes=1/No=0	First offer=1 /Negotiated=0
	(5)		(7)	(8)
Must retire=1	−22.576**	−14.730**	−0.131	0.153
	(9.979)	(6.455)	(0.079)	(0.141)
Age at start (-54)	12.699	4.769	0.063	−0.126*
	(9.704)	(4.734)	(0.053)	(0.074)
Must retire*age at start	−11.453	0.780	−0.106	0.143
	(14.211)	(6.545)	(0.084)	(0.114)
Entry year fixed effects	Yes	Yes	Yes	Yes
Observations	369	315	545	416
Pbar/Mean DV	18.97	21.69	0.247	0.291

Note: Models replicated Table 8.3 (Model 4) using alternative measures of tax incentives. Robust standard errors, clustered at People's Committee Chairmen, in parentheses.
*** p<0.01, ** p<0.05, * p<0.1

8.3 A Regression Discontinuity Approach in Vietnam

reduction, and 13% less likely to receive land fee reductions, although the last number falls slightly short of significance. For firms in retiring locations that did receive some incentives, the generosity was also less. CIT reductions were lower and lasted for shorter periods, and tax holidays were also shorter. The magnitude of this finding is substantially large. Firms investing in provinces with retiring PCOMS pay 22% points more in taxes and have tax holidays that are over a year shorter than firms investing in provinces with PCOMS with advancement potential. A final piece of evidence from Table 8.4 is that no difference exists between PCOMs about whether the tax incentive was offered originally or negotiated, which indicates that these results are derived from PCOM decisions and not strategic interactions with investors.

Summary of Vietnam Analysis

Our theory predicts that single-party regimes with imperfect meritocratic promotion are the most likely suspects for upward pandering. To test this theory directly, we took advantage of the retirement age in Vietnam, which exogenously assigns PCOMs close to the age of fifty-four into two groups. Those younger than fifty-four are still eligible for promotion, whereas those just on the other side have zero probability of promotion. Critically, officials above and below the line are roughly identical on over 100 potential individual, firm-level, and provincial-level confounders. By taking away the incentives for credit claiming, we hypothesized that officials who must retire would no longer be motivated to offer generous fiscal incentives to potential investors. These officials would be more concerned about the fiscal health of their localities and would favor investment attraction without superfluous giveaways.

To test our theory, we used a RDD around the age fifty-four cutoff, finding that retiring officials were 16% less likely to offer fiscal incentives. In particular, they were 28% less likely to offer tax holidays and 69% less likely to offer CIT reductions. These results were robust to a range of specification choices, bandwidth alterations, and placebo testing.

In essence, we find evidence consistent with our theory that when subnational officials in single-party regimes no longer have an incentive for promotion, they lose interest in upward pandering and follow their true preferences. Understanding single-party regimes is important since these countries represent the most economically successful and durable types of authoritarian countries.

8.4 Testing the Personalism Hypothesis in Putin's Russia

Our second empirical case study explores the relationship between personalism and tax incentives. In contrast to single-party regimes, personalist regimes depend on allegiance to an elite leader who has consolidated power around him or herself. As a result, signaling economic performance is less important than engaging in acts of loyalty towards the top leadership. As we noted above, stamping out popular discontent and mobilizing electoral victories, whether through electioneering or outright fraud, are more valuable. Thus, in countries characterized by pluralism, we expect less use of fiscal incentives.

Russia since 2000 provides a fascinating location to test this hypothesis in more depth because it not only offers a prime example of personalist leadership under Vladimir Putin (Geddes et al. 2014) but also, according to most experts, is characterized by growing personalism over time (Shevtsova 2007; Baturo and Elkink 2016). Critically for us, this personalism became firmly established by a specific institutional change in 2005 that replaced the direct election of governors of Russian regions with appointments by central authorities connected to the Kremlin (Sharafutdinova 2010). We take advantage of this structural break to test our theory using an interrupted time-series design.

Personalist Authoritarianism Under Putin

Due to the murkiness of authoritarian politics, some confusion exists about how to properly code the current Russian brand of authoritarianism. Hadenius and Teorell (2007) characterize Russia since 2000 as a hegemonic party system under United Russia, because the party has always controlled less than 75% of seats in parliament (2008=64.4%, 2011=50.2%) and because the chief executive has been elected with less than 75% of the vote (Putin won 64% of votes in 2012). Svolik (2012) does not consider the country to be authoritarian until 2005, and then lists the country as a contested autocracy – as opposed to an established autocracy – for similar reasons. In contrast, Geddes et al. (2014) code the country as strictly personalist throughout the time period and specifically do not classify it as a single-party or hegemonic party regime. Magaloni et al. (2013) agree with the hegemonic party coding throughout but argue that the multiparty system became infused with personalism beginning in 2007 – which, not coincidentally, coincided with the removal of regional elections.

Among Russian specialists, consensus is growing around the idea that executive control over the judiciary, legislature, and regions has expanded (Gel'man et al. 2003; Goode 2007), which is consistent with growing

8.4 Testing the Personalism Hypothesis in Putin's Russia

personalism. Shevtsova (2007, p. 40) puts it most elegantly. Since he took office in 1999, Putin slowly "set about building his 'pyramid of power,' emphasizing subordination, strengthening the role of the bureaucracy, bringing the members of the security services into the government, centralizing control, and eradicating opposition."[14] Increasing personalism in Russia has been best documented empirically by Baturo and Elkink (2016), who, using a network analysis of appointments and proximity to Putin, are able to document the precise timing of changes in his ability to exert control and consolidation of power. They conclude, "We find that as early as 2004, the Russian regime can be regarded as personalist, and is strongly so from 2006 onward" (p. 75).

Similar to the Magaloni et al. (2013) data, the 2006 date coincides precisely with the removal of elections for regional governorships.[15] According to Russian scholars, gubernatorial elections were quite competitive prior to the 2005 removal. Incumbent Russian governors possessed a range of administrative instruments that they used to win elections and were therefore able to carve out some independent policy space. Out of seventy-two elections between 2001 and 2004, Kremlin-backed (United Russia) candidates successfully challenged incumbent governors in only fifteen races (Goode 2007, p. 376). Moreover, Konitzer (2005) showed that economic performance played a major role in elections.

By contrast, there is evidence that promotion was based on loyalty after the 2005 elections (Konitzer and Wegen 2006; Goode 2007; Sharafutdinova 2010). Indeed, in a comprehensive analysis of gubernatorial appointments after 2005, Reuter and Roberston (2012) document that a wide range of economic performance indicators are uncorrelated with the Kremlin's decision to reappoint governors. Most important by far was the incumbent governors' ability to mobilize votes for the United Russia Party and Putin, in particular (p. 1032). Frye et al. (2014) document the efforts to mobilize votes on Russian factory floors after this time. In explaining the pattern of stuffed ballots in Russian elections post-2006, Myagkov et al. (2009) similarly conclude (p. 136):

Absent the usual signals that a true democracy, imbedded in a market economy, provides, the Kremlin needs ways to judge the loyalty and competence of those outside its walls, and elections serve that purpose. A weak showing, relative to the past, on the part of Putin, Medvedev, or United Russia in some oblast, rayon, or precinct signals a governor or local apparatchik who needs replacement if not outright incarceration.

---

[14] Quoted in Baturo and Elkink (2016, p. 80).
[15] Standard measures of constraints on executive decision making also decline around this time. See Figure 8.A2 for details.

A more recent study, which looked at the reappointment of vice-governors charged with the economic portfolio in Russia, draws a related but more nuanced conclusion by studying regional variation in the quality of electoral competition. While the authors confirm the strength of personalist appointments in the more authoritarian Russian regions with minimal electoral competition, they also find that vice-governors are more likely to be held accountable for poor economic performance in those same authoritarian regions. They conclude that in Russian regions where United Russia faces the greatest electoral competition, economic performance plays a secondary role to the ability to mobilize votes for the regime, again demonstrating the importance of loyalty (Reuter and Buckley 2015).

The bottom line is that the 2005 switch to gubernatorial appointments increased the role of personalism in the promotion and reappointment of Russian leaders. It is thus an ideal opportunity to explore how the exogenous increase in personalism increased the use of fiscal incentives among Russian governors. The aggregate effects of this phenomenon can be observed in Figure 8.9, where we see the sharp drop in the share of Russian governors presiding over changed tax laws after appointments began. In the four years prior to the change, 14.7% of Russian regions altered their tax policy as opposed to 9.8% afterward, a statistically significant difference (p=.03).

Model Specification and Data

The ideal specification for Hypothesis 8.3 would compare the changes in the use of incentives between elected and non-elected Russian governors in a difference-in-differences framework. This strategy, however, is unfortunately unavailable because the switch was applied to all regions at the same time, thus eliminating a potential control group. As a second-best alternative, we propose Equation 2 below, where we employ an interrupted time-series analysis with panel fixed effects (Cook and Campbell 1970; McDowall et al. 1980). Following Reuter and Robertson (2012), the treatment variable is y2005, which takes the value of 1 if year>=2005 and 0 if year<2005. To some extent, this creates a slight bias against finding a relationship since a lag is likely between the removal of elections and its effect on policy. Our estimation strategy treats the relationship as immediate.

$$PR(incentive_{gt} = 1) = \beta_0 + \beta_1 y2005_{it} + \gamma Region_{gt} + \pi Govenor_{gt} + \delta_g + u \quad (2)$$

One threat to causal inference is that appointed governors may vary dramatically in observable and unobservable features from their elected peers. For instance, it may take more competence, talent, or

8.4 Testing the Personalism Hypothesis in Putin's Russia

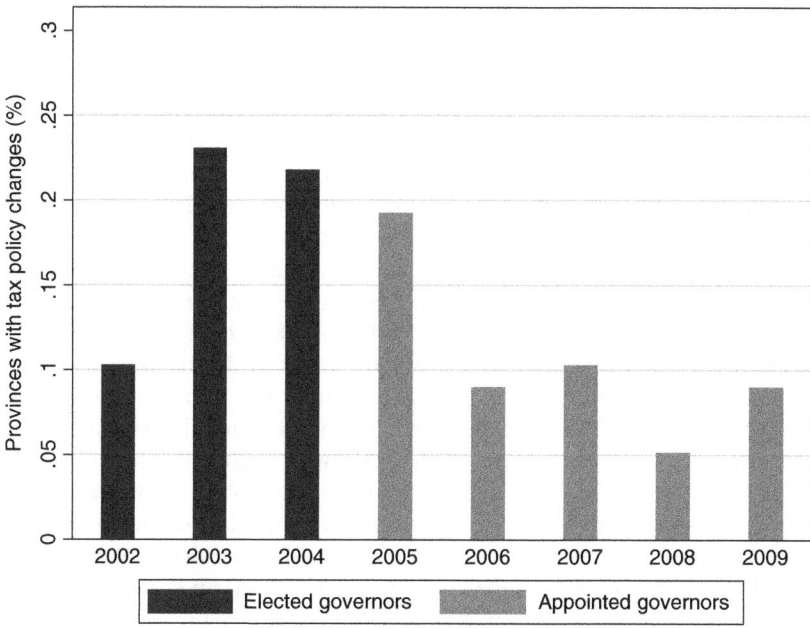

Figure 8.9 Share of Russian regions changing tax policy by year.
Note: Data on tax policy changes from Szakonyi and Nazrullaevay (2015).

entrepreneurialism to win an election in Russia than to finagle an appointment. To avoid this selection bias, we limit our analysis to only the 111 governors who both were elected at any point prior to the institutional change and who served as appointed governors after 2006, reducing our n from 780 governor years to 485 governor years. We believe that this choice is extremely conservative since we limit our analysis to the behavior of governors who were in power under both regimes.

Moreover, we introduce governor fixed effects (δ) so that the counterfactual we compare is the appointed governors to themselves. In essence, we hold constant all the time invariant personality features of governors to understand how their behavior was altered after institutional features changed their incentives. Since most governors only served in one location, this also indirectly applies regional fixed effects. The exception is promotion to Moscow or St. Petersburg, which we address by dropping in robustness tests. As the governor fixed effects only address time invariant features, we also test the robustness of our findings by applying vectors of time-variant regional variables γ, thought to be important in the literature, such as infrastructure (road density), urbanization (share of population in urban areas), and regional investment risk ratings. Time-variant governor characteristics (π) include variables found to be important in the extant literature – such as the governor's attachment to the region, measured as the number of years the governor has served in the locale (International Center for the Study of Institutions and Development 2015). This variable also captures region-governor time trends.

The dependent variable for the analysis comes from Szakonyi and Nazrullaevay (2015), who used a database of regional texts to construct a dataset of all laws passed from 2000 to 2008, which were related to investment initiatives in Russia's regions. Laws under regional jurisdiction include laws on (1) property, profit, land, and transportation taxes (only four types of taxes), (2) the participation of regional governments in investment funds, (3) the use of public-private partnerships, (4) investment tax credits, (5) direct subsidies to firms and state guarantees, and (6) the provision of expertise in the implementation of the proposed project. Based on only major regional laws, the authors constructed a variable called *tax policy changes*, which is 1 when (a) an entirely new bill on legislation was passed or (b) over 50% of the main legislation was revised, and 0 otherwise.

In our analysis, we use *tax policy change* to test our story of tax incentives. Although it is not a direct measure of firm-level targeting as it is in Vietnam, it does reflect changes in the governing laws that authorize the use of tax incentives. We expect that we will see a decline in these authorizations as governors no longer find it useful to employ targeted incentives.

Results

Our main results are presented in Table 8.5. Three models are presented. In Model 1, we study the main specification with only governor fixed effects and no time-variant controls. In Model 2, we add time-variant controls. In Model 3, we drop Moscow and St. Petersburg, a standard robustness check in the literature on subnational political economy in Russia.[16] The coefficient on the treatment variable is significant in all three models. In Model 3, the fully specified equation, we find an 8% reduction in the probability of tax changes after governors were switched

[16] As with the Vietnamese analysis, we subject our findings to a placebo test in Figure 8.A3. The results indicate that previous periods are not significant in a negative direction, indicating that 2005 is an exogenous shock, and we have simply picked up a portion of a pre-existing downward trend in tax incentive usage.

8.4 Testing the Personalism Hypothesis in Putin's Russia

Table 8.5 *Change in tax policy after institutional change*

Dependent variable = policy	Tax change			Other economic policy changes		
	Bivariate (1)	Controls (2)	Drop metros (3)	Bivariate (4)	Controls (5)	Drop metros (6)
Post 2005=1	−0.083**	−0.072*	−0.080**	0.043	0.054	0.051
	(0.036)	(0.039)	(0.039)	(0.035)	(0.038)	(0.038)
Years governor in region		−0.008	−0.009		0.006	0.006
		(0.039)	(0.039)		(0.038)	(0.038)
Road density		−0.001	−0.001		−0.001	−0.001
		(0.001)	(0.001)		(0.001)	(0.001)
Urban share (%)		0.012	0.014		−0.008	−0.008
		(0.022)	(0.022)		(0.021)	(0.021)
Investment risk rating		0.122**	0.104**		0.025	0.029
		(0.050)	(0.051)		(0.049)	(0.049)
Constant	0.171***	−0.770	−0.837	0.092***	0.593	0.572
	(0.025)	(1.542)	(1.536)	(0.024)	(1.507)	(1.500)
Governor FE	Yes	Yes	Yes	Yes	Yes	Yes
Observations	485	481	472	485	481	472
R-squared	0.117	0.135	0.138	0.095	0.097	0.098
RMSE	0.341	0.341	0.341	0.333	0.335	0.335

Note: Linear probability models with standard errors in parentheses. *** $p<0.01$, ** $p<0.05$, * $p<0.1$

from elected to appointed leadership. As a further placebo test, the next three models (4–6) run the same specifications but alter the dependent variable to include other economic policy changes, such as shifts in regulations or infrastructure outlays. Importantly, we see no difference among Russian governors after elections on these alternative policies, which strengthens our confidence in the tax incentives as pandering story.

In Table 8.6, we follow up the analysis by looking at the specific types of tax policies that were affected. We find that the coefficient is negative in eleven of the twelve specifications but is imprecisely estimated. The large standard errors result from our sample's small share of regions that made any changes to these specific tax laws; this can be seen in the coefficients on the constant in the unadjusted models, which recover the share of pre-treatment regions changing policy. The share of region

Table 8.6 Specific tax policies and tax incentives in Russia

Dependent variable = policy change	Profit tax		Property tax		Land tax		Investment fund		Tax credits		Subsidies	
	Bivariate (1)	Controls (2)	Bivariate (3)	Controls (4)	Bivariate (5)	Controls (6)	Bivariate	Controls	Bivariate	Controls	Bivariate	Controls
Post 2005=1	−0.007 (0.032)	0.011 (0.035)	−0.078** (0.033)	−0.060* (0.036)	−0.020 (0.014)	−0.011 (0.015)	−0.013 (0.023)	−0.006 (0.026)	−0.006 (0.020)	−0.003 (0.022)	−0.004 (0.028)	0.009 (0.031)
Years governor in region	−0.001		−0.007		−0.002		0.000		0.000		0.027	
Road density		(0.034)		(0.036)		(0.015)		(0.025)		(0.022)		(0.031)
		−0.001 (0.001)		−0.001 (0.001)		−0.000 (0.000)		−0.000 (0.000)		−0.000 (0.000)		−0.000 (0.001)
Urban share (%)		0.034* (0.020)		0.019 (0.020)		0.008 (0.008)		−0.016 (0.014)		−0.011 (0.013)		−0.011 (0.017)
Investment risk rating		0.052 (0.045)		0.075 (0.047)		−0.005 (0.019)		−0.016 (0.033)		−0.022 (0.029)		0.016 (0.040)
Constant	0.101*** (0.023)	−2.265 (1.387)	0.147*** (0.023)	−1.156 (1.435)	0.027*** (0.010)	−0.430 (0.594)	0.056*** (0.017)	1.228 (1.023)	0.040*** (0.014)	0.845 (0.891)	0.073*** (0.020)	0.536 (1.228)
Governor FE	Yes	Yes	Yes	Yes	Yes	Yes	Yes	Yes	Yes	Yes	Yes	Yes
Observations	494	474	494	474	494	474	494	474	494	474	494	474
R-squared	0.123	0.146	0.121	0.134	0.131	0.140	0.113	0.121	0.115	0.122	0.098	0.109
RMSE	0.302	0.307	0.311	0.317	0.128	0.131	0.221	0.226	0.192	0.197	0.265	0.271

Note: Linear probability models with standard errors in parentheses. *** $p<0.01$, ** $p<0.05$, * $p<0.1$

8.4 Testing the Personalism Hypothesis in Putin's Russia   165

years in the pre-treatment period that experienced one of the tax policy changes ranges from 2.7% to 14.7%. Not surprisingly, we observe significant change only where there was sufficient activity prior to 2005, such as with property taxes.

Summary of the Russian Analysis

Our theory predicted that personalized authoritarian regimes would have less need for targeted incentives, which was consistent with cross--national analyses. To test Hypothesis 8.3 more directly, we looked to local-central relations in Russia. Although Russia was already on its way to personalism, its impact was unambiguously increased with the cancellation of regional elections in 2005. Using an interrupted time-series approach to study how individual governors responded to the alteration in their career motivations, we find significant reductions in legal and tax policies underlying targeted incentives. These findings are consistent with our belief that personalism reduces the need for upward pandering to elite officials based on imperfect economic promotion criteria.

It is important to note that we are not stating that personalized promotion is normatively superior to imperfect meritocracy. As numerous Russian scholars have demonstrated (Reuter and Robertson 2012; Reuter and Buckley 2015; Beazer 2015), using loyalist criteria for retention and promotion removes the motivation for new policies that could enhance economic performance in the short to medium term, including investment in infrastructure, human capital, and general economic governance reforms. Along similar lines, personalist promotion by definition favors loyalty over competence, meaning that the proportion of low-quality leaders in high-ranking positions is large (Egorov and Sonin 2011). Finally, pandering does not go away under personalist promotion. The asymmetric information gap between principles and agents remains, as does the need to personally associate oneself with successful outcome criteria. The increase in ballot-box stuffing in Russian elections (Myagkov et al. 2009; Rundleet and Svolik 2015), for instance, may be a symptom of resorting to modes of electoral victory for which they have the greatest ability to claim credit.

What we find especially interesting is the complex transition in Russia from directly elected governors to politically appointed governors in an increasingly personalist regime. In our chapter on local elections in the United States, we showed that directly elected mayors were more likely to overuse incentives for credit claiming, whereas appointed city managers offered less generous incentives and had higher levels of oversight. In much of this literature, city managers are qualified technocrats making decisions without the constraints of direct elections, although they are appointed by elected officials. The Russian context gives us examples of appointed government officials – appointments that are seemingly less meritocratic, based on loyalty rather than performance. In these extremely different cases, we find a similar outcome relative to directly elected officials; appointments are associated with less generous use of incentives.

8.5 Conclusion

This chapter began with a puzzle. The theory of electoral pandering that we explored in the book is at odds with the empirical fact that authoritarian countries offer more, on average, than democracies. In this chapter, we extended the logic of our story to authoritarian regimes. We theorized that pandering is possible in authoritarian regimes when the principals (central elites) face the same asymmetric information disadvantage as voters in electoral systems – that is, the agents (subnational or lower level officials) understand the relationship between policy and outcome in attracting FDI better than they do. Thus, when motivating lower-level officials to pursue investment or growth by offering high-level positions, they also encourage credit-claiming behavior, whereby subnational officials attempt to associate themselves directly with the entrance of new firms. We have tested the logic of this argument cross-nationally and through empirical case studies of Vietnam and Russia. In doing so, we make three additional contributions to this book.

First, we offer nuance and rigor to the debates about the global race to attract investments and the utility of incentives in that effort. We are not convinced by the prevailing argument that authoritarian incentives substitute for governance and property rights protection (Li 2006), explaining why investors might prefer authoritarian locations over more secure democratic environments. This argument is based purely on the investor's sourcing decisions and does not take into account the preferences of local actors who must craft the incentive policy. This chapter helps flesh out why some authoritarian states might choose incentives, even when they appear to be damaging to long-term fiscal stability (IMF 2014).

8.5 Conclusion

Second, we demonstrate that the necessary conditions for upward pandering exist only in one type of authoritarian regime – single-party states with quasi-meritocratic institutions. We find evidence for the cross-national correlation and test the theory directly by illustrating how aging Vietnamese officials quickly abandon the use of tax incentives once they become ineligible for promotion. The need to claim credit for attracting firms no longer exists, allowing them to pursue their true preferences – economic growth of their home regions without damaging revenue giveaways. This finding helps us better understand how single-party organization works and why it is considered to be the most stable and economically successful form of authoritarianism (Magaloni and Kricheli 2010).

Third, we show that regimes that do not have quasi-meritocratic promotion do not experience the overuse of incentives since there is little relationship between economic performance and advancement. Thus, the entire authoritarian empirical finding of greater incentives use is accounted for by single-party states. In fact, personalist regimes – where loyalty trumps performance in retaining and advancing officials' careers, and where performance-based promotion is not credibly guaranteed – actually offer far less in incentives. We show this most clearly in our interrupted time-series approach in Russia, which demonstrates that after subnational elections were removed, the very same governors were 7% less likely to exploit tax policy changes in working with investors.

Finally, the extension of this work to additional countries with different political climates and less democratic institutions helps us contend with alternative mechanisms driving incentive use. Our work has shown that electoral pandering shapes incentive use, but an alternative argument (see the studies in Chapter 6) is that elected politicians may be harnessing the power of incentives to extract campaign contributions for electoral gain. Extending our work to authoritarian regimes allows us to more closely focus on how political accountability through nondemocratic promotion shapes incentive use. There is no reason to believe that campaign contribution motivations would affect our analysis in this chapter. Thus, we find evidence that is consistent with the general logic of pandering.

APPENDIX

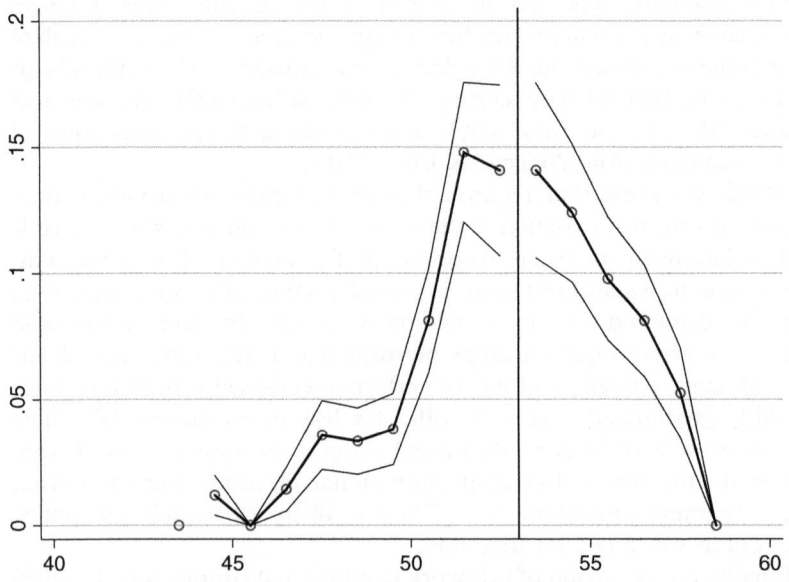

Figure 8.A1 McCrary density test of age at start.
Source: is McCrary, Justin. "Manipulation of the running variable in the regression discontinuity design: A density test." *Journal of Econometrics* 142.2 (2008): 698–714.

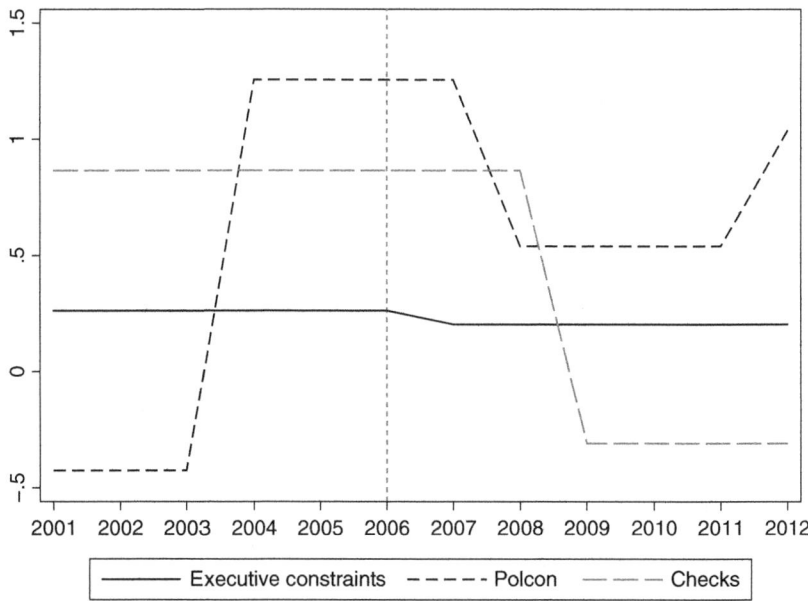

Figure 8.A2 Standard measures of executive constraints in Russia over time.

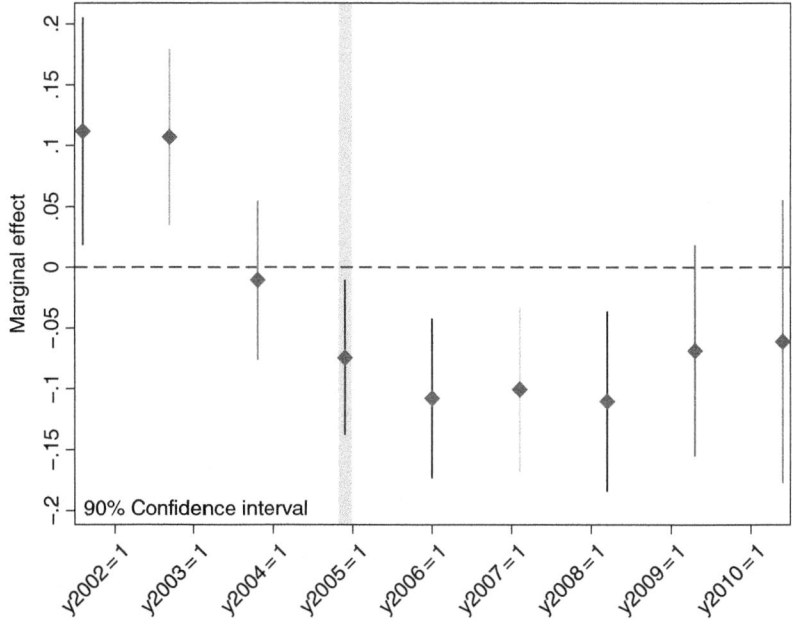

Figure 8.A3 Placebo test of Russian analysis.
Note: This graph replicates the fully specified Russian Incentives Model but alternates the cutoff year. Diamonds represent coefficient estimates, and range bars represent 90% confidence intervals.

Table 8.A1 Balance between officials eligible for promotion and who must retire

Potential confounders	Source	Survey question	Must retire (n=47)		Promotion eligible (n = 50)			Significance tests				MANOVA	
			Mean	SD	Mean	SD	P-Value	T-Statistic	Wilcoxon Z	Fisher's P		F	P
Forcing variables													
Age when appointed chairman	NGTCHC		55.32	1.08	51.62	1.12	0.00	−15.88	−6.97	0.00		82.35	0.00
Current age of chairman	NGTCHC		56.85	1.48	53.68	2.22	0.00	−7.84	−4.42	0.00			
Chairman promoted (Yes=1)	NGTCHC		9.5%	29.7%	26.0%	44.3%	0.04	2.05	1.14	0.25			
People's Committee Chairperson	NGTCHC												
Characteristics													
Chairman has MBA (Yes=1)	NGTCHC		0.0%	0.0%	6.0%	24.0%	0.11	1.62	1.81	0.07		0.50	0.81
Member of Central Committee (Yes=1)	NGTCHC		9.5%	29.7%	8.0%	27.4%	0.80	−0.26	−0.26	0.80			
Chairman serving in hometown (Yes=1)	NGTCHC		61.9%	49.2%	64.0%	48.5%	0.84	0.21	0.29	0.98			
Years of education	NGTCHC		15.90	2.27	16.08	2.05	0.69	0.40	0.09	0.98			
Leader does not favor foreign-invested enterprises (share of firms)	PCI	H3	37.0%	10.4%	36.6%	8.8%	0.84	−0.20	−0.49	0.92			

Variable	Source	Hypothesis											
Leader does not favor state owned enterprises (share of firms)	PCI	H4	34.1%	5.3%	33.6%	4.6%	0.65	−0.45	0.28	0.92		0.62	0.65
People Council confidence Votes													
Share of high confidence votes	ONA		73.6%	11.8%	73.3%	11.8%	0.93	−0.08	0.23	0.92	0.75		
Share of medium confidence votes	ONA		21.6%	10.6%	22.6%	9.4%	0.72	0.36	0.12	0.75	0.43		
Share of low confidence votes	ONA		4.9%	4.5%	4.4%	5.2%	0.75	−0.32	−0.63	0.43	0.52		
Abstention in confidence votes	ONA		0.6%	1.9%	2.0%	5.0%	0.17	1.39	0.50	0.52			
Infrastructure													
Number of electricity outages	PCI	E3	27.90	17.69	25.52	15.65	0.54	−0.62	−0.63	0.17		0.21	0.97
Telephones per capita	GSO	Infrastructure	64.28	41.08	60.02	35.38	0.63	−0.49	0.50	−0.02	0.42		
Share of road asphalted	GSO	Infrastructure	6.9%	1.7%	7.0%	1.8%	0.64	0.46	0.50	0.62			
Internet subscription rate	VINIC		6.0%	7.7%	5.5%	6.6%	0.74	−0.33	1.03	0.26			
Share of IZ land allocated	MPI	PCI Hard Data	49.6%	23.7%	51.7%	26.2%	0.76	0.30	0.25	0.65			
Number of industrial zones	MPI	PCI Hard Data	4.90	5.50	4.76	6.70	0.94	−0.08	−0.16	0.81			
Development													
Economic development													
GDP per capita (ln)	GSO	PCI Hard Data	3.24	0.58	3.13	0.42	0.40	−0.85	−0.08	0.65		0.33	0.8903
Share of country's industrial output	GSO	Industry	1.67	2.55	1.67	3.58	1.00	−0.01	−0.48	0.85			

Table 8.A1 (cont.)

Potential confounders	Source	Survey question	Must retire (n=47)		Promotion eligible (n = 50)			Significance tests				MANOVA	
			Mean	SD	Mean	SD	P-Value	T-Statistic	Wilcoxon Z	Fisher's P		F	P
Output from construction sector (billions of VND)	GSO	Industry	12874.65	26719.80	10939.95	18830.49	0.75	−0.32	0.26	0.85			
Nominal provincial GDP (billions USD)	GSO	PCI Hard Data	45225.42	61158.48	41391.45	79300.22	0.82	−0.23	0.02	0.42			
Inflation (GDP deflator)	GSO	PCI Hard Data	10.19	5.94	9.95	5.48	0.85	−0.18	−0.71	0.42			
Business development													
Private enterprises per 1000 citizens (ln)	GSOC	LHDN	5.64	0.96	5.27	0.73	0.10	−1.68	−0.59	0.42		0.98	0.47
Private enterprises per 1000 citizens	GSOC	LHDN	2.37	1.57	2.31	3.79	0.94	−0.08	−0.63	0.42			
Retail sales (billions of VND)	GSO	Industry	34046.99	48316.32	44742.04	106941.50	0.63	0.49	0.40	0.85			
Number of FDI projects (ln)	GSO	Investment	3.81	1.96	3.95	1.95	0.78	0.28	0.52	0.67			
Capital size of FDI projects (billions of VND, ln)	GSO	Investment	3.81	1.96	3.95	1.95	0.78	0.28	0.52	0.67			
Average trade fairs held in province	MOIT	PCI hard data	8.91	4.17	10.11	4.91	0.22	1.25	1.31	0.32			
Private service providers/total service providers	GSOC	nganh_kd	1.0%	0.8%	1.0%	0.8%	0.88	0.16	0.32	1.00			
Average enterprise profit (billions VND)	GSOC	kqkd9	6.05	1.26	6.04	1.02	0.95	−0.07	−0.72	0.66			
Human capital													
Population (1000s)	GSO	LHDN	1347.24	1162.49	1476.18	1203.42	0.69	0.40	0.77	0.65		0.61	0.78
Population (1000s, ln)	GSO	LHDN	6.92	0.50	7.11	0.38	0.10	1.65	2.01	0.10			

Variable	Source	Category										
Services provided – vocational training centers (% good or very good)	PCI	E8	35.3%	7.7%	37.2%	8.5%	0.28	1.09	1.35	0.13		
Literacy rate	GSO	Education	92.4%	7.8%	93.8%	5.1%	0.42	0.81	0.12	0.85		
Net migration into province	GSO	Population & employment	-0.16	9.31	-1.34	5.76	0.56	-0.59	-0.32	0.85		
Skilled labor in workforce (%)	GSO	Population & employment	15.3%	6.8%	14.5%	5.7%	0.62	-0.50	0.04	0.85		
Services provided – general education (% good or very good)	PCI	E7	53.4%	9.1%	53.7%	8.4%	0.88	0.15	-0.14	0.62		
High school graduation rate (%)	GSO	Population & employment	97.1%	2.1%	97.0%	2.5%	0.89	-0.14	0.00	0.85		
Employment rate	GSO	Population & employment	58.9%	4.2%	58.8%	3.1%	0.90	-0.13	-0.37	0.85		
Geography												
Distance from Hanoi (km)	GSO	Administrative unit	821.17	733.35	946.24	760.03	0.43	0.80	0.24	0.49	0.77	0.63
Distance from Hanoi (km, ln)	GSO	Administrative unit	6.10	1.34	6.21	1.37	0.69	0.39	0.08	0.55		
Central highlands region	GSO	Administrative unit	2.4%	15.4%	10.0%	30.3%	0.14	1.48	0.34	0.73		
North southeast region	GSO	Administrative unit	7.1%	26.1%	16.0%	37.0%	0.20	1.30	2.22	0.03		
South central coast region	GSO	Administrative unit	14.3%	35.4%	8.0%	27.4%	0.34	-0.96	-0.32	0.75		

Table 8.A1 (cont.)

Potential confounders	Source	Survey question	Must retire (n=47)		Promotion eligible (n = 50)		Significance tests				MANOVA	
			Mean	SD	Mean	SD	P-Value	T-Statistic	Wilcoxon Z	Fisher's P	F	P
Northern mountains region	GSO	Administrative unit	26.2%	44.5%	18.0%	38.8%	0.35	−0.94	−1.04	0.30		
Mekong delta region	GSO	Administrative unit	23.8%	43.1%	20.0%	40.4%	0.66	−0.44	−1.24	0.21		
Red River delta region	GSO	Administrative unit	16.7%	37.7%	20.0%	40.4%	0.69	0.41	0.27	0.79		
North central coast region	GSO	Administrative unit	9.5%	29.7%	8.0%	27.4%	0.80	−0.26	0.26	0.79		

Note: Must Retire= 1 if >=54; Promotion eligible= 1 if >=50 & <54.

Sources: (NGTCHC) Nien giam tS chu-c hanh chinh ViSt Nam (Vietnam Administrative Handbook). Multiple Years. Statistical Publishing House: Hanoi, Vietnam (www.nxbthongke.com.vn/?page=bookdetail&id=517); (PCI) Provincial Competiveness Index. Multiple Years. Province-level Dataset. Vietnam Chamber of Commerce and Industry, Hanoi, Vietnam (www.pcivietnam.org/du-lieu-pci-c16.html); (ONA) Office of National Assembly 2 012. Dataset on Provincial People's Council Confidence Voting. Supplied Directly to Author; (GSO) General Statistical Office. Multiple Years. Statistical Handbook Online (https://www.gso.gov.vn/Default_en.aspx?tabid=766); (GSOC) General Statistical Office Enterprise Survey. Multiple Years. (http://catalog.ihsn.org/index.php/catalog/3 209/study-description); VNINIC. Multiple Years. Report on Vietnam Internet Resources. Hanoi, Vietnam (www.vnnic.vn/sites/default/files/whitebook/ReportOnVietNamInternetResources2014.pdf); MPI (Ministry of Planning and Investment); MOIT (Ministry of Industry and Trade); MONRE (Ministry of Natural Resources and Environment). Data listed as PCI Hard Data was supplied directly to the PCI research team by the sources and is available in the PCI provincial datasets.

Table 8.A2 *Balance between officials eligible for promotion and who must retire*

Potential confounders	Source	Survey question	Must retire (n=42)		Promotion eligible (n = 50)			Significance tests			MANOVA	
			Mean	SD	Mean	SD	P-Value	T-Statistic	Wilcoxon Z	Fisher's P	F	P
Institutions & governance												
General governance												
Final score in PCI governance ranking	PCI	Annual Report	58.05	3.28	58.55	3.44	0.48	0.70	0.87	0.62	0.22	0.88
Ranking in PCI governance index	PCI	Annual Report	31.85	16.86	30.09	15.86	0.61	−0.52	−0.83	0.32		
Attitude of provincial government towards private business (% good or very good)	PCI	H1	43.5%	6.4%	44.1%	8.4%	0.71	0.38	0.80	0.62		
Regulation												
Time spent to comply with government regulations (>10%)	PCI	D6	23.9%	8.6%	22.2%	7.1%	0.30	−1.05	−1.00	0.13	0.62	0.71
Negotiations with tax authority are normal (% agree or strongly agree)	PCI	D14.3	42.7%	8.1%	44.0%	6.2%	0.37	0.90	1.07	1.00		
Total inspections (median)	PCI	D1	1.24	0.34	1.31	0.34	0.38	0.87	1.12	0.44		
Firms registered within 1 month	PCI	C5	15.1%	6.6%	15.7%	6.7%	0.64	0.47	0.68	0.32		
Days to register business	PCI	C1	10.65	2.29	10.60	2.06	0.91	−0.11	0.33	0.62		

Table 8.A2 (cont.)

Potential confounders	Source	Survey question	Must retire (n=42)		Promotion eligible (n = 50)			Significance tests				MANOVA	
			Mean	SD	Mean	SD	P-Value	T-Statistic	Wilcoxon Z	Fisher's P		F	P
Registration officials have professional knowledge (Yes=1)	PCI	C3.1.3	39.8%	8.0%	40.0%	6.8%	0.91	0.11	−0.87	0.85			
Property rights & contracting institutions														
Land use rights certificate (share of firms holding (%))	PCI	B4	66.0%	13.3%	69.7%	10.8%	0.14	1.50	1.12	0.32		0.39	0.88
Share of land with land use rights	MONRE	PCI Hard Data	85.3%	9.9%	87.4%	9.3%	0.29	1.07	0.71		0.62	
Wait for land title (median days)	PCI	B4.2	45.04	32.76	41.51	18.64	0.52	−0.65	0.70	0.38			
Expropriation risk (mean on 1–5 scale)	PCI	B4.3	2.59	0.22	2.62	0.23	0.50	0.68	1.94	0.05			
Share of cases in local courts filed by private firm (%)	SPC	PCI Hard Data	76.1%	21.6%	78.8%	16.0%	0.50	0.68	0.15	1.00			
Used courts or other legal institutions to resolve disputes (%)	PCI	G6	24.7%	12.9%	23.5%	10.5%	0.70	−0.39	0.26	0.67			
Transparency														
Average access to provincial legal documents (1–5)	PCI	F1.1–1.12	3.03	0.11	3.07	0.15	0.21	1.25	−0.06	0.62		0.42	0.84

Variable	Source	Sub-source									
Average access to provincial planning documents (1–5)	PCI	F1.1–1.12	2.40	0.12	2.43	0.18	0.39	0.87	0.80	0.62		
Average website openness (1–20)	PCI	PCI hard data	21.53	5.31	22.44	6.09	0.46	0.75	0.85	0.32		
Transparency sub-index (PCI)	PCI	Annual report	5.83	0.39	5.88	0.50	0.58	0.55	0.81	1.00		
Relationship is necessary to obtain provincial documents (%)	PCI	F2	67.3%	7.2%	66.5%	7.5%	0.61	−0.52	−0.92	0.62		
Corruption												
Percentage of revenue in informal payments (% >10%)	PCI	G10	9.3%	5.4%	8.1%	3.9%	0.21	−1.27	−1.07	0.62	1.24	0.30
Corruption control sub-index (PCI)	PCI	Annual report	5.96	1.04	6.16	0.80	0.29	1.06	1.21	0.13		
Commissions on government contracts (%)	PCI	G13	51.0%	7.8%	50.3%	10.6%	0.72	−0.36	−0.32	0.62		
Firms in my line of business pay bribes (% Strongly Agree or Agree)	PCI	G9	56.4%	10.2%	56.5%	8.4%	0.96	0.05	−0.61	0.32		
Growth in year before chairman's tenure												
Development growth												
Avg. GDP growth	GSO	PCI hard data	11.0%	5.6%	11.9%	5.3%	0.49	0.69	0.57	0.79	0.36	0.83
Avg. growth in FDI projects	MPI	PCI hard data	27.1%	60.0%	25.7%	32.0%	0.92	−0.11	0.08	0.64		
Avg. growth in FDI capital	MPI	PCI hard data	321.5%	890.2%	412.8%	801.6%	0.70	0.39	1.18	0.65		
Avg. growth in employment	GSO	Population & employment	1.4%	1.2%	1.1%	1.2%	0.42	−0.81	0.52	0.30		

Table 8.A2 (cont.)

Potential confounders	Source	Survey question	Must retire (n=42) Mean	SD	Promotion eligible (n = 50) Mean	SD	Significance tests P-Value	T-Statistic	Wilcoxon Z	Fisher's P	MANOVA F	P
Avg. growth in private enterprises	GSO	Investment	19.8%	16.8%	20.5%	7.0%	0.85	0.19	0.56	0.30		
Human capital growth												
Avg. growth in population	GSO	Population & employment	1.0%	0.8%	0.9%	0.7%	0.93	−0.08	0.75	0.10	0.27	0.90
Avg. change in literacy	GSO	Population & employment	0.4%	0.5%	0.4%	0.6%	0.86	0.18	−0.12	0.85		
Avg. change in graduation rates	GSO	Population & employment	2.4%	4.0%	2.9%	3.8%	0.57	0.56	−0.21	0.85		
Governance growth												
Avg. change in PCI scores	PCI	Annual report	−0.21	1.81	−0.07	1.45	0.67	0.42	0.67	0.13	0.43	0.65
Avg. change in PCI rank	PCI	Annual report	−0.14	6.21	0.32	6.24	0.73	0.35	−0.20	0.62		

Note: Must retire= 1 if >=54; Promotion eligible= 1 if >=50 & <54.

Sources: (NGTCHC) Nien giam tS chu-c hanh chinh ViSt Nam (Vietnam Administrative Handbook). Multiple Years. Statistical Publishing House: Hanoi, Vietnam (www.nxbthongke.com.vn/?page=bookdetail&id=517); (PCI) Provincial Competiveness Index. Multiple Years. Province-level Dataset. Vietnam Chamber of Commerce and Industry Vietnam, Hanoi, Vietnam (www.pcivietnam.org/du-lieu-pci-c16.html); (ONA) Office of National Assembly 2012. Dataset on Provincial People's Council Confidence Voting. Supplied Directly to Author; (GSO) General Statistical Office. Multiple Years. Statistical Handbook Online (www.gso.gov.vn/Default_en.aspx?tabid=766); (GSOC) General Statistical Office Enterprise Survey. Multiple Years. (http://catalog.ihsn .org/index.php/catalog/3 209/study-description); VNINIC. Multiple Years. Report on Vietnam Internet Resources. Hanoi, Vietnam (www.vnnic.vn/sites/def ault/files/whitebook/ReportOnVietNamInternetResources2014.pdf); MPI (Ministry of Planning and Investment); MOIT (Ministry of Industry and Trade); MONRE (Ministry of Natural Resources and Environment). Data listed as PCI Hard Data was supplied directly to the PCI research team by the sources and is available in the PCI provincial datasets.

9 The Distributional Effects of Investment Incentives

On August 9, 2014, the city of Ferguson, Missouri, erupted after the shooting of Michael Brown by police officer Darren Wilson. This shooting, while tragic, helped spark a national debate about issues ranging from police tactics to racial inequality. One factor largely left out of the discussion, however, was the underlying contribution of state and local incentive policies to the incident by exacerbating economic and racial inequality in the region.

These issues were brought to the fore in a provocative *Atlantic Monthly* article by Walter Johnson on the city of Ferguson's inability to raise tax revenue. Johnson (2015) uncovered that Ferguson's Fortune 500 company, Emerson Electric, paid only $68,000 in property taxes for its headquarters, not owing to formal economic development policies but to an extremely low tax assessment of their headquarters and new data center. Despite a global headquarters and brand new $50 million building on their 152-acre campus, Emerson's property values assessment never exceeded $15 million. In fact, the taxes paid by Emerson were so low that even the company's leaders noticed it and therefore rejected formal tax abatements from the St. Louis Economic Development Partnership.

The revenue shortfall from these low tax assessments in Ferguson was exacerbated by a policy of TIF, used to lure retail operations.[1] These TIFs were funded with municipal bonds, so as the localities' revenue dipped, they found themselves struggling deeper to find resources to make the interest payments.[2] In short, the city's aggressive pursuit of big investors had placed them in a double bind.

Johnson went on to explicitly link the city's tax incentives and abatements to attract large companies to aggressive policing and socioeconomic inequality. According to Johnson, the tremendous giveaways in tax incentives left Ferguson with a budget shortfall that could only be

---

[1] Details on Ferguson's use of TIFs can be found in the city's comprehensive financial report (Department of Finance, City of Ferguson 2014).

[2] For example, the city's Downtown TIF fund decreased 41% in 2014 due to weaker tax collections and debt obligations (Department of Finance, City of Ferguson 2014, p. 7).

balanced by aggressive policing to enforce and collect municipal fines, which totaled 20% of the city's budget in 2013 (Johnson 2015). This example is an extreme case of funding economic development through regressive revenue measures. Without a wealthy personal-income tax base, mining the city's poor residents for fines appeared to be an escape.

From a methodological perspective, Ferguson could be an outlier. It is a notoriously poorly governed city that received the glare of the national spotlight after an explosive event. We argue in this chapter, however, that Ferguson's plight is actually indicative of a larger phenomenon that can be observed at all levels of governments that use incentives as part of an economic development strategy. Even under the most successful conditions, incentives reduce the short-term revenue that is available from new corporations – either fully, in the form of tax holidays, or partially, in the form of corporate income tax reductions. The costs of the new investment projects, however, do not disappear in the short term. New corporations increase demands on infrastructure, which must be maintained and upgraded. The projects may increase pollution or waste, or may have other environmental consequences that require attention and expenditures from local officials. Even the bureaucratic costs of licensing, land registries, and regulatory enforcement are not trivial for new entrants. When companies relocate to a city but do not pay for themselves in initial revenue, where do politicians find the funds to plug the short-term financial shortfalls?

Identifying the costs or benefits of incentives is difficult in that the implications of incentives not only depend on the effectiveness of attracting investment or encouraging expansions, but also the spillovers to other business. In some theoretical works, such Ellis and Rogers (2000), incentive offers are modeled as a prisoner's dilemma, arguing that incentives make all states worse off. Other works, such as that of Kline and Moretti (2014), model the economic benefits of place-based economic development policies, illustrating the potential economic development and tax-revenue generation benefits of incentives. An empirical study by Hanson and Rohlin (2011) shows that incentives often have negative spillovers in communities, undercutting the argument that incentives generate additional tax revenues through indirect increases in employment and the expansion of the tax base. In general, the literature on the fiscal costs of incentives is less developed than the work exploring the direct impact of incentives on targeted firms.

In this chapter, we examine the link between economic development incentives and tax inequality. We suggest that incentives are costly to governments, requiring conscious policy decisions on how to fund these programs. Elected officials regularly choose regressive taxation and spending policies that disproportionately affect the poor and middle class to fund their incentive programs. Next, we directly examine the two main mechanisms of shifting the costs of economic development politics. We show that politicians choose to fund economic development programs through regressive sales taxes. Indeed, many states have laws that actually require economic development programs to raise additional revenue through sales taxes. We show a statistically significant correlation between sales taxes and incentives, but also provide qualitative evidence of a clear causal relationship. Politicians are enacting new regressive taxation policies precisely to fund incentive programs.

Next, we examine how politicians cut back expenditures on social programs and public services to balance the books, leading to cuts in important services for the poor or equalizing institutions such as education. While finding a clear link between government spending cuts and incentives is challenging, few patterns are clearer than the relationship between incentives and local education funding. It is no surprise, therefore, that school districts show strong opposition to incentives, generating some high-profile lawsuits that we discuss later in this chapter.

9.1 Incentives Increase Tax and Spending Inequality

Numerous studies have examined the efficiency (or inefficiency) of place-based policies. This chapter deviates from the cost-benefit analysis of incentives at the firm level that we documented in Chapter 4 to explore the fiscal costs of incentives to governments. What are the fiscal costs of these incentives to state and local governments? In a remarkable self-study of economic development policies in the region, the East-West Gateway – an economic development organization that represents the St. Louis area and boasts the mayor of St. Louis and the mayor of Florissant (neighboring Ferguson) as members of its board of directors – criticized its own local economic policies. The report reached a devastating conclusion about the aggregate effect of St. Louis tax incentive programs (2011, p. iii):

> This research documents that the use of these tax incentives has been ineffective both as a way to increase regional sales tax revenue or to produce a significant increase in quality jobs. It also clearly has not helped municipalities avoid fiscal stress or had a general beneficial economic impact on the region.

In line with Johnson's thesis on Ferguson, the report stressed that the costs were not just inefficiency and ineffectiveness: "tax incentives have exacerbated economic development and racial disparity in the St. Louis region" (East-West Gateway 2011, p. iv). The report found that poor cities had actually further injured themselves by trying to compete with the deals offered by rich municipalities. The authors concluded that the programs do not pay for themselves from additional tax revenues, and they merely serve to generate greater fiscal strain.[3] The self-study illustrates the broad awareness of the inequalities caused by these incentives, including awareness on the part of elected mayors and other government officials. And yet, incentives, including TIFs, are still common among municipalities in the state (Missouri Department of Revenue 2015).[4]

This example summarizes our broader concerns about the distributional impact of incentives. In the rest of this this chapter, we outline the ways in which economic development policies can be funded, focusing on the distributional impact of incentives. We first critically assess the argument of economic development organizations, state and local agencies tasked with increasing investment and revenue, that incentives generate additional revenues. Then, we explore how cities and states pay for incentives in the short and long run by reducing other spending, raising taxes, or issuing debt.

The best-case scenario, articulated by supporters, is that economic development programs, which are primarily comprised of tax incentives and other giveaways, provide a net positive taxpayer return, where investments in economic development lead to future increases in tax revenues.[5]

As we illustrate in the rest of this chapter, governments have made clear decisions on how to fund these incentives which helps reveal their costs. This is because even the most successful incentive programs impose short- to medium-term budget shortfalls on governments. After all, tax incentives, particularly tax holidays, specifically limit revenue collection from new investors at the same time that those projects generate bureaucratic, regulatory, and infrastructure costs for local governments. As we show below, localities generally pay for these budget shortfalls in two ways: (1) tax base broadening or (2) expenditure cuts.

Ironically, one of the motivations for location-specific incentives is to reduce regional inequalities; economic development policies are targeted at firms to encourage them to move to specific locations or to encourage activities that can reduce wage inequality. Unfortunately, existing research has found little support for incentives reducing poverty

---

[3] For academic work on the use of TIFs, see Felix and Hines (2013). They find that cities with per capita incomes below $25,000 rarely use TIFs.

[4] One example is the city of St. Louis' creation of the Cortex business district in 2012. This business district has channeled millions in incentives to companies, including a $32 million TIF for IKEA in 2014 (Bryant 2014).

[5] Our discussion of the GASB 77 in the next chapter provide evidence that numerous pro-incentive organizations make the argument that tax incentives increase government revenues.

rates, introducing other measures of economic inequality, or decreasing inequality.[6]

We argue that incentive use can lead to an increase in *tax inequality* through the shifting of tax burdens. In the next three sections, we provide an empirical analysis of the link between incentives and inequality. As noted above, the incredible heterogeneity of government decisions on funding incentives requires some care and modesty in the determination of the fiscal impact of incentives. A comprehensive analysis of the topic requires a mixture of quantitative and qualitative analysis. The quantitative analysis in sections 9.2 and 9.3 allows us to establish patterns of taxation inequality and incentive use that are consistent with governments choosing regressive taxation policies to fund incentive programs. In Section 9.2, we show that incentive use is indeed correlated with higher levels of aggregate tax inequality. In Section 9.3, we show that this tax inequality is likely caused by the strong correlation between the use of regressive sales taxes and incentive use.

At the end of Section 9.2 and continuing in Section 9.3, we largely draw on qualitative analysis to help explore the plausibility of a causal link between incentives and fiscal inequality. In Section 9.3, we show that the incentive programs are, at least frequently, the *cause* of higher levels of regressive taxation. This is due to a legal requirement in many states that incentive programs be paid for by enacting new taxes. In Section 9.4 we show that incentives are associated with major reductions in revenues for school districts. This pattern has been formally established in a number of court cases.

9.2 General Patterns of Tax Inequality and the Use of Incentives

The variety of types of incentives, as well as the abatement of future tax revenues for tax incentives makes direct comparisons of the cost of incentive programs fraught with measurement error. Fortunately, existing research by Patrick (2014) has argued that incentives, specifically non-tax incentives, at the state and local level are constrained by state constitutional provisions. A large number of states have detailed rules on the types of support that can be offered to business. Patrick uses these constitutional rules to estimate the impact of incentives on state employment and growth.

We harness Patrick's Incentive Environment Index (IEI) to examine how a state's ability to offer incentives affects the fiscal choices of elected officials. Patrick examines how state constitutions shape states' ability to

---

[6] See Mason and Thomas (2010) for a review of the literature on TIFs and inequality. Mason and Thomas find that TIF use in Missouri increased inter-municipal inequality.

raise debt, use general government revenue, or use equity provisions such as public-private partnerships for the public to take ownership positions in a firm.[7]

Our own International City/County Management Association data (see Chapter 5) finds that there is a correlation of 0.37 between municipalities offering direct subsidies and the offering of tax incentives. Thus, we feel comfortable drawing on the work of Patrick (2014), which overcomes many of the methodological problems with other incentive studies by focusing on legal limits to offering non-tax incentives.

Patrick (2014) generates her index by examining state constitutional provisions on providing direct aid to firms. The IEI score ranges from 31 to 129, with higher scores indicating a greater ability of the state to offer incentives to business.[8] She provides systematic evidence that these policies shape the ability of localities to offer non-tax incentives to firms, arguing that a state's ability to offer cash incentives or low-interest financing is limited by three type of restrictions: credit clauses, appropriation clauses, and stock clauses (Patrick 2014, p. 17). For example, credit clauses limit the ability of states to use their credit to aid private firms, but potential restrictions on their use vary tremendously. Some states limit the ability of governments to raise industrial revenue bonds, the proceeds of which can be used for cash incentives or abatements. Credit clauses are one of the most common forms of restrictions, and can also constrain the ability of states or municipalities to directly offer credit to firms in the form of low-interest loans or other forms of financing. As Patrick (2014) outlines, states vary in their use of credit clauses, sometimes restricting industrial revenue bonds at the state level, at other times restricting only at the local level. This rich variation in state constitutional limits often amounts to state constitutions excluding very specific forms of support to private firms.

What is most compelling about this measure is that it can be harnessed to examine how states' ability to offer upfront incentives to firms shapes tax policy decisions. Note that we argue that even if these incentives are non-tax incentives (cash grants, for example), they will have long-term consequences for states and municipalities struggling to fund these programs. In the next section, we examine in more detail the use of regressive sales taxes to fund incentives. In this section, we simply examine the

---

[7] These constraints are largely about non-tax incentives, so the forgiving of future tax revenues is not captured in this measure, although government spending that requires additional taxes in the future clearly is. There is at least suggestive evidence that these incentives are complements, not substitutes. Patrick (2014) shows that most "megadeals" include both grant and tax abatement components, and other work has noted that many tax incentive programs are tradable, allowing firms to monetize incentives.

[8] Patrick (2014) provides a detailed discussion of this index.

9.2 General Patterns of Tax Inequality and the Use of Incentives

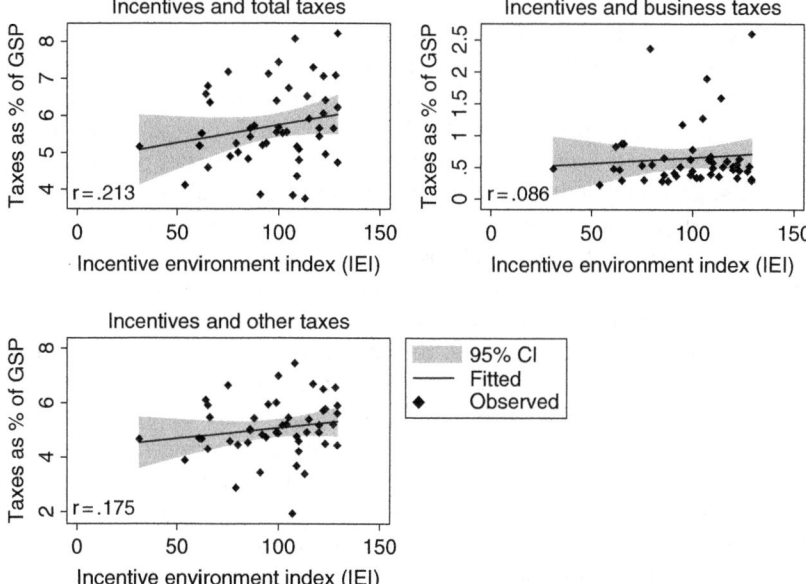

Figure 9.1 Constitutional ability to offer incentives and total taxation. Note: The IEI measures the state incentive rules through constitutional limits on raising debt, using general government revenues, or using equity provisions for incentives in 2000. Larger numbers represent a greater ability to offer incentives. The state tax shares as a percentage of gross state product are from the US Census Bureau, State Government Tax Collections 2006. We measure total taxes in the upper left panel, business taxes (corporate income tax, property tax, corporate licensing tax, and occupational licensing tax) in the upper right panel, and all other taxes (including personal income taxes) in the lower left panel.

overall relationship between states that offer incentives and the progressivity (or regressiveness) of their tax code.

Figure 9.1 graphically illustrates this pattern using the IEI from 2000 and state taxation from 2006 that builds on the work of Prilliman and Meier (2014). Prilliman and Meier (2014) use data from the US Census Bureau – state government tax collections from 1977 to 2006 – to calculate the total state taxes as a percentage of gross state product, as well as breakdowns of business taxes (corporate income tax, property tax, corporate licensing tax, and occupational licensing tax). Their study uses data on tax burdens to examine how state taxes affect economic activity.

Their main finding is that taxes have little impact on gross state product, employment, or business establishment.

We use their coding and the original data source (US Census) to calculate state taxes, business taxes, and non-business taxes as a percentage of gross state product in 2014. This research design allows us to examine how past constraints on incentives shape current tax decisions. Our first graph presents the relationship between the ability of a state to offer incentives and total state taxes as a percentage of state gross product.

The first panel of Figure 9.1 presents a positive relationship between the ability to offer incentives and state taxes as a percentage of gross state product. In the top right and lower left panels of Figure 9.1 we also present the relationship between the ability to offer incentives and business taxes as a percentage of state gross product and non-business taxes as a percentage of gross state product. In both panels, there is an association between incentives and higher tax burdens, although variance around the predications is relatively wide for both panels. These three panels provide suggestive evidence that the ability to harness incentives to attract private business is clearly not a way to lower overall taxes on business and labor.

To complement this analysis we now focus on actual dollars of incentives announced by state and local governments and how this affects the overall distribution of taxation. We again draw on data from IncentivesMonitor. We aggregate incentive dollars provided by state and local governments to the state level from 2010 to 2014. To reduce the influence of outliers and skew, we measure incentives as the natural log of total dollars of incentives as a percentage of the (log) state's population.

To measure the progressivity of the taxation at the state and local levels, we draw on the Institute on Taxation and Economic Policy (ITEP) database of the progressivity of state and local tax burdens (ITEP 2015). ITEP collects micro data from multiple sources, including the American Community Survey, Consumer Expenditure Survey, Current Population Survey, IRS Individual Public Use Tax Files, and US Census data, combining these with aggregated data from sources such as state tax and revenue departments to create simulated tax burdens. These simulations model projected personal income taxes, consumption taxes, and corporate taxes, which serve as inputs into the ITEP index using a straightforward aggregation strategy.[9]

---

[9] The index for each state equals 1 minus the average of the following ratios: (1) the after-tax income of the richest 1% as a share of pretax income over the after-tax income of the poorest 20% as a share of pretax income; (2) the after-tax income of the richest 1% as a share of pretax income over the after-tax income of the middle 60% as a share of pretax income; and (3) the after-tax income of the best-off 20% as a share of pretax income over the after-tax income of the poorest 40% as a share of pretax income, half-weighted. For

9.2 General Patterns of Tax Inequality and the Use of Incentives

In short, the index calculates the inequality of taxation. Negative values indicate regressive tax burdens on individuals stemming from state and local tax policies. In fact, all states have negative values, ranging from the least unequal at -0.5 (Delaware) to the most unequal at -12.5% (Washington).

Consistent with the theory that states fund incentives through regressive taxation policies, the states with the most unequal tax burdens are those that are most active in providing incentives. Texas, the subject of our analysis in Chapter 6, is the second most unequal state. As we outline in the next section, the relationship is mechanical since some states such as Texas levy sales taxes at the local level explicitly to fund incentive programs. Also on the list of most regressive jurisdictions are Washington, the site of the largest incentive in US history (Boeing), and Illinois, a state notorious for the use of TIFs.

In Figure 9.2 we present the relationship between incentives allocated from 2010 to 2014 and tax inequality in 2014. Again, we should be cautious about making causal claims. In aggregate, it is tricky to tie individual incentive policies to immediate increases in regressive taxes. Some incentives in this time period may have been funded with immediate tax changes, while other incentive programs lead governments to forgo future tax revenue and thus required cuts in spending, increased revenue collection, or bond issues, which led to debt and higher interest.

Figure 9.2 reveals that greater incentive use (dollars allocated in 2010–2014) is associated with higher levels of tax inequality in 2014. This inequality is a key measure of the progressivity of the tax system. States that provide more incentives have more regressive tax systems.

What is driving the association between incentives and unequal tax burden? ITEP (2015, p. 6) presents a summary of the main components of state and local tax policies and how they contribute to the regressive nature of taxation:

> Sales and excise taxes are very regressive. Poor families pay almost eight times more of their incomes in these taxes than the best-off families, and middle-income families pay more than five times the rate of the wealthy.

Following this line of argument, the correlation between incentives and tax inequality is mostly likely generated by the funding of incentives through regressive sales and excise taxes. In the next section, we not only reveal a correlation between sales taxes and incentives; we demonstrate a clear causal relationship between the two. Many incentive programs were funded

more details on the ITEP methodology, see Institute on Taxation and Economic Policy. ITEP Microsimulation Tax Model Overview. Accessed June 15, 2016. www.itepnet.org/about/itep_tax_model_simple.php.

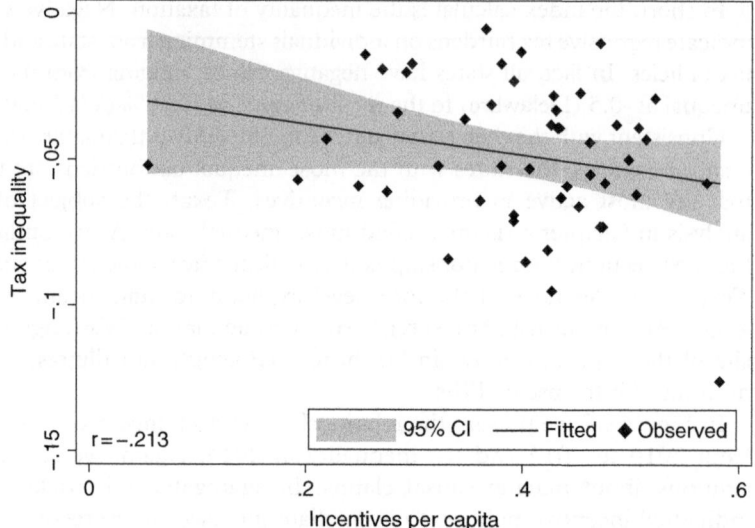

Figure 9.2 Incentives allocations and tax inequality (2010–2014). Note: Tax inequality is the ITEP (2015) measure of the level of tax inequality in 2000. Larger numbers represent more equal taxation. The x-axis presents incentives per capital as the natural log of total dollars of state and local incentives from IncentivesMonitor (www.incentivesmonitor.com) as a percentage of the natural log of state population. Accessed August 5, 2017.

by creating new sales taxes dedicated specifically for the purpose of making up for budget shortfalls caused by tax giveaways.

9.3 Increasing Sales Taxes to Pay for Tax Incentives

One of the clearest and most common mechanisms for funding fiscal incentives and other components of economic development programs are sales taxes at the state or local level. How common are incentives associated with sales taxes? Focusing on cities, as opposed to states, gives us a large sample of very diverse communities to examine.

Descriptive Statistics and Bivariate Relationships

To answer this question, we return to the 2009 ICMA survey data of local economic development that we analyzed in Chapter 5. This survey

9.3 Increasing Sales Taxes to Pay for Tax Incentives

queries municipalities about their economic development policies and about the types of existing taxes these jurisdictions have in place. A total of 844 municipalities answered the survey in 2009, providing information on their incentive policies, growth in incentive usage, how incentives are funded, and existing tax policies.

Descriptive statistics provides detail on these programs. First, municipalities were asked the percentage of incentives that are locally funded. According to municipal leaders, 88% of economic development dollars came from local public sources, and only 6% came from private (local- or state-level) sources. The most telling response was to the question of how economic development was financed, presented in Figure 9.3.

As Figure 9.3 illustrates, incentive programs are paid using a variety of sources, including many specialized fees, such as hotel (or casino) taxes. Most relevant for this chapter is the use of sales taxes to help pay for economic development. This number can be complicated to calculate, as some municipalities vary in the flavor of the sales taxes that they use.

Figure 9.3 shows that 23% of municipalities use sales taxes to fund economic development. This percentage may seem modest, but many cities do not have any sales taxes at all. Obviously, cities that do not have

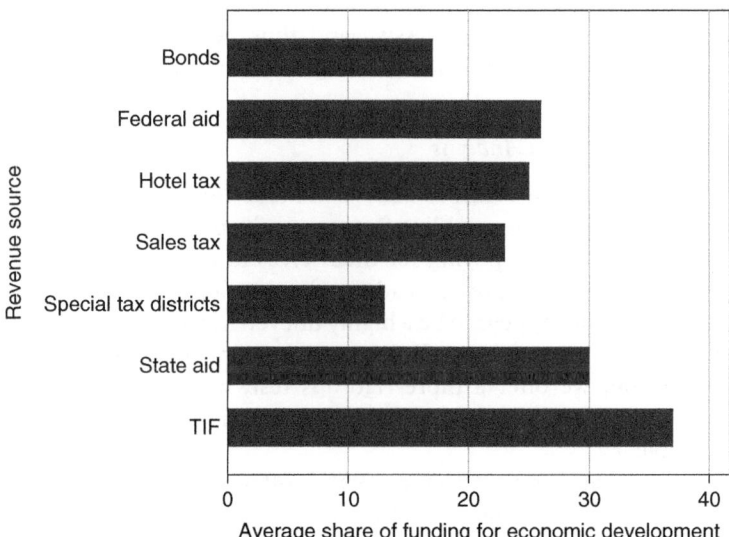

Figure 9.3 Funding for economic development.
Note: Percentages are based on municipality self-reports on the sources of funding for economic development from ICMA (2009).

any sales taxes cannot use these taxes to fund economic development. Our data reveals that just over half of the respondent municipalities have some form of sales taxes. When we only examine municipalities with sales taxes, 44% of these municipalities use sales tax revenues for economic development purposes.

The widespread use of sales taxes has important implications for the distribution of taxes across income groups. Politicians know that sales taxes bite harder for the poorest, as the ITEP (2015) report indicated. Sales taxes have long been known to be regressive (Suits 1977), and this position is not particularly controversial. Sales taxes account for a large portion of a poor person's income, simply because the denominator is smaller. Thus, the poor end up paying 7% of their income in sales taxes, compared to only 4.5% for wealthier citizens. When politicians raise sales taxes rather than other forms of revenue, they are making an explicit choice to shift larger burdens onto their poorest taxpayers. Because of this, many state sales taxes programs now exempt certain items, such as food, to minimize the regressivity of the taxes.

What is less clear is why sales taxes, as opposed to other more progressive forms of taxation, are popular with voters. As noted by Slemrod (2006), sales taxes are relatively popular despite the fact that these taxes are regressive. He argues that individual perceptions of the existing tax system shape support for sales taxes. Individuals already perceive the current tax system as regressive and thus believe that a shift towards sales taxes would lead to a more progressive overall tax system.

Regression Analysis

The ability of politicians to enact sales taxes to pay for economic development incentives is troubling from an equity perspective. If incentives do not end up actually paying for themselves in future medium- and long-term revenue and are instead funded through regressive taxes, this situation would appear to be a highly uneven transfer from a city's poorest residents to its wealthiest. Because of the controversial nature of such a conclusion, we offer a more rigorous test, where we formally test the relationship between incentives and economic development sales taxes, in Table 9.1.

Given that almost all cities (95%) offer some type of incentive we examine a question fielded on the growth of incentives as the key independent variable. This question asked municipalities to assess how much the average dollar amount of incentives changed in the past five years on a 1 (much less) to 5 (much greater) scale. Twenty-one percent of municipalities indicated increases in incentives, while 13% indicated declines in

9.3 Increasing Sales Taxes to Pay for Tax Incentives

Table 9.1 *Sales taxes funding economic development*

	(1)	(2)	(3)	(4)	(5)
Incentive growth	0.071***	0.060**			0.054***
	(0.02)	(0.02)			(0.02)
Local sales tax		0.308***			
		(0.04)			
Tax incentives			0.086**		
			(0.04)		
Subsidies				0.103***	
				(0.04)	
Log population					−0.006
					(0.02)
Economic growth					−0.015
					(0.01)
Economic dev. plan					0.033
					(0.04)
Foreign competition					0.00
					(0.04)
Region dummies	No	No	No	No	Yes
Observations	519	466	710	710	507
R-squared	0.02	0.12	0.01	0.01	0.13

Note: Logit models with sales taxes as the dependent variable. Marginal probabilities with standard errors in parentheses.
*** $p<0.01$, ** $p<0.05$

the average value (66% remained unchanged). Our main question is whether the municipalities with the greatest increase in the use of incentives resort to regressive sales taxes to fund their economic development programs.

In Table 9.1, we present a logit model where cities that fund incentives with sales taxes are coded as 1.[10] For ease of interpretation, we present marginal probabilities with robust standard errors in parentheses. In the first model, we include the key independent variable of the growth in incentives. In the second model, we include a control if the municipality has a sales tax, independent of whether or not this is used for economic development. In both models, we find that cities with the greatest growth in incentives are more likely to self-report funding economic development

---

[10] The wording of the question is as follows: "Which of the following sources of government revenue are used to fund your economic development programs? *(Check all applicable.)*." All models are logit models with robust standard errors.

through sales taxes. The substantive impact is quite large. Each 1-point increase in the use of incentives (1–5 scale) leads to an additional 6%–7% increase in the probability of using sales taxes to fund economic development. In the next two models, we examine if cities that provide incentives are more likely to enact sales taxes for economic development. We code a dummy variable for municipalities that use some form of tax incentives and direct subsidies to firms as 1, and cities without such programs as 0.[11] In the final model, we include controls for population, economic growth, whether the municipality has a formal economic development plan, and whether the municipality considers foreign locations to be the main competitors for investments.[12] The findings are similar. Municipalities that provide tax incentives or direct subsidies to firms are substantially more likely to enact sales taxes to fund economic development. In other words, municipalities fund fiscal incentives by broadening their tax base and introducing more regressive taxation.

In that light, tax incentives represent a transfer from the poorest citizens to wealthier corporations. This would be fine if there was a connection between incentives and investment and employment growth, but as we showed in Chapter 4, there is very little evidence for such a relationship.

Qualitative Evidence from Legal Authorizations of Incentive Programs

The strong correlation between sales taxes and incentive programs should be treated with caution. It is plausible that that some other unobserved factor is leading to a correlation between sales taxes and incentive programs. We know from the survey that municipalities are funding economic development with sales taxes, but did they *raise* these taxes specifically to fund these programs?

Fortunately, proving causation here does not require a complicated research methodology. All we have to do is read the legislation authorizing these incentive programs. Many of these sales taxes were specifically created to fund economic development programs, including over 500 municipalities in Texas. The cities in Texas levied sales taxes as part of legislation authorizing Texas 4A economic development corporations (TexasAhead

---

[11] In our sample of 844 local governments, 579 and 549 municipalities offered tax incentives and direct subsidies to firms; 446 municipalities offered both types of incentives to firms.

[12] Population is the natural log of the population in 2009, economic growth is a 1–7 range of self-reported economic growth rates in the past five years, the economic development plan variable is coded as 1 if the municipality has a written economic development plan for the attracting of investment, and foreign competition is coded as 1 for municipalities that see foreign locations as their primary competition for investment.

2016). The 1979 Texas Development Corporation Act authorized municipalities to raise sales taxes in order to fund economic development incentive programs, and these programs have been further expanded through amendments in 1989 and 1991.

The programs require voter approval and are *only* used for economic development (i.e., incentives), not for funding the general budget, paying municipal debt, building schools, or any other public purpose, with the exception of cleaning up contaminated property.

Resorting to the sales tax option is a widely used option; over 1,400 municipal sales taxes have been levied to fund economic programs since the Act's passage.[13] While it is possible that these programs could generate jobs, economic development, and tax revenues in other ways, their very creation through sales taxes provides transparency regarding their expected costs and who pays for them. In short, regressive sales taxes are specifically used to mobilize funds for incentive programs aimed at corporations.

While no systematic database exists on the funding mechanisms for incentive programs, news searches of economic development sales taxes initiatives yield numerous examples outside of Texas. In Arkansas, the cities of Booneville, Camden, Crossett, Eldorado, Newport, and Russellville, along with a handful of counties, have passed sales taxes ranging from 0.25% to 1% to fund economic development (Gillian 2009).

The pattern is clear; many cities fund economic development through the use of sales taxes. Using data and the actual wording of legislation, we have demonstrated that not only do municipalities use sales taxes to fund economic development, but many cities specifically create sales taxes with the goal of offsetting the budgetary holes caused by incentive schemes.

9.4 What Are the Fiscal Trade-Offs? School Districts and Economic Development Incentives

> But now, as we head into 2014, we know we have more work to do. That's why today I'm laying out a five-year blueprint for jobs and economic growth in Illinois. It's a blueprint that builds on the foundation we have laid these past five years.
>
> And it's a blueprint that recognizes that a truly strong economy relies not just on jobs, but also on fairness and inclusion. If we follow this blueprint, we'll do three things: create more jobs, deliver stronger education and build an economy that works for everyone.
>
> Illinois Governor Pat Quinn, 2014 State of the State Address

---

[13] For a list, see Glenn Hegar: Texas Comptroller of Public Accounts, List of Cities Who Have Adopted an Additional Local Sales and Use Tax. Accessed June 10, 2016. http://comptroller.texas.gov/taxinfo/addit.html.

In the annual Illinois State of the State Address, Governor Quinn outlined his priorities for the years and his many accomplishments. The accomplishments included claiming credit for business expansions and relocations from programs such as Advantage Illinois and Illinois Jobs Now!, along with more encompassing claims of "partnering with Chrysler" to expand jobs in the state. The goal of further job creation was presented as a complement to providing educational opportunities for children and adults.

Yet, despite the soaring rhetoric from elected officials on the self-funding nature of incentives and their positive effects on education, the academic literature on economic development incentives, and TIF in particular, has linked incentives with reductions in school funding. In a review of the literature on TIFs, Greenbaum and Landers (2014) highlight a number of studies showing that TIFs are costly for municipalities in the short and long run. Weber's (2003) study of TIFs in Illinois finds that TIFs had a major negative impact on school funding, which was only partially offset by additional transfers from the state. In this subsection, we show that the negative relationship between incentives and school funding has been recognized by courts and state legislatures.

Academic work highlights that revenue declines force trade-offs for state and local governments. Once money is allocated through incentives to firms, other programs, which depend on the revenue, must be cut or scaled back. This is clear to many stakeholders. Indeed, among the most vocal opponents of incentive programs, particularly local property abatements, are educational institutions and associations.[14]

Educators have long argued that economic development incentives have a negative impact on education funding. The American Federation of Teachers has generally been antagonistic towards what it termed "corporate welfare" in one of its resolutions urging for reform of economic subsidy programs (American Federation of Teachers 2000). In its 2009 guide to reforming state fiscal systems, it made changes in economic development policies an important component of its proposed reforms, including greater oversight, clawbacks, and the outright cutting of some subsidy programs. The union also highlights that many local economic development programs, such as TIF, by relying on municipal bonds, directly reduce the revenue base of school districts (American Federation of Teachers 2009). Similar criticisms have been levied by the National Education Association.[15]

---

[14] In a 1991 New York Times article, numerous education scholars and individual teachers voiced concerns on the fiscal costs of education (Celis 1991).

[15] The National Education Association of the United States produced a study with Good Jobs First descriptively titled "Protecting Public Education from Tax Giveaways to

9.4 What Are the Fiscal Trade-Offs?

The opposition of teachers and education associations to incentives along with the academic work linking incentives to reductions in school funding provide evidence of the trade-offs between incentives and schools. Our final piece of evidence provides four illustrative examples from Massachusetts, Illinois, Maryland, and California. Of special note is the case of California, where a landmark court case essentially repealed TIFs due to their negative impact on schools.

Our first illustrative example is the state of Massachusetts' audit of its ongoing Film Tax Credit. In the audit, the state auditor noted the extremely high cost of the program, totaling over $118,000 per local job created (including out-of-state jobs created, the number drops to $64,000).[16] According to the report, Massachusetts' balanced budget law requires spending cuts to offset these tax credits.[17] Thus, politicians in Massachusetts are *required* by law to make spending cuts to adjust for these expensive tax credits.

Even in cases where budget balance requirements do not directly require spending cuts, the fiscal strain on state budgets is obvious to state and local governments. One clear example is that some states reimburse local governments for the lost revenue from property tax abatements (Kenyon et al. 2012). State governments are often required to compensate municipalities that use tax incentives, causing a potential strain on state finances. But do these cuts come at the expensive of education institutions, as claimed by education interest groups?

A second example comes from the state of Illinois. A recent proposal to cancel seven TIF districts in Illinois would increase revenues over $250 million over five years, with half of these revenues dedicated to Chicago schools (Spielman 2015). This was not a technical point lost on politicians. Chicago Mayor Rahm Emanuel made clear that the very *purpose* of canceling these incentives was to generate additional revenue for cash-starved Chicago schools (Spielman 2015).

Our final example is perhaps the most compelling. In a recent lawsuit, school districts in California sued the state of California for lost property tax revenue from incentives. The schools had a major ally. In an effort to shore up the state's budget, Governor Jerry Brown proposed shutting down the state's 400 or so TIF districts. These districts imposed a tremendous cost on the state, as the state budget was required to compensate local municipalities for lost tax revenues. Governor Brown proposed shutting

---

Corporations: Property Tax Abatements, Tax Incremental Financing, and Funding for Schools" (National Education Association 2003).
[16] Massachusetts Department of Revenue (2014).
[17] Massachusetts Department of Revenue (2014).

down these districts and allowing property tax revenues to go directly to school districts (Dolan et al. 2011).

The fight over economic development went to the courts, with the California Redevelopment Association and others representing cities versus the California Director of Finance. Many cities, economic development associations, and broader organizations representing regions in California filed amicus curie briefs in support of these incentive programs.[18] On the other side were public interest groups such as the California Professional Firefighters association, the California Teachers' Association, and a number of local school districts. The 2012 ruling by the California Supreme Court shut down the 400 or so TIF districts in California.

The finding that TIFs cost school districts revenue was recognized by the California Supreme Court and has now been codified in many economic development programs (Kenyon et al. 2012). Numerous TIF programs now require approval from local school boards, and many states include grants to local school districts for lost property tax revenue. While the issuing of grants solves the school funding issue, it also means that the local development cost gets passed to the state, and in many cases can lead school districts to shift from opposition to TIFs to the overuse of TIFs to maximize grants.

9.5 Conclusion

Economic development has a number of goals, and the use of taxpayer money to fund quality employment, alternative energy, or amenities are important policy decisions for cities and states. Moreover, leadership is hard and always requires difficult choices, especially when politicians must choose how to allocate scarce budgetary resources. These decisions are made even more difficult by the fact that they are intertemporal and intergenerational. Politicians must choose how to balance policies that create the conditions for future economic growth against the needs of the public today. In the minds of many voters and some politicians, incentives are considered part of a strategy of planning for the future. Forgone revenue today will lead to more productive companies and more jobs down the road. In Chapter 4, we showed that these claims about future economic fortune were dubious at best, which generated the core premise of our argument in the book. If the payoffs are so uncertain, why offer them? In this chapter, we push beyond uncertainty and provide evidence

---

[18] A list of briefs in the case can be found at Stanford Law School: Robert Crown Law Library, Cal. Redevelopment Assoc. v. Matosantos. Accessed June 10, 2016. scocal.stanford.edu/opinion/cal-redevelopment-assoc-v-matosantos-34044.

9.5 Conclusion

that incentives have clear costs today that could undermine economic prospects.

Using a mix of quantitative and qualitative evidence, we document that cities and states that use investment incentives exhibit higher levels of economic inequality, which is fueled by a reliance on regressive taxation (through sales taxes) to pay for them and cuts to vital public services such as education. One could go so far as to make the argument that incentives serve as a transfer from a jurisdiction's middle class to its richest residents. In the case of Ferguson, the city filled the budget hole generated by expensive incentives by increasing the share of revenue accounted for by fines and penalties, fueling the already intense racial acrimony through increased policing. The explosive result was captured by newspaper headlines and television screens throughout the world.

The Ferguson riots were an anomaly, however. In most cases, the effect of incentives is a slow march to increased inequality and the degrading of the public services that might ameliorate inequality by increasing opportunity and general human capital. As we show in the final section of this chapter, a large proportion of the fiscal costs fall disproportionately on school districts.

The bottom line is that using incentives as a tool for political pandering is extremely costly. Politicians are exchanging short-term political gain for the long-term economic health of their populaces. When confronted with the high costs to school districts, what is the response of politicians? As we document in the next chapter, organizations representing economic development agencies, state financial officers, and election officials maintain that these incentive programs generate tax revenues for their districts. In a public battle over a proposed rule increasing the transparency of the costs of economic development programs, educational associations took the position that local governments should disclose the amount of tax revenues forgone from incentive programs. The opposition took the position that reporting would be too onerous a burden and that, in fact, most of these programs increased tax revenues through these abatements.

This debate motivates are final empirical exploration. Could transparency about the true economic costs of incentives reduce their utility as a political credit-claiming tool?

10 Potential Policy Solutions to the Pandering Problem

Our research was meant to contribute to academic debates on the competition for capital and how domestic politics shape economic policy in even the most globalized of countries. Ironically, the governments that are most dependent on mobile capital for investment may see the biggest impact of domestic politics on their economic development efforts. Far from making domestic politics irrelevant, the competition for capital – domestic or international – provides tremendous opportunities for politicians to take credit or reduce blame for economic outcomes.

Yet, our book also has very obvious links to public policy in the United States and beyond. Central to our work is voters' beliefs that incentive programs work, and this belief provides opportunities for pandering. Public beliefs that do not square with expert opinions are common in American politics, and there is always a temptation to focus on educating voters as a means of ending bad policy outcomes. Voters believe these policies work. In a few cases they are right, but in the vast majority, their beliefs appear to be incorrect from a long-term economic perspective. Moreover, the more complex and subtle the incentive policy, the more rationally ignorant voters are likely to be since the time invested in really understanding the policies is simply not worth the costs for each individual (Tullock 1958). Yet, as we have shown in Chapter 9, incentive policies may directly harm the interests of voters, reducing resources available for public services and contributing to inequality.

What can be done? There is already some movement to correct some of the more egregious uses of economic policies for credit claiming. Actions include backlashes against lucrative tax credits and incentive programs for TV and movie production. Nonprofit groups across the political spectrum, such as Good Jobs First, along with exposés by the *New York Times*, have publicized problematic incentives in attempts to shed further light on the opaque use of economic development policies.

Rather than speculate on the potential reforms, we identify two current types of reforms that have been enacted or proposed. First, we explore the use of clawback provisions as a way to safeguard taxpayer money.

10.1 The Ineffectiveness of Clawbacks

Clawback provisions police incentive programs by using the threat of cancellation and recouping of incentive payments or credits when firms do not live up to the incentive agreements. For example, firms may agree to particular numbers of jobs created in pre-specified time periods. If they fail to generate these jobs, more and more incentive programs now have the ability to reduce awards or may even require repayment of incentives. In Section 10.1, we examine the effectiveness of clawbacks in one of the main Missouri incentive programs. Unfortunately, we find very little evidence that clawbacks improve the performance of the incentive program.

A second reform is to provide greater transparency in the allocation of incentives, both on the specific firms receiving incentives and the fiscal costs to communities. In Section 10.2, we explore a recent ruling by a government oversight body that would require states and municipalities to disclose the fiscal costs of incentives. This ruling by the Government Accounting Oversight Board (GASB) first came into effect on December 15, 2015, and thus we cannot yet evaluate this ruling's effect on incentive allocations. Multiple interest groups have become active in the fight over GASB rules. We show that clear patterns are made by the actors that voice opposition to increased transparency of incentives (those most likely to benefit politically) and by those that voice support for increased transparency (from those groups that view incentives as costliest).

In Section 10.3, we test the impact of such transparency efforts directly by returning to our survey experiments from Chapter 7, where voters appeared to support politicians who offered incentives, whether or not they actually won the project. In this analysis, we employ virtually the same design with one small exception. This time, we remind voters of what they must give up in order to provide an incentive to new investors. We show that voters are very sensitive to the costs of these incentive programs. Providing information on the trade-offs for these programs negated many of the political benefits of their use for US and Canadian citizens that we observed in Chapter 7. Will the GASB reforms lead to less political pressure to use incentives? Given that this rule was recently enacted, we can only speculate on the direct impact of this increase in transparency. Based on our survey experiments, however, we believe that increasing transparency on the costs of incentives seems like a more promising route for reform rather than the use of clawbacks.

10.1 The Ineffectiveness of Clawbacks

In the last chapter, we established that incentive programs impose substantial costs to cities, states, and countries. The goal of this final part of the project is to complement the earlier analysis of incentives that focused on the Kansas PEAK program, summarized in Chapter 4, by extending it to the flagship incentive program in Missouri, the Missouri Quality Jobs program. We provide full details of our analysis in Appendix and only summarize the main findings here.

Expanding this study to an additional incentive program allows us to examine the generalizability of the first study and provides an additional evaluation that is extremely relevant for the study of the fiscal costs of incentives. Missouri clearly documents incentives that have been canceled or "clawed back" from firms that failed to comply with the incentive agreement.

As we document in the appendix, 45% of the Missouri incentives were subject to cancellation or clawbacks, which could have an impact on the overall performance of Missouri Quality Jobs Program. This situation allows us to compare the overall job creation of firms that received incentives and to perform secondary analysis to examine how the job creation performance of the program improves by removing underperforming firms from the program.

We use the same research design that we discussed in Chapter 4 to examine job creation of the flagship Missouri economic development program. Our analysis of the Missouri Quality Jobs Program is similar to our analysis of the Kansas PEAK program, with one addition. Using coarsened exact matching we estimate the impact of job creation in Missouri for firms that received incentives and those that did not. We also separate the firms that were subject to clawbacks and those that fulfilled their job creation commitments.

Our estimates, presented in detail in Appendix, illustrate that incentives in Missouri are associated with only an additional 1.31 jobs per incentive package as compared to the control group. Thus, the average cost per job of incentives exceeds $1 million. This estimate pools both the nonperforming, clawed-back firms as well as firms that continued in the program. What happens when we separate these two types of firms? As expected, the clawed-back firms created *fewer* jobs than the control group (with no incentives). Nevertheless, the remaining firms, which were judged to be compliant with the Missouri Quality Jobs Program, still created a trivial amount of jobs (see Appendix for more precise estimates). Even these best performing firms only created one–two more jobs per $1.6 million in incentives.

Our analysis of Missouri suggests that the fundamental problem with these programs is not that firms fail to comply with incentive agreements. The far bigger issue is the redundancy of incentives that has been documented throughout this book. As we noted in previous chapters, on average, two-thirds of firms report that they would have invested or expanded even without incentives. Clawbacks can thus police fraud or legitimate poor performance of investments, but they do not address that many incentive dollars are duplicative, wasted on firms that would have come anyway.

10.2 Can Transparency Improve Economic Development?

Given the ineffectiveness of clawbacks, an alternative strategy for improving the use of incentives is to increase these programs' transparency. Yet transparency can come in a number of forms, ranging from details on individual incentive offers to states and municipalities providing estimates of the aggregate costs of incentive programs. Although this reform is too recent to undergo analysis of its effectiveness, we can observe how political actors responded to a proposed rule change.

In 2013, GASB, a professional association that sets standards for state and local accounting, proposed a draft proposal that could reshape the debate over economic development policy. GASB is not a government entity, but GASB rules are largely followed by local governments in order to access capital (GASB 2008). After many years of taking no clear positions on the transparency of incentives, GASB issued a draft that would require transparency in the reporting of tax abatements, which included documenting the cost of abatements in government Comprehensive Annual Financial Reports. In short, municipalities would need to fully report the costs of incentives to their stakeholders.

The motivation for the GASB draft was that "[t]ax abatements are primarily viewed in the context of reducing tax revenues" (GASB 2014, p. 6), and a study that it commissioned highlighted the deficiencies in most states' collection and dissemination of data. This study included not only an evaluation of current abatement reporting but also surveys of numerous actors involved in abatements, including municipal bond raters. After circulating its draft text, GASB invited public comments on its draft, receiving almost 300 comments in total (GASB 2016).[1] This call for public comments provides a clear window into who supports or opposes incentives, their arguments, and their views on transparency of these programs.

Some of the comments are far from surprising. Public interest organizations – including those tracking incentives and, more generally, organizations pushing for transparency of government policies – voiced supportive comments, in many cases encouraging even stricter disclosure

---

[1] Nathan Jensen contributed to comment 180 with a number of other academics.

Potential Policy Solutions to the Pandering Problem

rules.[2] Many foundations, such as the Ford Foundation (GASB 2014, comment 178), voiced their support for increased transparency.[3]

Other major supporters included organizations representing state employees and teachers, in particular. For example, the American Federation of Teachers (AFT) submitted detailed comments, expressed its concerns about incentive programs, and encouraged the GASB to go farther by requiring other types of incentive programs to comply with these increased reporting standards (GASB 2014, comment 209). Other educational associations commented in support, expressing similar criticisms about the draft's limited scope.[4] In comment after comment, these agencies pointed out how these economic development policies divert revenues from educational funding using the same evidence that we documented in Chapter 9. Other unions and labor organizations, from the American Federation of Labor and Congress of Industrial Organizations (AFL-CIO) to the Memphis Firefighters Association, submitted comments about the fiscal costs of incentives and applauded the move towards greater transparency.[5]

Numerous government agencies also supported this transparency, with many agencies offering their own experiences as a model for disclosure. Both the Independent Budget Office New York City (GASB 2014, comment 221) and the Minnesota State Legislature (GASB 2014, comment 197) expressed support for the draft based on their own experiences. Many state auditors and comptrollers urged for even stronger standards.[6]

---

[2] For example, multiple organizations submitted comment 110. US PIRG supported this draft in comment 230 (GASB 2014).
[3] For joint comments from a number of foundations, see comments 242 and 245 (GASB 2014).
[4] New York State United Teachers (GASB 2014, comment 181), Washington Education Association (GASB 2014, 184), Education Law Center (GASB 2014, 185), Illinois Federation of Teachers (GASB 2014, 191), Louisiana Federation of Teachers (GASB 2014, 210), Ohio Federation of Teachers (GASB 2014, 211), AFT New Mexico (GASB 2014, 212), Jefferson County and Birmingham AFT (GASB 2014, 213), New York State School Boards Association (GASB 2014, 259), Alabama Education Association (GASB 2014, 286), School Superintendents of Alabama (GASB 2014, 285), Tennessee Teachers Association (GASB 2014, 287).
[5] American Federation of State, County, and Municipal Employees AFL-CIO (GASB 2014, comment 204), the Teamsters (GASB 2014, comment 216), Memphis Firefighters Association (GASB 2014, comment 229), Service Employees International (GASB 2014, comment 238), AFL-CIO (GASB 2014, comment 268).
[6] The State of Tennessee, Division of Audit recommended including a broader set of incentives (GASB 2014, comment 175). State Auditor of Vermont (GASB 2014, comment 232), Comptroller of Maryland (GASB 2014, comment 233), the Cook County Illinois Clerk (GASB 2014, comment 237), State Auditor of New Mexico (GASB 2014, comment 263) all voiced support for this draft. The Comptroller of the City of

10.2 Can Transparency Improve Economic Development? 203

While the vast majority of comments were supportive,[7] a cluster of critical comments was submitted from organizations representing elected officials and economic development professionals. These groups complained vociferously of the onerous burden disclosure would put on city and state officials, and the technical difficulties of collecting some of this data. National and state government financial officer's associations alone submitted seven comments[8] along with numerous other agencies and cities.[9]

The most prominent argument made by these agencies was that many of these economic development policies have a positive return on investment, including the increase of tax revenues in the future. Among their comments, a representative of the International Economic Development Council submitted:

> It is worth noting that tax abatements, or incentives, as they are commonly referred to in the economic development profession, are utilized with the intention of increasing the tax base over time. They represent an investment in the economic future of the community. Agreements are not entered into with the goal of losing money. Indeed, increasing the tax base is one of the most important objectives of economic development, next to job creation and improving the quality of life within a community.[10] (GASB 2014, comment 279)

A similar position was taken by the National Association of State Auditors, Comptrollers and Treasurers (GASB 2014, comment 225), the Georgia Economic Developers Association (GASB 2014, comment 226), and, in a joint letter, by the Government Finance Officers Association, International City/County Management Association, National League of Cities,

---

Philadelphia supported the proposal and gave examples of barriers in obtaining local economic development incentive data (GASB 2014, comment 217).

[7] The few general business associations submitting comments supported increased transparency. Most prominent was the Advocates for Independent Business (GASB 2014, comment 241). Its logic was that "[m]any cities, for example, have provided tax abatements to new big-box retail projects that compete directly with the Main Street businesses that we represent, sometimes leading to business closures and job losses."

[8] The Government Finance Officers Association (GASB 2014, comment 173), Florida Government Finance Officers Association (GASB 2014, comment 194), Illinois Government Finance Officers Association (GASB 2014, comment 199), Georgia Government Finance Officers Association (GASB 2014, comment 248), Virginia Government Finance Officers Association (GASB 2014, comment 250), Government Finance Officers Association of Texas (GASB 2014, comment 266), New York Government Finance Officers Association (GASB 2014, comment 295).

[9] Three cities submitted critical comments: City of Papillion, Nebraska (GASB 2014, comment 247), City of Dubuque, Iowa (GASB 2014, comment 264), City of Nebraska City, Nebraska (GASB 2014, comment 291).

[10] The Washington State Auditor offered a more complicated set of suggestions, focusing on the lack of a clear definition of an abatement (GASB 2014, comment 214).

National Association of Counties, and US Conference of Mayors (GASB 2014, comment 192). All of these comments claimed that the very premise of disclosing the costs of incentives made little sense. The Auditor of Delaware Country, Ohio, made the clearest point: "I would like to point out that in Ohio, tax abatements are approved on the local level and do not result in a reduction in tax revenues" (GASB 2014, comment 267).

These public comments on proposed transparency of incentives reveal two patterns. First, for the most part, the pro-incentive and anti-incentive camps are quite clear. The strongest supporters of incentives are the organizations representing government finance officers and economic development, along with associations representing elected mayors. A much larger number of critical voices emerged, including progressive and centrist NGOs, groups representing teachers, and public-sector unions. Government comptrollers and auditors are more mixed in their pattern of support.

What is also interesting is the lack of voice from many business interests. Business associations and conservative think tanks were silent on these issues,[11] with the exception of Advocates for Independent Business, who supported greater transparency. This mirrors the lack of support for these incentive policies from conservative and libertarian groups.[12]

Second, what is also revealing in these comments is the core debate on the fiscal costs of incentives. Interests representing higher education provided numerous details on how incentives are costly for school districts. These comments were mirrored by firefighters and public-sector unions, along with foundations and public-interest groups, all making claims about the fiscal costs of these incentives. As noted above, critical comments largely came from economic development professionals and elected officials. One of the most common arguments was that incentive programs generate long-run revenues.

On December 15, 2015, the GASB rule went into effect, leading to changes in the way states and municipalities report the fiscal consequences of incentives.[13] As Chapter 9 shows, two major consequences of incentives are the shifting of the burden of taxation to regressive sales taxes and through reductions of education funding.

---

[11] For a critical comment, see Novogradac & Company LLP (GASB 2014, comment 277).
[12] For example, see testimony critical of incentives to the Subcommittee on Federal Spending Oversight and Emergency Management from the Research Manager from the Heritage Foundation (Boccia 2015). A report by the American Legislative Exchange Council labels economic development subsidies as tax cronyism (Freeland et al. 2014).
[13] The impact of this ruling will not be apparent until cities release their 2016 and 2017 annual reports, which are still not fully complete as of this writing.

10.3 Testing the Benefits of Transparency in the United States and Canada

The GASB reform is consistent with the evidence in this book. The asymmetry between citizens, firms, and governments makes it incredibly difficult to identify redundant incentives, and our survey experiments indicate that voters provide additional credit (at least in the United States) for the excessive use of incentives. Politicians do not hide the fact that they are providing incentives, and in many cases, the dollars allocated to a firm are made clear in newspaper headlines and even in some governors' press releases. However, politicians rarely explain the opportunity costs of the incentives, the expenditures forgone in an attempt to lure new investors. In this final empirical analysis, we wondered whether the political benefits of investment incentives could be reduced by simply letting voters understand the true costs of the policy. Would this reduce their utility for credit-claiming and pandering?

As readers may recall, the focus of Chapter 7 was a survey experiment fielded in 2009 specifically designed to test our core theoretical model. In it, we showed that governors can effectively claim credit or avoid blame by using investment incentives. Our question mirrored the types of messages that governors use when communicating their economic development efforts to constituencies. As a result, the question wording purposely hid any trade-offs between incentives and other potential uses for scarce fiscal resources. But as we showed in Chapter 9, these incentives are not costless. They have dramatic effects on tax equality, income distributions, and public services. If trade-offs are presented in line with the GASB transparency recommendations above within the experimental design, how might this affect support for incentive policies?

Testing Transparency About the Costs of Incentives in the United States

To test the transparency policy solution, we fielded a follow-up survey in 2012 as part of Washington University's The American Panel Survey (TAPS). TAPS is similar in structure to the survey experiment from Chapter 7. It is an Internet-based survey of a representative population of 2,000 respondents. The specific question we fielded is almost identical in wording to our question from Chapter 7, with the addition of only two sentences on trade-offs in italics:

> Your state competed with a number of other states over a new manufacturing plant with 1,000 employees. With the support of the governor, your state offered a tax incentive (break/reduction) package that was equal or less than that of other states. As with all government policies, tax incentives come with trade-offs. *The money dedicated to tax incentives would not be available for government spending or tax cuts for individuals.*
>
> If your state does not receive this investment, how would this affect your evaluation of your governor's performance in office?
>
> (1) I would be much more likely to vote for the governor in the next election.
> (2) I would be slightly more likely to vote for the governor in the next election.
> (3) My vote choice would not be altered.
> (4) I would be slightly less likely to vote for the governor in the next election.
> (5) I would be much less likely to vote for the governor.

We present a simple table of these results in Table 10.1. For presentation purposes we again collapse "much more likely" and "slightly more likely" into a single variable coded 1 if the respondent is more likely to vote for the governor and 0 otherwise. In Table 10.1, the first row corresponds to the percentage of respondents indicating that they are more likely to vote for the governor if receiving the investment condition. The columns indicate when the respondent was treated with an incentive program that was greater than the other states or equal to, or less than, other states. The obvious implication is that the presentation of trade-offs between incentives and either tax cuts or spending increases has a dramatic impact on support for incentive programs.

Offering incentives becomes a losing strategy for governors when the trade-offs between incentives and either general tax reductions or spending increases. While we find no discernable difference between preferences when governors do not receive the investment, we observe a major difference in effect size when governors do receive the investment. Governors who attract investment without offering

Table 10.1 *Percentage of respondents supporting governor*

	Incentive	No incentive
Investment	0.2871	0.4326
	(.2261,.3569)	(.3535,.5154)
No investment	0.2265	0.2364
	(.1582,.3133)	(.1616,.3322)

Note: 95% confidence intervals in parentheses.

10.3 Testing the Benefits of Transparency

incentives receive 14.6% more support than governors who attracted investment with incentives, although this difference is not statistically significant.

This simple act of adding one sentence, which completely reverses the effects we observed in Chapter 7, has important implications for our project. Essential to any politicians' effective economic development strategy – at least in the context of credit claiming and blame avoidance using investment incentives – is message control. We know that politicians can pander to the public by offering lucrative investment incentives to firms, and these politics are an effective strategy to gain votes. Yet, this strategy backfires if politicians provide sincere information on the trade-offs between governments' selective support for investments and the other potential uses of government revenue. Transparency initiatives like the GASB, therefore, which are designed to make these trade-offs explicit, could go a long way towards reducing the pandering problem.

These results fit within the broader literature on inefficient redistribution in international trade policy. As Kono (2006) shows, democratic countries are more likely to use less transparent policy instruments, such as health and safety regulations, in an effort to provide trade protection for their constituencies. Central to Kono's argument is that politicians are purposely selecting complicated policy instruments that are difficult for opposing politicians to criticize.

We argue that politicians, rather than hiding incentives, tout their use of incentives to attract investment. Nevertheless, while they tout the benefits to all listeners, they obfuscate the costs. They can then do some legwork to minimize the potential criticisms of their programs. For example, one of the most common incentive programs is the tax holiday, which politicians argue has no direct cost to the state. Firms locate in a region with a tax holiday, generating jobs and other spillovers to the investment; their profits are exempt from taxation, but government officials can argue that the state revenues are unaffected.

As we know from the empirical evidence in Chapter 4, however, in many cases firms have already decided to locate in a district and are maximizing the incentives they can collect. This does provide a clear opportunity cost to the state coffers, for it is likely that the investor would have still come, allowing the state to collect income taxes. However, this argument is more complicated to make, and politicians and firms both have reasons to publicly voice the importance of incentives as a driving factor for firms' investment location choices.

Testing Transparency About the Costs of Incentives in Canada

In this chapter's final section, we explore credit claiming and transparency regarding the trade-off from incentives in the Canadian context. This final online survey experiment was fielded in 2015, after the US experiments, and thus had the benefits of testing additional mechanisms compared to the previous efforts.[14] In this survey experiment, we focused our design on two provinces, Ontario and Quebec, through the Local Parliament Project.[15]

Canadian provinces have been in competition for investment with provincial governments and have offered incentives across industries, ranging from automobile producers to film production. Our focus on Ontario and Quebec allowed us to select – using data from IncentivesMonitor[16] – a real and pertinent incentive. In both provinces, we observed an incentive of roughly $27 million and 350 employees, so we consider this example to be a realistic incentive treatment. Our research design included three elements: (1) the size of the investment, (2) whether or not the province received the investment, and (3) whether or not we provided information on the potential fiscal trade-offs.

Imagine the following scenario:

Your province competed with a number of other provinces over a new manufacturing plant with 350 employees. [Your province offered a financial incentive package of $27 million that was larger than that of other provinces/Another province offered a financial incentive package of $27 million that was substantially larger than that of your province.]

If your province [receives/does not receive] this investment, how would this affect your evaluation of the Liberal Party's performance in office?

(1) I would be much more likely to vote for the Liberals in the next provincial election.
(2) I would be slightly more likely to vote for the Liberals in the next provincial election.
(3) My vote choice would not be altered.
(4) I would be slightly less likely to vote for the Liberals in the next provincial election.
(5) I would be much less likely to vote for the Liberals in the next provincial election.

---

[14] Our hypotheses and research design were registered at the Evidence in Governance and Politics Design Registry (Design 20150914AA).
[15] www.localparliament.ca (Accessed August 5, 2017).
[16] www.incentivesmonitor.com. (Accessed August 5, 2017).

10.3 Testing the Benefits of Transparency

Our sample included a total of 2,000 respondents. For the first treatment, with two treatment dimensions (size of incentive and whether the province received the investment), we provided roughly 1,000 respondents with the following vignette. The remaining 1,000 respondents received the second treatment: information on the fiscal costs of incentives. We provide the treatment values in brackets.

As with the TAPS survey in the United States above, this experiment has an additional treatment, one that helps us test how support for the incumbent party is shaped by the trade-offs of incentives. We provide the exact wording of the question below. The trade-off treatment is italicized.

Imagine the following scenario:
Your province competed with a number of other provinces over a new manufacturing plant with 350 employees. Your province offered a financial incentive package of $27 million that was larger than that of other provinces.

As with all government policies, incentives come with trade-offs. The money dedicated to incentives would not be available for government spending or tax cuts for individuals.

If your province receives this investment, how would this affect your evaluation of the Liberal Party's performance in office?

(1) I would be much more likely to vote for the Liberals in the next provincial election.
(2) I would be slightly more likely to vote for the Liberals in the next provincial election.
(3) My vote choice would not be altered.
(4) I would be slightly less likely to vote for the Liberals in the next provincial election.
(5) I would be much less likely to vote for the Liberals in the next provincial election.

We randomized this trade-off across all four scenarios presented above (large incentive/small incentive, received investment/did not receive investment). In Table 10.2, we present all of our treatment combinations for increases in support for the Liberal Party. The first two columns present the findings from respondents who did not see the trade-off – that is, that respondents reward politicians for attracting investment. If the province offers a large incentive, support for

Table 10.2 Increased support for the Canadian Liberal Party

	All respondents (N=2171)								
	Larger incentive				Smaller incentive				
	No trade-off		Trade-offs		No trade-off		Trade-offs		TOTAL
	FDI	No FDI	FDI	No FDI	FDI	No FDI	FDI	No FDI	
	0.279	0.1826	0.209	0.1248	0.2582	0.1625	0.222	0.1755	0.2004
	(.2342,.3287)	(.1453,.227)	(.17,.2541)	(.0945,.1632)	(.212,.3105)	(.1278,.2045)	(.1805,.2699)	(.1369,.2223)	(.1858,.216)

	Moderates (N=1083)								
	Larger incentive				Smaller incentive				
	No trade-off		Trade-offs		No trade-off		Trade-offs		TOTAL
	FDI	No FDI	FDI	No FDI	FDI	No FDI	FDI	No FDI	
	0.2709	0.1709	0.195	0.1232	0.2191	0.1681	0.2159	0.124	0.1852
	(.2069,.3461)	(.1223,.2337)	(.1406,.2641)	(.0817,.1817)	(.1644,.2859)	(.1186,.2327)	(.161,.2833)	(.0791,.1891)	(.1653,.207)

Note: 90% confidence intervals in parentheses.

Table 10.3 Decreased support for the Canadian Liberal Party

All respondents (N=2171)

	Larger incentive				Smaller incentive				
	No trade-off		Trade-offs		No trade-off		Trade-offs		TOTAL
	FDI	No FDI	FDI	No FDI	FDI	No FDI	FDI	No FDI	
	0.1179	0.2087	0.1206	0.1686	0.131	0.2296	0.1051	0.1486	0.1553
	(.0874,.1573)	(.1698,.2538)	(.899,.16)	(.1325,.2121)	(.0974,.1741)	(.1885,.2767)	(.0759,.1438)	(.1138,.1918)	(.142,.1696)

Moderates (N=1083)

	Larger incentive				Smaller incentive				
	No trade-off		Trade-offs		No trade-off		Trade-offs		TOTAL
	FDI	No FDI	FDI	No FDI	FDI	No FDI	FDI	No FDI	
	0.1361	0.207	0.1031	0.1846	0.108	0.205	0.0816	0.1391	0.1469
	(.0892,.2021)	(.1556,.27)	(.0641,.1616)	(.1328,.2507)	(.0697,.1637)	(.1511,.2719)	(.0501,.1303)	(.092,.205)	(.1289,.1669)

Note: 90% confidence intervals in parentheses.

the Liberal Party increases, and this increase is especially large if the province receives the investment (0.279). What happens to this support if respondents are treated with the simple information that these incentives generate trade-offs? In the third and fourth columns we show that support for the Liberal Party drops. In the context of receiving investment, there is a seven-percentage-point decrease in the number of respondents indicating that they were more likely to vote for the Liberal Party in the next election.

In short, clearly presenting the trade-offs of incentive policies mitigates much of the positive impact of offering them.

Table 10.2 presents the data for all eight of our treatment combinations for all respondents and only moderates. The main finding here, both intuitive and consistent with our work, is that presenting trade-offs is especially damaging to the support of the Liberal Party when the party is offering large incentives. Thus, the fiscal costs become especially salient when the party is offering incentives larger than their competitors'.

In Table 10.3, we present the same information, but this time coding for decline in support for the Liberal Party. The main finding here, also intuitive, is that presenting trade-offs mitigates the blame in provinces not receiving investment. Whether a province offers a large or small incentive, presenting information on the trade-off dramatically reduces the negative elector impact of not receiving an investment – the blame-avoidance mechanism. For example, districts that offered large incentives are punished if they do not receive investments; there is an almost ten-percentage-point difference in the amount of respondents indicating that they will vote for another party if the province receives the investment (11.79%) and if the province does not receive the investment (20.87%). If voters are presented with information about trade-offs, the difference in blame (i.e., decline in vote share) decreases to 4.8% (a loss of 16.86% of votes if the province does not receive the investment versus 12.06% if the province does receive the investment).

Our findings from Canada collaborate our previous results that presenting trade-offs has a moderating influence on credit and blame. We find that presenting the fiscal trade-offs of incentives limits the credit and blame that politicians receive for attracting investment, and therefore should reduce incentives to pander.

10.4 Conclusions

Throughout this book, we have argued that there is a political logic to the use of economic development incentives, which exploits the uncertainty of their benefits for political gain. In Chapter 9, however, we showed that incentive programs have real fiscal costs, often leading to either an increase in regressive sales taxes or spending cuts on vital services like education. These spending decisions lead to greater inequality, and in extreme cases, can affect political stability. At their worst, the choices appear to be a transfer from the poor and middle class to some of the world's wealthiest corporations. In this final empirical chapter, we ask whether these negative implications can be mitigated.

In particular, we explore the effectiveness of two policy solutions that have already been tried in the United States. First, we study the effectiveness of clawbacks, clauses in incentives contracts that allow governments to cancel incentives if companies fail to meet agreed upon employment or revenue targets. Clawbacks could reduce the negative effect of pandering by creating opportunities for jurisdictions to recoup resources that did not live up to their political billing. Taking advantage of the Missouri Quality Jobs program data, we empirically test whether clawbacks have led to more effective allocation of resources. We find evidence for a significant but small effect. Companies with clawbacks in their contracts created slightly more jobs than those that didn't. The effects are smaller than advocates might hope, because clawbacks do not adequately address selection bias and redundancy in the original allocation. As Chapter 4 showed, roughly two-thirds of firms receive incentives for investments they planned to make anyway. These projects might create jobs, but they are the same jobs that would have been generated even without an incentive. Threatening cancellation does not alter these original projections. Clawbacks are meant to deal with egregious waste and abuse, and that is important; but on the whole, redundancy offers are the far more pernicious fiscal cost.

The second policy approach we study is simple transparency. Our work, presented in the many chapters of this book, highlights that central to the political benefits of incentives is a hiding of the costs. Our work on local incentives in Chapter 5 suggests that the politicians most likely to harness incentives have the least transparency and the most limited oversight of these programs. If citizens, media, and civil society were made aware of the true costs of incentives, would they be less likely to support them, reducing their benefits as a tool for pandering? One promising route for reform is the GASB Statement No.77 (2015), which requires exactly this type of public disclosure.

Unsurprisingly, given our analysis, the partisans in this fight over transparency are NGOs fighting for more progressive policies and education associations worry about further cuts to education spending versus associations of economic developers and elected officials. We do not yet know how this transparency rule will affect states and municipalities. In theory, it could lead to a reigning in of the number or size of incentives. Conversely, this rule may be simply ignored by some municipalities, or the information provided (on the costs of incentives) will be presented in each municipality's Comprehensive Annual Finance Report in the footnotes.

Is this enough transparency to reshape the use of incentive programs? To test the impact of disclosure, we examined how altering our survey experiments from Chapter 7 by detailing opportunity costs affected support in the United States and Canada. The clearest finding is that presenting information on the trade-offs – in terms of higher taxes or lower spending – moderates the positive electoral impact of using incentives. Voter support for incentives plummets when the questions makes costs transparent to voters. From a theoretical perspective, transparency reduces the asymmetric information advantage that politicians have over voters and thereby reduces the political benefits of pandering.

While it is too early to claim victory, the finding points towards a solution to pandering and wasteful allocations. Future research should move beyond survey experiments to rigorous field evaluations that seek to determine true behavioral responses of voters. We remain optimistic that transparency will reduce the deleterious motivations of politicians to pander.

APPENDIX   DETAILED ANALYSIS OF CLAWBACK PROGRAMS IN MISSOURI

The empirical analysis that we present in this appendix suggests that the Missouri Quality Jobs program has a similar impact to the Kansas PEAK program. Neither incentive program has a statistically significant impact on job creation. The use of clawbacks does improve the overall job creation of the Missouri program by canceling some of the worst performance companies. After removing these companies from the analysis, we find that the Quality Jobs program has a statistically significant impact on job creation in Missouri. Unfortunately, the size of this impact is tiny. This finding means that although companies that receive Quality Jobs incentives are creating jobs faster than a "control" group of firms, our estimates suggest that this program is not at all cost effective.

Clawbacks and the Missouri Quality Jobs Program

States and municipalities can use such controls to mitigate the risks associated with these economic development policies, potentially reducing the risk that scarce economic development dollars are wasted (Sullivan and Green 1999). Sullivan (2002) finds that municipalities that make the most extensive use of incentives are also the localities that employ the strongest controls.

Unfortunately, variation in the implementation of clawbacks calls into question how effective these provisions are in reducing the costs of incentive programs and in ensuring compliance with the conditions of incentive agreements (Peters 1993).

The potential importance of clawbacks and concerns about their usage justifies further exploration of how clawbacks improve the performance of incentives in a single state. Missouri's extensive use of clawbacks provides us with the ability to examine how the monitoring of post-incentive performance can improve incentive programs' job creation.

The Missouri Quality Jobs program was the flagship Missouri incentive program created in 2005. It was eventually replaced by the Missouri Works program in August 2013.[17] This latter program allows companies to retain the state income taxes withheld for qualified jobs along with other forms of tax incentives, and includes strong clawback provisions.

As a mechanism for job creation, Missouri Quality Jobs has a number of stipulations. First, to be eligible for this incentive, the jobs created must exceed the county average wage, which ranges from just over $19,000 in Ripley and Ozark Counties to over $53,000 in St. Louis. Second, employers must offer health insurance.

Beyond the quality of the jobs, the Department of Economic Development establishes a baseline employment number for established

---

[17] For program details, see Missouri Department of Economic Development (2014).

Table 10.A1 *Descriptive statistics*

Number of incentives	Average credits	Average witholding	Investment	Jobs
597	0.89	0.82	12.6	138
Only approved incentives				
242	1.4	1.2	22.8	171
Only disqualified incentives				
269	0.41	0.45	4.6	99
Only closed incentives				
61	0.95	0.89	10	137

Note: Credits, withholding, and investment are expressed in natural log of dollars.

firms by requiring previous employment and payroll information from companies prior to applying for the incentive. All applications are expected to create the proposed jobs within two years of receiving the incentive.

Analysis of the Missouri Quality Jobs Program

In Table 10.A1 we provide summary statistics of Missouri Quality Jobs allocations to date. Through an FOIA request, we identified 597 total incentive applications. Twenty-five of these incentives were withdrawn before receiving incentives. The remaining incentives can be broken down into incentives that have been allocated (approved), canceled or clawed back (canceled), or now closed either due to program completion or other cancellations.

Despite the heavy monitoring of incentives and use of clawbacks, the program is controversial. In an audit of the program, the Missouri State Auditor found that the program's economic development impact and job creation were overstated, and that the underlying quality of the data was suspect. The report summarized this first point (Schweich 2012, p. 8):

Data used to project the economic impact of the Missouri Quality Jobs (MQJ) program are significantly overstated. Significant weaknesses also exist in the manner in which actual program data is obtained, maintained, verified, and reported to the legislature. Actual program data is not timely and is not verified to ensure accuracy and compliance with program requirements, and therefore, the data presented to the public and the legislature is outdated and not reliable. As a result of these deficiencies, the overall economic impact of the MQJ program cannot be accurately assessed.

Similar criticisms of major economic development programs are common. In fact, in many ways Missouri's economic development data availability and evaluation of incentive performance is better than many other states. The Pew Foundation's study of state-level incentive evaluations places Missouri in the top category along with twelve other states (Pew Center on the States 2012). Thus, criticisms of the quality of the data and oversight of incentives in Missouri is at least representative of other states and quite possibly less acute than the rest of the country.

Taking this data at face value, it seems obvious that companies that received incentives created jobs. Otherwise, companies that fail to generate jobs are removed from the program. But the major methodological hurdle in evaluating this program is the problem of establishing a valid counterfactual. Would the company have created the jobs even without the incentive?

Following our analysis in Chapter 4, we outline a research design strategy to ameliorate these concerns by using matching methods to compare companies that received incentives with a control group of firms that did not receive incentives. As noted in Chapter 4, the first methodological hurdle in evaluating incentive programs is the comparison of firms that received incentives to those that did not. For example, in 2006 the average firm that did not receive incentives in Missouri had a total of sixteen employees. Firms that received incentives had an average 2006 employment of 295 workers. This is a tremendous difference. But this difference emerged before these firms eventually participated in the Missouri Quality Jobs program. In 2012, the average firm that did not participate in the Missouri Quality Jobs program had 12 employees compared to 251 employees of firms participating in the incentive program.[18]

To address this imbalance on observable confounders, we again turn to coarsened exact matching (Iacus et al. 2012) to compare Missouri Quality Jobs recipients with a matched set of control firms. We specifically match firms based on their pre-Quality Jobs program employment (log of employment in 2006), the three-digit Standard Industrial Classification (SIC) code, and a dummy variable if the firms was a subsidiary of a parent company. We present the results of this study in

---

[18] This decline in the average employment could be due to the great recession or the entrance of a number of new, small firms in the sample.

Table 10.A2 Matching estimates of job creation (2006–2012)

	All firms		Disqualified		Approved
	(1) OLS	(2) OLS	(3) CEM	(4) CEM	(5) CEM
Incentive	2.778***	0.318***	0.269**	0.015	0.599***
	(0.068)	(0.029)	(0.128)	(0.176)	(0.207)
2006 Employment		0.952***			
		(0.001)			
Constant	0.96	0.101***	3.384***	3.384***	3.384***
	(0.002)	(0.001)	(0.006)	(0.006)	(0.006)
N	471,728	251,304	124,208	124,208	124,208

Note: Models 1 and 2 are ordinary least squares regressions with the natural log of 2012 employment as the dependent variable. Models 3–5 present coarsened exact matching estimates using the natural log of 2006 employment, a dummy for subsidiary (as opposed to a parent firm), and three-digit SIC dummy variables.
*** $p<0.01$, ** $p<0.05$

Table 9.2. The first model takes the naïve approach and simply examines the relationship between jobs in 2012 and whether or not the firm received incentives. This model does not control for the fact that the firms that applied for Quality Jobs incentives were already larger than non-incentivized firms, nor does it account for other factors that could affect employment.

The results from this naïve approach finds that firms that received incentives had an additional sixteen jobs (natural log of 2.78 jobs) compared to firms that did not receive incentives. In firm applications for this program, the average firm proposed creating seventy-one jobs. Thus, even the naïve specification with a bias towards uncovering large effects shows that firms performed below expectations.

However, as noted, most of these companies actually began the incentive program with a larger number of employees. Model 2 includes a variable for the natural log of employment in 2006. The estimated coefficient shrinks considerably, whereby firms that received incentives employed only an additional forty-five jobs.

These simple regressions are illustrative, but as noted, a number of factors can shape employment performance. Model 3 presents our coarsened exact matching estimates using previous employment, three-digit industry code, and a dummy variable for whether or not the company is a subsidiary of a parent company for matching. The estimates of the impact of incentives is even more modest. Incentives are associated with an additional 1.31 jobs (natural log of 0.269). As is to be expected, reducing the selection bias into treatment through matching reduces the size of the estimated effect.

This number of new jobs is very small compared to the program costs. The average tax credit authorized and average withholding authorized were both over $800,000. The total authorization for the firms in this sample, adding tax credits and withholdings, was $1.68 million.

As we mentioned above, Missouri is active in the monitoring of incentives. Clawback provisions are central to this program, and Missouri is rated as one of the best states in terms of the use of clawbacks (Mattera, Cafcas, et al. 2012).

In this data, 198 of 409 Missouri Quality Jobs incentives were disqualified, although we do not have information on when they were disqualified, how much was spent on incentives for these firms, and what was eventually recaptured. However, we can perform the same analysis and split the sample between the firms that were disqualified and those that were not, essentially assuming that no incentives were given to the disqualified firms.

In Model 4, we estimate the impact of participating in the incentive program on employment for the disqualified firms. The estimates are not statistically distinguishable from zero, and the estimates are incredibly small. These results mean that the firms that were disqualified generated jobs at no faster rate than the control groups. The use of clawbacks effectively identified firms that were not creating jobs faster than the control group.

In Model 5, we perform coarsened exact matching that no longer includes the disqualified firms in the estimates. The employment creation of these firms more than doubles compared to Model 3. The use of clawbacks is effective in weeding out the worst-performing firms and thus in substantially improving the overall performance of the incentive program in the stated goal of generating jobs.

Unfortunately, the overall performance is still well below expectations, generating just under an additional two jobs for each incentive offered. Thus, the doubling of the performance in job creation means very little from such a low baseline.

These final results provided mixed evidence for the utility of policing incentive programs through clawbacks and monitoring. The disqualification of firms participating in the Missouri program clearly saved taxpayers' money; incentives were halted to firms that were creating jobs at no faster rate than firms that had received no incentives.

Table 10.A3 *Summary statistics of approved versus disqualified firms*

	Approved	Disqualified
2006 Employment	527.94	185.61
2012 Employment	509.77	217.45
Percent change	−0.03	0.17
Size of incentive	$2,831,231	$1,028,006
Number of incentives	77	103

Nevertheless, this ex-post monitoring was not enough to improve the overall quality of the program. Our best back-of-the-envelope calculation is that this program is paying almost $1 million per job created (compared to the job creation of a control group of firms).

In a final analysis, we examined the descriptive characteristics of companies that were approved relative to those that were disqualified in Table 10.A3. These simple summary statistics show that the disqualified firms actually generated more jobs in the 2006–2012 time period than the approved incentives, although this is partially driven by a number of outliers. In a number of preliminary analyses, we examined attributes such as the sector and the use of campaign contributions by recipient firms.

The only predictive factor, easily observed in this summary table, is that larger incentives are much less likely to be disqualified than smaller incentives. This finding is open to multiple interpretations. An optimistic view is that the largest incentives are vetted in a way that dramatically increases the probability of complying with the program's conditions. A pessimistic view is that the discretion allowed in the enforcement of clawbacks can lead economic development officials to enforce clawbacks only on the smaller firms. Without more data on the actual process of determining clawbacks, these are simply conjectures.

The conclusion of this analysis is that although some claim that Missouri's active use of clawback provisions has the potential to improve the program's performance, our empirical evidence suggests that clawbacks cannot dramatically increase incentive programs' effectiveness. The costs of this program, despite the clawbacks, are roughly estimated at $1 million per job created.

Thus, the fundamental problem with these programs is that the firms that are already considering expanding or relocating are those most likely to apply for incentives. These firms may have already made their investment decisions, and the incentives lower the costs for the firms but do not really "create" any new jobs. Our unfortunate conclusion is that one of the most promising reforms of incentives – the use of clawbacks – does not compensate for the fundamental flaw of these programs' redundancy. Clawbacks can be an effective way to recoup some of the lost money from incentive programs, but they do not turn incentive programs into effective economic development tools.

11 Final Thoughts

11.1 The Biggest Incentive Deal of All Time?

In the fall of 2013, the Boeing Company triggered the biggest incentive war in US history. The iconic aircraft maker – with its corporate headquarters in Chicago and colossal production facilities in the state of Washington – was in a major dispute with the machinists' union in Washington. With the making of the new 777X on the horizon, Boeing began negotiations with the union and the state for better labor conditions and incentives to keep production in the Seattle area. Reportedly, at least twenty-two states expressed interest and submitted bids. Few of the states' locations, however, had the resources to meet all Boeing's criteria, and most that came close already had existing Boeing production facilities. Thus, we can narrow the true set of potential locations to the twelve to fifteen states that Boeing contacted for bids.

Why would states with such marginal chances of winning a Boeing investment bother to go through the formalities of putting together an offer sheet? As we have argued throughout this book, even for the long shots, incentives are a win-win proposition when it comes to political strategy. If the state of Missouri's largely front-loaded $1.7 billion incentive package, passed through a special legislative session, had somehow swung Boeing, the result would have been a coup for the state. However, even if it failed, it provided a strong signal to Missouri's voters that the Missouri leadership was promoting growth since it was doing everything it could to attract big investment projects (Lieb 2013).

11.2 Incentives for Economic Development

The Boeing ordeal both highlights the main thesis of our book and illustrates the complexity of national, state, and local economic development policies. Economic incentives, used to attract investment, share many of the same attributes as the larger class of economic development policies. Policy instruments such as tax incentives minimize the future obligations for firms in exchange for real investment. These investment projects hopefully employ workers that pay local taxes and can lead to other economic spillovers. Cash incentives, the purchasing of land, or improving infrastructure for firms can also be a catalyst for economic development. Each job directly created by the incentives could create a number of indirect jobs. Economic development specialists therefore argue that incentives can be long-term investments that generate outsized returns.

Nevertheless, economists have long asked the question of whether the same returns could be obtained much more cheaply. In doing so, they ask, "Were these policies necessary to attract investment or would firms have invested anyway?"

If the economists are right, valuable resources could have been used in other ways. They could used for general reductions in taxes or regulations that do not discriminate among firms, used for public goods such as improvements in education and infrastructure, or even spread to all firms through across-the-board tax reductions for companies and individuals. Are these incentives cost effective, or are there better uses for this scarce capital than incentives to individual firms?

11.3 Debating the Use of Incentives

Before we even start to debate the proper incentive policies, we have to tackle the obvious questions that economists are asking. Were these incentives necessary in the first place? Would the firm have invested without the incentives? Did the firm distort its type of investment to fit into the parameters set by government economic development policies?

These questions are extremely hard to answer definitively, but we reviewed the substantial work on the subject in Chapter 4. The bulk of the evidence clearly points to the fact that the vast majority of firms would not have changed their investment plans in the absence of incentives. The net result has been costly redundancy rates – the term used by economic analysts for giveaways to firms that have already made up their minds – which usually hovers around 66%, but have as high as 90% in some cases.

In the cases of incentive offers that were large enough to actually change firms' plans, the costs have far outweighed the benefits in terms of job creation and long-term economic growth. Our analysis of the PEAK incentive program perfectly illustrates this point. We found that these incentives had no impact on job creation in Kansas. If anything, they were associated primarily with firms switching their mailboxes back and forth across the Kansas-Missouri border. The expected job growth never materialized. In the few cases where large benefits of incentive programs have been claimed, extensive audits have identified a disturbing pattern – reported job creation was, at best, exaggerated and, at worst, a fiction based on outright fraud. Audits of Programs in Ohio, Utah, and South Africa (see Chapter 4) have reached shockingly similar conclusions when experts have looked beneath the hood of hyperbolic job claims.

Thus, the proper use of incentives probably requires extremely talented economic development officers who have the type of information to judiciously offer incentives, price discriminating between those firms that would come anyway and those firms that require incentives to make their investments. Such a strategy also requires a careful pricing strategy, where politicians must be careful to not pay too much to get an investment.

In this book, we have argued that politicians have little political reason to be careful and discriminating. Politicians often want to spin their economic development strategies as positively as possible, making their policies seems both necessary and highly effective. Firms have little reason not to go along with politicians' tall tales since they are likely to receive cash or credit for a decision they would have made anyway. Through manipulating the information available and not allowing for a systematic cost-benefit analysis, politicians can take credit for the firms that were going to locate in their jurisdiction anyway.

We have provided numerous stories of incentives gone bad, yet we are careful to note that these examples are not direct evidence of these policies being systematically flawed. We argue that only through systematic empirical analysis can we adjudicate important debates on the use of incentives. In making our case, we specifically examined the political logic of incentives, exploring when politicians wanted to use these levers despite the large empirical uncertainty.

11.4 A Final Reflection on Theory and Evidence

In Chapter 2, we outlined our theory, based on previous work on politicians "pandering" to voters. Our key insight was that politicians can use economic policies to claim credit for good outcomes (investment in their locality) and to reduce blame for bad outcomes (the failure to attract investment or the loss of an existing firm).

The core logic is that if voters believe that incentive policies can be used to attract capital, but they cannot directly observe if an incentive was necessary for an investment, politicians can exploit this information asymmetry. In applying this tactic, politicians overuse incentives so that they can "show" voters their efforts in attracting investment – by providing incentives to

11.4 A Final Reflection on Theory and Evidence

firms that were going to come anyway and by offering incentives to firms that were never going to come in the first place.

We show that the proclivity to overuse incentives increases when electoral pressure is most fierce, such as when politicians are in the midst of reelection battles or when the electoral institutions are shaped so that a particular politician is held directly accountable by the electorate. For instance, we hypothesized that directly elected politicians – as many US mayors are – should offer far more generous incentive packages than indirectly elected politicians. We also argued that these directly elected mayors would attempt to decrease the amount of oversight and scrutiny of their incentive programs because they want to be able to offer excessive incentives and to claim success for even the most wasteful of economic development efforts.

This theory chapter provides a very clear logic on the overuse of incentives and includes a number of falsifiable hypotheses on the use of incentives. However, as we noted at the start of Chapter 2, finding examples of incentives that fit our causal logic is easy, but this is a far cry from rigorously testing our theory or the systematic pattern of overuse of incentives for political reasons.

In Chapter 3, we provide examples of the prevalence of economic development strategies that harness tools aimed at picking winner and loser firms, and provide generous financial incentives for their attraction, expansion, or retention. Countries across the world provide these incentives, although the United States is an outlier in both the generosity of incentives and the prevalence of local and state (rather than national) incentive programs.

Our tour of incentives was admittedly spotty and incomplete. While politicians around the world tout the government policies that are used to attract investment, often claiming credit for these programs by linking investments with incentives, systematic data is lacking. Despite the data limitations, we provide evidence of the use of incentives across the world. Most countries have some type of incentive programs on the books, and we can identify a number of cases of massive incentives from every region in the world.

In Chapter 4, we document the voluminous economic literature that is highly critical of these programs on a number of grounds. The most obvious is that there is very little evidence that these incentive programs actually retain or attract investment. When they may sometimes "work" in the sense that they marginally increase the probability of entrance by an investors, these programs are incredibly costly, and the fiscal competition for capital is another form of winners' curse. The locations that attract firms with incentive programs are often doing more harm than good to the long-run performance of their economies.

The details of these two criticisms and further problems with governments picking winners with taxpayer money are documented in Chapter 4. We also illustrate the lack of effectiveness of incentives by examining the impact of the main Kansas incentive program on job creation by comparing incentives firms with very similar firms that did not receive incentives.

This insight leads us to examine the political logic of these programs, which accounts for the bulk of the empirical work that follows, demonstrating that even economically inefficient policies can be fantastic political tools for incumbent politicians. In Chapter 5, we provide a more systematic analysis of incentive programs by focusing on the large incentive programs of US cities. Using variation in electoral institutions in US cities and a database of 2,000 incentives in the United States, we show that cities with directly elected mayors (mayor-council systems) are much more likely to overuse incentives than alternative forms of government. In line with our theory, we also find that these directly elected politicians have substantially weaker oversight of these incentive programs.

These findings on the overuse of incentives in cities with elected mayors are as close to a smoking gun as can be, given our use of observational data on incentives. However, at least one other alternative theory exists. It is entirely plausible that elected politicians are allocating incentive dollars, not to pander to voters and claim credit for investment but as a quid pro quo whereby politicians offer firms taxpayer-funded handouts and firms generously reward politicians with campaign contributions. This alternative has sometimes been called the patronage or campaign-finance hypothesis. A firm gives (legal) campaign contributions and governments write (legal) checks to help subsidize the firm's investment.

In Chapter 6, we highlight a number of prima facie problems with this alternative theory. The most telling is that politicians, far from hiding these payments "under the table," tout the use of incentives in press releases, reelection campaigns, and public debates. Such flaunting is inconsistent with most existing theories of exchange of campaign contributions for private benefits.

This chapter's major contribution is our analysis of the largest state-level incentive program, the TEF. We use public records requests to obtain information on the incentives offered and the applications rejected. Ultimately, we find no evidence that firms that provided campaign contributions to Texas Governor Perry had any impact on the allocation of incentives. If anything, we find evidence that the fund is not very discerning at all, offering incentives to nearly all of the firms that apply.

We show that similar patterns emerge in the border war between Kansas and Missouri. There is very little evidence that the expensive

11.4 A Final Reflection on Theory and Evidence

incentives offered to investors, often jumping back and forth across the Kansas and Missouri border, were at all related to campaign contributions. Clearly, this example does not present a definitive test of the impact of campaign contributions on incentive programs, but it offers some evidence that pandering provides the most reasonable account for much of the incentive use in the United States.

Chapter 7 most directly tests our theory from Chapter 2, from the perspective of voters. We hypothesize that voters reward politicians for the use of incentives and test our prediction by harnessing a series of survey experiments in the United States and United Kingdom. In these experiments, we use the power of randomization to examine how voters respond to different hypothetical investment scenarios. Do voters reward or punish their incumbent governors for the use of incentives?

We find robust evidence that voters reward the overuse of incentives in the United States. An investment coming to a state without incentives provides some boost to a governor's reelection prospects, but offering an incentive to attract this investment adds even more. Thus, even if the governor knows that the investor is coming with 100% probability, providing financial incentives to the firm allows the governor to claim additional credit for the investment. We find even stronger evidence when the state fails to attract the investment. A governor losing an investment to a competitor state has a great likelihood of losing the reelection, but this downside is largely mitigated by offering incentives. In other words, the governor can claim to have done all he could to win the project.

In short, a governor cannot lose by offering incentives. Voters will give extra credit to elected politicians if an investment comes with taxpayer-funded incentives. And if the firm chooses an alternative location, the use of incentives mitigates the blame for failing to attract the investment. Thus, incumbent politicians who are interested in reelection have a dominant strategy – offering incentives to firms. These three chapters provide compelling evidence for the political use of incentive programs in US cities and states. Politicians publicly use incentive programs in a way that is tremendously costly for voters; they offer too many checks, and the individual amounts are excessive.

In Chapter 8, we extend our empirical analysis to a nondemocratic context, focusing on how credit claiming can drive incentive use even in authoritarian countries. Here, we must account for an inconvenient empirical fact: nondemocratic countries tend to offer more generous incentives than their democratic peers. How can electoral pandering account for incentives in countries without free and fair elections to stimulate pandering to voters? We argue that our theory of "pandering upward" can help account for the use of incentives in authoritarian regimes. In the chapter, we suggest that local political elites can use incentives to claim credit (or reduce blame) for firms' investment location decisions before their central government benefactors.

Harnessing cross-national data on incentive use, we show that previous research, which identified authoritarian regimes as using more incentives than democratic regimes, is driven by a very specific type of regime. Single-party states, as opposed to personalistic regimes, account for the entire difference between democratic and authoritarian regimes. In particular, single-party regimes – where local leaders have motivations for investment promotion for career advancement – are associated with greater use of incentives. We then turn to two country studies, arguing that Vietnam and Russia provide contrasting political environments for the importance of credit claiming. In the Vietnamese case, local leaders provide excessive incentives up to the point when age restrictions make promotion no longer feasible. When career advancement remains an option, politicians harness incentives despite evidence that the vast majority of these incentives have no impact on investment decisions. They do so because they are attempting to pander upward towards central leaders who might promote them. Russia is a regime that is characterized by increasing personalism since governance reforms were enacted in 2005 causing a shift from directly elected governments to politically appointed governors. In the period prior to this shift, we observe aggressive changes in tax incentives to capture investment. After the reforms, we find that the very same governors that were active in investment promotion are dramatically less active in passing incentive legislation.

While the political benefits of incentives are positive, what are the economic costs of the usage? Chapter 9 provides both quantitative and qualitative evidence that incentives lead to increases in tax inequality through the use of regressive sales taxes and spending cuts, specifically in local education budgets. In fact, most of the time, the legislation allowing for the use of incentives is specifically authorized to make up for revenue shortfalls by broadening the tax base through sales taxes or cutting public services. Economic development advocates claim that these effects are short term and that eventually economic and revenue growth will be more than enough to compensate voters and enhance public services. We find little evidence to justify these assertions. What we find instead is that incentives tend to benefit corporations while increasing the revenue demands on citizens through regressive sales taxes and cuts to services their children depend upon.

Finally, Chapter 10 builds on these inequality results to empirically test two potentially policy solutions. First, we explore the use of clawback provisions as a way to safeguard taxpayer money. Second, we analyze whether providing increased transparency to citizens might reduce the political benefits of using incentives to claim credit. By tweaking our original survey experiments, we show that voters in the United States and Canada are very sensitive to the costs of these incentive programs. Providing information on the trade-offs for these programs negated many of the political benefits of their use. In short, pandering is the result of an asymmetric information advantage that the politician has over voters. Because they do not know about the opportunities forgone, voters tend to support the idea that incentives create growth and jobs. Politicians leverage the uncertainty, therefore, to claim credit for attracting new investments. When we remove the idea that the programs are costless and that other, perhaps more popular, public benefits must be sacrificed, voters are far less likely to support the initiatives.

It remains to be tested whether politicians will change their behavior in such an environment, but we believe that the evidence points to them making a rational calculation to reduce incentive usage.

11.5 America and Beyond

Our theoretical argument on credit claiming applies to a large number of cities, states, provinces, and countries around the world. Most of our work centers on the United States for two important reasons. First, the United States is the Wild West of incentive programs. With a very weak national investment promotion agency, subnational governments engage in the bulk of incentive programs. Love it or hate it, America's vaunted federalism and laboratory of democracy allows for a tremendous amount of authority on the part of state and local governments to use incentives for the attraction and retention of business. Second, our aim was to provide as definitive a test as possible of the political use of incentives. We sought out the highest quality incentive data, requested government documents for US cities, and engaged in a number of original survey experiments.

Yet our attempt at rigor comes at the cost of lacking systematic empirical tests outside of the United States. While we provide some basic data on other incentive programs in Chapter 3, we do not perform any rigor analysis of incentive programs outside of the United States in the first seven chapters of this book (although our survey experiments include the United Kingdom in Chapter 7 and Canada in Chapter 9). Nonetheless, our theory should travel across countries, helping to explain the perplexing use of a largely flawed economic development strategy.

Our strongest cross-national evidence can be found in Chapter 8, where we show that our theory on pandering can even apply to nondemocratic regimes. This point is broader than illustrating how the use of incentives in Vietnam and Russia is driven by political factors. We show that the wide variance in the use of incentives maps onto the political motivations of politicians.

More broadly, the professional motivations of politicians are the key driver. Politicians and bureaucrats who can lose their jobs through apparent poor effort in the tough job of attracting investments will look for ways to show that they are doing their best to attract investment. The use, or overuse, of financial incentives, while not cost effective, is one way to demonstrate effort.

As we noted above, it is very difficult to change the opinions of everyday voters. However, the policy-makers that oversee economic development programs may be more malleable to persuasion. We hope that this book provides some lessons for public officials. Economic development agencies *may* overuse incentives as a means of showing effort in the attraction of investment. Yet, as elites become more skeptical of these policies, they may demand more rigorous evidence that these policies are effective. These sorts of reforms are technically feasible, politically practical, and could be very effective in the overuse of incentives.

Recent initiatives, such as those proposed by the Pew Charitable Trusts, have the ability to make these economic development programs more transparent, accountable and ultimately more effective. We hope that our book also goes some way towards swaying at least a few of these policy-makers to reconsider the use of incentives as a primary means of attracting votes.

References

Abrevaya, Jason. 1997. The Equivalence of Two Estimators of the Fixed-Effects Logit Model. *Economics Letters* 55: 41–43.
Ahern, William. 2010. Economic Development Teams in VA, MD, and DC Bid for Northrop Grumman Headquarters. http://taxfoundation.org/blog/economic-development-teams-va-md-and-dc-bid-northrop-grumman-headquarters. Accessed August 25, 2017.
Aldrich, John H., John L. Sullivan, and Eugene Borgida. 1989. Foreign Affairs and Issue Voting: Do Presidential Candidates "Waltz Before a Blind Audience?" *American Political Science Review* 83: 123–141.
American Federation of Teachers. 2000. AFT Resolution: Corporate Welfare Reform.
American Federation of Teachers. 2009. State Revenue Systems: Options for the Current Fiscal Crisis. https://www.aft.org/sites/default/files/staterevenuesurvey1109.pdf. Accessed August 25, 2017.
Angrist, Joshua and Jorn-Steffen Pischke. 2010. *Mostly Harmless Econometrics*. Princeton N.J.: Princeton University Press.
Ansolabehere, Stephen. 2010. CCES, MIT PORTL Module, 2005. Harvard Dataverse, V2. hdl.handle.net/1902.1/14620. Accessed August 25, 2017.
Ansolabehere, Stephen, John M. de Figueiredo, and James M. Snyder Jr. 2003. Why Is There So Little Money in Politics? *Journal of Economic Perspectives* 17: 105–130.
Arceneaux, Kevin. 2006. The Federal Face of Voting: Are Elected Officials Held Accountable for the Functions Relevant to Their Office? *Political Psychology* 27: 731–754.
Auerbach, Alan J and James R. Hines. 1988. Investment Tax Incentives and Frequent Tax Reforms. *American Economic Review* 78(2): 211–16.
Bai, Matt. 2013. Curt Schilling, Rhode Island and the Fall of 38 Studios. *New York Times* (April 20).
Bailey, David and Alex de Ruyter. 2012. Re-examining the BMW-Rover Affair: A Case Study of Corporate, Strategic and Government Failure? Applied Research Centre for Sustainable Regeneration (SURGE) Working Paper Series, No. 1, Coventry University.
Barlett, Donald L. and James B. Steele. 1998. Corporate Welfare: The Empire of Pigs. *Time Magazine*. (November 30).
Baron, David P. 1989. Service-Induced Campaign Contributions and Electoral Equilibrium. *Quarterly Journal of Economics* 104: 45–72.

Barrell, Ray and Nigel Pain. 1999. Domestic Institutions, Agglomerations and Foreign Direct Investment in Europe. *European Economic Review* 43: 925–934.
Bartels, Larry M. 2000. Partisanship and Voting Behavior. *American Journal of Political Science* 44: 35–50.
Bartik, Timothy J. 2005. Solving the Problems of Economic Development Incentives. *Growth and Change* 36: 139–166.
Baruch, Yehuda and Brooks C. Holtom. 2008. Survey Response Rate Levels and Trends in Organizational Research. *Human Relations* 61: 1139.
Basinger, Scott J. and Mark Hallerberg. 2004. Remodeling the Competition for Capital: How Domestic Politics Erases the Race to the Bottom. *American Political Science Review* 98: 261–276.
Basinger, Scott J. and Harold Lavine. 2005. Ambivalence, Information, and Electoral Choice. *American Political Science Review* 99: 169–184.
Bateman, Thomas and Charles Schwenk. 1986. Biases in Investor Decision Making: The Case of John DeLorean. *American Journal of Business* 1: 5–12.
Baturo, Alexander and Johan A. Elkink. 2016. Dynamics of Regime Personalization and Patron-Client Networks in Russia, 1999–2014. *Post-Soviet Affairs* 32: 75–98.
Baturo, Alexander and Julia Gray. 2009. Flatliners: Ideology and Rational Learning in the Adoption of the Flat Tax. *European Journal of Political Research* 48: 130–159.
Beazer, Quintin. 2015. Who's to Blame? Punishing Poor Economic Performance in a Centralized Political System. Paper presented at the European Association for Comparative Economic Studies – Higher School of Economics Workshop, Moscow, Russia (June 29).
Bell, Daniel A. 2015. *The China Model: Political Meritocracy and the Limits of Democracy*. Princeton N.J.: Princeton University Press.
Bernstein, Peter W. 1984. States Are Going Down Industrial Policy Lane. *Fortune* (March 5).
Bishop, Mac William. 2012. Border War: Kansas City. *New York Times* (December 1).
Blaydes, Lisa. 2010. *Elections and Distributive Politics in Mubarak's Egypt*. New York: Cambridge University Press.
Blomstrom, Magnus and Ari Kokko. 2003. The Economics of Foreign Direct Investment Incentives. National Bureau of Economic Research Working Paper Series, No. 9489.
Bobonis, Gustavo J. and Howard J. Shatz. 2007. Agglomeration, Adjustment, and State Policies in the Location of Foreign Direct Investment in the United States. *The Review of Economics and Statistics* 89: 30–43.
Boccia, Romina. 2015. Corporate Welfare Wastes Taxpayer Resources. Testimony Before the Subcommittee on Federal Spending Oversight and Emergency Management. www.heritage.org/research/reports/2015/06/corpo rate-welfare-wastes-taxpayer-and-economic-resources. Accessed August 25, 2017.
Boix, Carles and Milan W. Svolik. 2013. The Foundations of Limited Authoritarian Government: Institutions, Commitment, and Power-Sharing in Dictatorships. *The Journal of Politics* 75: 300–316.

Bollinger, Christopher R. and Keith R. Ihlanfeldt. 2003. The Intraurban Spatial Distribution of Employment: Which Government Interventions Make a Difference? *Journal of Urban Economics* 53 (3): 396–412.

Bondonio, Daniele and Robert T. Greenbaum. 2007. Do Local Tax Incentives Affect Economic Growth? What Mean Impacts Miss in the Analysis of Enterprise Zone Policies. *Regional Science and Urban Economics* 37: 121–136.

Bratton, Michael and Nicolas Van de Walle. 1994. Neopatrimonial Regimes and Political Transitions in Africa. *World Politics* 46: 453–489.

Brennan, Geoffrey and James M. Buchanan. 1980. *The Power to Tax: Analytical Foundations of a Fiscal Constitution*. New York: Cambridge University Press.

Bronzini, Raffaello and Guido de Blasio. 2006. Evaluating the Impact of Investment Incentives: The Case of Italy's Law 488/1992. *Journal of Urban Economics* 60: 327–349.

Brooker, Paul. 2014. *Non-Democratic Regimes*. New York: Palgrave MacMillan.

Brownlee, Jason. 2007. *Authoritarianism in an Age of Democratization*. New York: Cambridge University Press.

Bryant, Tim. 2014. IKEA Gets the Green Light as TIF is Approved. *St. Louis Post-Dispatch* (February 8).

Buettner, Thiess and Martin Ruf. 2007. Tax Incentives and the Location of FDI Evidence from a Panel of German Multinationals. *International Tax and Public Finance* 14: 151–164.

Burke, Fred and Nguyen Vinh. 2005. Provincial Tax Incentives Subject to Review. *Tax Notes International* (June 8).

Buss, Terry F. 2001. The Effect of State Tax Incentives on Economic Growth and Firm Location Decisions: An Overview of the Literature. *Economic Development Quarterly* 15: 90–105.

Busso, Matias, Jesse Gregory, and Patrick M. Kline. 2010. Assessing the Incidence and Efficiency of a Prominent Place Based Policy. National Bureau of Economic Research Working Paper Series, No. 16096.

Byrnes, Nanette and Coleman Cowan. 2007. The High Cost of Wooing Google. *Businessweek* (July 23).

Canes-Wrone, Brandice, Michael C. Herron, and Kenneth W. Shotts. 2001. Leadership and Pandering: A Theory of Executive Policymaking. *American Journal of Political Science* 45: 532–550.

Caplan, Bryan. 2007. *The Myth of the Rational Voter*. Princeton NJ: Princeton University Press.

Caplan and Associates 2009. Analysis of State-Level Economic Development Contingency Funds. http://cdm16884.contentdm.oclc.org/cdm/singleitem/col lection/p16884coll54/id/61/rec/2 (report prepared for Kansas Inc.). Accessed August 25, 2017.

Carlstrom, Gregg. 2012. Candidates Fail to Connect in N Carolina town. *Aljazeera* (October 30). www.aljazeera.com/indepth/spotlight/us2012/2012/09/20129301 0563616163.html. Accessed August 25, 2017.

Carter, Brandon. 2017. "Layoffs Set to Begin Next Month at Carrier Plant Trump Struck Deal With," *The Hill*, June 22. http://thehill.com/homenews/administra tion/339036-layoffs-set-to-begin-next-month-at-carrier-plant-trump-struck-deal. Accessed August 25, 2017.

Calonico, Sebastian, Matias D. Cattaneo, and Rocio Titiunik. 2014. Robust data-driven inference in the regression-discontinuity design. *Stata Journal* 14(4):909–946.

Celis, William. 1991. Business Tax Breaks Are Hurting Schools, Educators Complain. *New York Times* (May 22).

Chapman, Dan. 2001. Jobs Carry High Price Tag. *Atlanta Journal Constitution*, at A1 (August 5).

Charron, Nicholas and Victor Lapuente. 2010. Does Democracy Produce Quality of Government? *European Journal of Political Research* 49: 443–470.

Cheibub, José Antonio, Jennifer Gandhi, and James R. Vreeland. 2010. Democracy and Dictatorship Revisited. *Public Choice* 143: 67–101.

Chen Ye, Hongbin Li, and Li-An Zhou. 2005. Relative Performance Evaluation and the Turnover of Provincial Leaders in China. *Economics Letters* 88: 421–425.

Chen, Ting and James K. Kung. 2016. "Do Land Revenue Windfalls Create a Political Resource Curse? Evidence from China." Working Paper Hong Kong University of Science and Technology. www.jameskung.net/#!workingpaper/c1etn. Accessed August 26, 2017.

Cheng, Tun-Jen, Stephan Haggard, and David Kang. 1998. Institutions and Growth in Korea and Taiwan: The Bureaucracy. *The Journal of Development Studies* 34: 87–111.

Chibber, Vivek. 2002. Bureaucratic Rationality and the Developmental State. *American Journal of Sociology* 107: 951–989.

Clingermayer, James C. and Richard C. Feiock. 2001. *Institutional Constraints and Policy Choice: An Exploration of Local Government*. Albany, NY: State University of New York Press.

Coase, Ronald and Ning Wang. 2012. *How China Became Capitalist*. New York: Palgrave Macmillan.

Cockerham, Sean. 2010. Parnell Seeks Investment Incentives for Oil Companies. *Alaska Dispatch News* (January 15).

Cohen, Jeffrey E. and James D. King. 2004. Relative Unemployment and Gubernatorial Popularity. *Journal of Politics* 66: 1267–1282.

Cohn, Scott. 2017. "Trump's Carrier Deal is Not Living Up to the Hype – Jobs Still Going to Mexico," *CNBC* (June 24).

Collier, Kiah. 2013. Abbot expands on his view of Perry's incentive program. *Houston Chronicle* (July 13).

Converse, Philip E. 1964. The Nature of Belief Systems in Mass Publics. In David Apter (ed.), *Ideology and Discontent*. New York: Free.

Converse, Philip E. 1974. Comment: The Status of Nonattitudes. *American Political Science Review* 68: 650–660.

Cook, Shadish and Donald Cambell. 1970. *Experimental and Quasi-Experimental Designs for Generalized Causal Inference*. Boston: Houghton Mifflin.

Coupe, Tom. 2005. Bias in Conditional and Unconditional Fixed Effects Logit Estimation: A Correction. *Political Analysis* 13: 292–295.

Cummings, Ronald G., Glen W. Harrison, and Elisabet E. Rutström. 1995. Homegrown Values and Hypothetical Surveys: Is the Dichotomous Choice Approach Incentive-Compatible? *American Economic Review* 85: 260–266.

Cycyota, Cynthia and David A. Harrison. 2006. What (Not) to Expect When Surveying Executives. A Meta-Analysis of Top Manager Response Rates and Techniques over Time. *Organizational Research Methods* 9: 133–160.

Davies, David G. 1959. An Empirical Test of Sales-Tax Regressivity. *Journal of Political Economy* 67: 72–78.

Davies, Ronald B. 2004. Tax Treaties and Foreign Direct Investment: Potential Versus Performance. *International Tax and Public Finance* 11: 775–802.

Davies, Ronald B. and Carsten Eckel 2010. Tax Competition for Heterogeneous Firms with Endogenous Entry. *American Economic Journal: Economic Policy* 2(1): 77–102.

Davis, Mark. 2015. Applebee's to Move Headquarters to California, Lay Off Some Area Employees. *Kansas City Star* (September 4).

de Blasio, Guido, Davide Fantion, and Guido Pellegrini. 2015. Evaluating the Impact of Innovation Incentives: Evidence from an Unexpected Shortage of Funds. *Industrial and Corporate Change* 24(4): 1285–1314.

Deno, Kevin T. and Stephen L. Mehay. 1987. Municipal Management Structure and Fiscal Performance: Do City Managers Make a Difference? *Southern Economic Journal* 53: 627–642.

Department of Finance, City of Ferguson. 2014. City of Ferguson, Missouri: Comprehensive Annual Financial Report for the Year Ending June 30, 2014. www.fergusoncity.com/DocumentCenter/View/1752. Accessed August 25, 2017.

Department of Trade and Industry, Republic of South Africa. 2012a. Financial Assistance. 12I Tax Allowance Incentive: Offerings (12I TAI). www .thedti.gov.za/financial_assistance/financial_incentive.jsp?id=45&subthe meid=26. Accessed August 25, 2017.

Department of Trade and Industry, Republic of South Africa. 2012b. Media Statements: Minister Davies Approves Projects Worth Billions of Rands. www.thedti.gov.za/editmedia.jsp?id=2341. Accessed August 25, 2017.

Diaz-Cayeros, Alberto. 2006. *Federalism, Fiscal Authority, and Centralization in Latin America*. New York: Cambridge University Press.

Dolan, Maura, Jessica Garrison, and Anthony York. 2011. California High Court Puts Redevelopment Agencies out of Business. *Los Angeles Times* (December 29).

Doner, Richard F., Bryan K. Ritchie, and Dan Slater. 2005. Systemic Vulnerability and the Origins of Developmental States: Northeast and Southeast Asia in Comparative Perspective. *International Organization* 59(2):327–361.

Downs, Anthony. 1957. An Economic Theory of Political Action in a Democracy. *The Journal of Political Economy* 65: 135–150.

Dunning, John H. 1977. Trade, Location of Economic Activity and the MNE: A Search for an Eclectic Approach. In Bertil G. Ohlin, Per-Ove Hesselborn, and Per Magnus Wijkman (eds.), *The International Allocation of Economic Activity*. London: Macmillan, 395–418.

Easson, Alex. 2004. *Tax Incentives for Foreign Direct Investment*. The Hague: Kluwer Law International.

East-West Gateway: Council of Governments. 2011. An Assessment of the Effectiveness and Fiscal Impacts of the Use of Development Incentives in the

St. Louis Region: Final Report (January). ewgateway.org/pdffiles/library/dirr/TIFFinalRpt.pdf. Accessed August 25, 2017.

Eder, Stephen. 2013. For ESPN, Millions to Remain in Connecticut. New York Times (December 26).

Egorov, Georgy and Konstantin Sonin. 2011. Dictators and Their Viziers: Endogenizing the Loyalty-Competence Trade-Off. *Journal of the European Economic Association* 9: 903–930.

Eligon, John. 2013. Missouri's Governor Calls for End to Contest of Incentives. *The New York Times* (November 12).

Ellis, Stephen and Cynthia Rogers. 2000. Local Economic Development as a Prisoners' Dilemma: The Role of Business Climate. *The Review of Regional Studies* 30(3): 315–330.

European Commission. 2016. "Transparency System" for Regional Aid for Large Investment Projects. http://ec.europa.eu/competition/state_aid/register/msf_2016.pdf. Accessed August 25, 2017.

Evans, Peter and James E. Rauch. 1999. Bureaucracy and Growth: A Cross-National Analysis of the Effects of Weberian State Structures on Economic Growth. *American Sociological Review* 64(5): 748–765.

Faulk, Dagney. 2002. Do State Economic Development Incentives Create Jobs? An Analysis of State Employment Tax Credits. *National Tax Journal* 55: 263–280.

Feiock, Richard C., Moon-Gi Jeong, and Jaehoon Kim. 2003. Credible Commitment and Council-Manager Government: Implications for Policy Instrument Choices. *Public Administration Review*, 63: 616–625.

Feiock, Richard C., Annette Steinacker, and Hyung Jun Park. 2009. Institutional Collective Action and Economic Development Joint Ventures. *Public Administration Review* 69: 256–270.

Felix, Alison R. and James R. Hines Jr. 2013. Who Offers Tax-Based Business Development Incentives? *Journal of Urban Economics* 75: 80–91.

Ferejohn, John. 1974. *Pork Barrel Politics: Rivers and Harbor Legislation 1947–1968*. Palo Alto, CA: Stanford University Press.

Fox, William F. and Matthew N. Murray. 2004. Do Economic Effects Justify the Use of Fiscal Incentives? *Southern Economic Journal* 71: 78–92.

Frazier, Eric and Henderson, Bruce. 2013. Google Announces $600M Lenoir Data Center Expansion. *Charlotte Observer*.

Frederickson, H. George, Gary A. Johnson, and Curtis H. Wood. 2004. *The Adapted City: Institutional Dynamics and Structural Change*. Armonk, NY: ME Sharpe.

Freeland, William, Ben Wilterdink, and Jonathan Williams. 2014. The Unseen Costs of Tax Cronyism: Favoritism and Foregone Growth. State Factor. (July 23). www.alec.org/publication/taxcarveouts/. Accessed August 25, 2017.

Frye, Timothy, Ora John Reuter, and David Szakonyi. 2014. Political Machines at Work: Voter Mobilization and Electoral Subversion in the Workplace. *World Politics* 66: 195–228.

Gabe, Todd and David Kraybill. 2002. The Effect of State Economic Development Incentives on Employment Growth of Establishments. *Journal of Regional Science* 42: 703–730.

Gaines, Brian J., James H. Kuklinski, and Paul J. Quirk. 2007. The Logic of the Survey Experiment Reexamined. *Political Analysis* 15: 1–20.

Gandhi, Jennifer. 2008. *Political Institutions Under Dictatorship*. New York: Cambridge University Press.

Gandhi, Jennifer and Adam Przeworski, 2007. Authoritarian Institutions and the Survival of Autocrats. *Comparative Political Studies* 40:1279–1301.

Garrett, Geoffrey. 1998. Global Markets and National Politics: Collision Course or Virtuous Circle? *International Organization* 52: 787–824.

Gattiker, Urs E. 1995. Firm and Taxpayer Returns from Training of Semiskilled Employees. *Academy of Management Journal* 38: 1152–1173.

Geddes, Barbara. 1990. How the Cases You Choose Affect the Answers You Get: Selection Bias in Comparative Politics. *Political Analysis* 2: 131–150.

Geddes, Barbara. 1999a. What Do We Know About Democratization After Twenty Years? *Annual Review of Political Science* 2: 115–144.

Geddes, Barbara. 1999b. Authoritarian Breakdown: Empirical Test of a Game Theoretic Argument. Presented at the annual meeting of the American Political Science Association, Atlanta, GA (September 2–5).

Geddes, Barbara, 2008. Party Creation as an Authoritarian Survival Strategy. In Conference on Dictators: Their Governance and Social Consequences. Princeton, NJ: Princeton University Press.

Geddes, Barbara, Joseph Wright, and Erica Frantz. 2014. Autocratic Breakdown and Regime Transitions: A New Data Set. *Perspectives on Politics* 12: 313–331.

Gehlbach, Scott and Philip Keefer. 2012. Private Investment and the Institutionalization of Collective Action in Autocracies: Ruling Parties and Legislatures. *The Journal of Politics* 74: 621–635.

Gel'man, Vladimir, Sergei Ryzhenkov, and Michael Brie. 2003. *Making and Breaking Democratic Transitions: The Comparative Politics of Russia's Regions*. Lanham, MD: Rowman and Littlefield.

Ghanem, Dalia and Junjie Zhang. 2014. Effortless Perfection: Do Chinese Cities Manipulate Air Pollution Data? *Journal of Environmental Economics and Management* 68: 203–225.

Gillian, Frankie. 2009. Sales Tax for Economic Development in Arkansas. wt-dc-prod.astate.edu/a/deltaced/files/LocalTaxforEconomicDevelopmentnewversion.pdf. Accessed August 25, 2017.

Glaeser, Edward L. 2001. The Economics of Location-Based Tax Incentives. Discussion Paper No. 1932, Harvard Institute of Economic Research. scholar.harvard.edu/files/glaeser/files/hier1932.pdf?m=1360042861. Accessed August 25, 2017.

Glass, Ira. 2011. *This American Life*: Episode 435: "How to Create a Job." Transcript. May 13. www.thisamericanlife.org/radio-archives/episode/435/transcript. Accessed August 25, 2017.

Goode, Paul. 2007. The Puzzle of Putin's Gubernatorial Appointments. *Europe-Asia Studies* 59: 365–399.

Gordon, Colin. 2009. *Mapping Decline: St. Louis and the Fate of the American City*. Philadelphia: University of Pennsylvania Press.

Gordon, Sanford C. and Catherine Hafer. 2005. Flexing Muscle: Corporate Political Expenditures as Signals to the Bureaucracy. *American Political Science Review* 99: 245–261.

Gordon, Sanford C. and Catherine Hafer. 2007. Corporate Influence and the Regulatory Mandate. *The Journal of Politics* 69: 300–319.

Gordon, Sanford C., Catherine Hafer, and Dimitri Landa. 2007. Consumption or Investment? On Motivations for Political Giving. *The Journal of Politics* 69: 1057–1072.

Goss, Ernest Preston and Joseph M. Phillips. 1994. State Employment Growth: The Impact of Taxes and Economic Development Agency Spending. *Growth and Change* 25: 287–300.

Goss, Ernest Preston and Joseph M. Phillips. 2001. The Impact of Tax Incentives: Do Initial Conditions Matter? *Growth and Change* 32: 236–250.

Government Accounting Standards Board (GASB). 2008. GASB Research Brief: State and Local Government Use of Generally Accepted Accounting Principles for General Purpose External Financial Reporting. gasb.org/resources/ccurl/3 36/337/GAAP_Research_Brief.pdf. Accessed August 25, 2017.

Government Accounting Standards Board (GASB). 2014. Exposure Draft – Tax Abatement Disclosures. GASB Exposure Draft. tinyurl.com/mqx4s7f. Accessed August 25, 2017.

Government Accounting Standards Board (GASB). 2015. Statement No. 77: Tax Abatement Disclosures. Governmental Accounting Standards Series, No. 353 (August). www.gasb.org/jsp/GASB/Document_C/GASBDocumen tPage?cid=1176166283745&acceptedDisclaimer=true. Accessed August 25, 2017.

Government Accounting Standards Board (GASB). 2015. Online Comment Letters. Project 19-20E. Tax Abatement Disclosures. Accessed June 25, 2016. http://tinyurl.com/ob74ofy. Accessed August 25, 2017.

Greenbaum, Robert T. and Jim Landers. 2009. Why Are State Policy Makers Still Proponents of Enterprise Zones? What Explains Their Actions in the Face of a Preponderance of the Research? *International Regional Science Review* 32: 466–479.

Greenbaum, Robert T. and Jim Landers. 2014. The Tiff over TIF: A Review of the Literature Examining the Effectiveness of Tax Increment Financing. *National Tax Journal* 67(3): 655–674.

Greenblatt, Alan. 2011. Kansas City Businesses Want to End the "Economic Border War." *Governing*. (August).

Greene, William. 2004. The Behaviour of the Maximum Likelihood Estimator of Limited Dependent Variable Models in the Presence of Fixed Effects. *Econometrics Journal* 7: 98–119.

Greenstone, Michael and Enrico Moretti. 2003. Bidding for Industrial Plants: Does Winning a "Million Dollar Plant" Increase Welfare? National Bureau of Economic Research Working Paper, No. 9844. www.nber.org/papers/w9844. Accessed August 25, 2017.

Grieco, Joseph M. 1982. Between Dependency and Autonomy: India's Experience with the International Computer Industry. *International Organization* 36: 609–632.

Grimmer, Justin, Solomon Messing, and Sean J. Westwood. 2012. How Words and Money Cultivate a Personal Vote: The Effect of Legislator Credit Claiming on Constituent Credit Allocation. *American Political Science Review* 106: 703–719.

Grossman, Gene M. and Elhanan Helpman. 2001. *Special Interest Politics*. Cambridge: MIT Press.

Guisinger, Alexandra. 2009. Determining Trade Policy: Do Voters Hold Politicians Accountable? *International Organization* 63: 533–557.

Guo, Gang. 2009. China's Local Political Budget Cycles. *American Journal of Political Science* 53: 621–632.

Gura, David. 2012. Google Search in North Carolina: Jobs. *Marketplace.org*. (November 13). www.marketplace.org/topics/tech/google-search-north-caro lina-jobs. Accessed August 25, 2017.

Hadenius, Axel and Jan Teorell. 2007. Pathways from Authoritarianism. *Journal of Democracy* 18: 143–157.

Hagan, Ken. 2015. Commentary: Keep Hillsborough and Florida in Film Game by Continuing Tax Credit Program. *Tampa Tribune*. (May 31).

Hainmueller, Jens. 2012. Entropy Balancing for Causal Effects: A Multivariate Reweighting Method to Produce Balanced Samples in Observational Studies. *Political Analysis* 20: 25–46.

Hainmueller, Jens and Yiqing Xu. 2013. Ebalance: A Stata Package for Entropy Balancing. *Journal of Statistical Software* 54: 1–18.

Hancock, Jason. 2011. Mo. Senate Committee Launches Probe of Mamtek Deal. *St. Louis Post-Dispatch*. (October 6).

Hanson, Andrew and Shawn Rohlin. 2011. Do Location-Based Tax Incentives Attract New Business Establishments? *Journal of Regional Science* 51 (3): 427–449.

Harrington, Joseph E. 1993. Economic Policy, Economic Performance, and Elections. *American Economic Review* 83: 27–42.

Harris, Aisha. 2013. The Incredible Story of the Film-Tax Fraudsters. *Slate*. www.slate.com/blogs/browbeat/2013/03/27/film_tax_fraud_in_uk_landsca pe_of_lies_scammers_sent_to_jail.html. Accessed August 25, 2017.

Hays, Jude C. 2003. Globalization and Capital Taxation in Consensus and Majoritarian Democracies. *World Politics* 56: 79–113.

Head, Keith, John Ries, and Deborah Swenson. 1995. Agglomeration Benefits and Location Choice: Evidence from Japanese Manufacturing Investments in the United States. *Journal of International Economics* 38: 223–247.

Head, Keith C., John C. Ries, and Deborah L. Swenson. 1999. Attracting Foreign Manufacturing: Investment Promotion and Agglomeration. *Regional Science and Urban Economics* 29: 197–218.

Hellwig, Timothy. 2008. Globalization, Policy Constraints and Vote Choice. *The Journal of Politics* 70: 1128–1141.

Hellwig, Timothy and David Samuels. 2008. Electoral Accountability and the Variety of Democratic Regimes. *British Journal of Political Science* 38: 65–90.

Hetherington, Marc J. 2001. Resurgent Mass Partisanship: The Role of Elite Polarization. *American Political Science Review* 95: 619–631.

Hickey, Jason. 2013. Federal and State Legislative Moves to Boost Competitiveness & Business Climate. *Area Development*. www.areadevelopment.com/EconomicsGovernmentPolicy/Q1-2013/state-federal-legislation-boost-business-climate-2727261.shtml. Accessed August 25, 2017.

Hicks, Michael J. and Michael LaFaive. 2011. The Influence of Targeted Economic Development Tax Incentives on County Economic Growth: Evidence from Michigan's MEGA credits. *Economic Development Quarterly* 25: 193–205.

Hines, James R, Jr, 1996. Altered States: Taxes and the Location of Foreign Direct Investment in America. *American Economic Review* 86(5): 1076–1094.

Huang, Haifeng, 2013. Signal Left, Turn Right Central Rhetoric and Local Reform in China. *Political Research Quarterly* 66(2): 292–305.

Huber, Greg. A. and Sandy C. Gordon. 2004. Accountability and Coercion: Is Justice Blind When It Runs for Office? *American Political Science Review* 48: 247–263.

Iacus, Stefano M., Gary King, and Giuseppe Porro. 2012. Causal Inference Without Balance Checking: Coarsened Exact Matching. *Political Analysis* 20: 1–24.

Illinois Tax Increment Association. 2016. About TIF: The TIF Concept. www.illinois-tif.com/about-tif/. Accessed August 25, 2017.

Imbens, Guido and Karthik Kalyanaraman. 2012. Optimal Bandwidth Choice for the Regression Discontinuity Estimator. *The Review of Economic Studies* 79: 933–959.

Institute on Taxation & Economic Policy (ITEP). 2015. Who Pays? A Distributional Analysis of the Tax Systems in All 50 States. 5th ed. www.itep.org/pdf/whopaysreport.pdf. Accessed August 25, 2017.

International Center for the Study of Institutions and Development. 2015. Research Project: Institutions and Economic Development: The Role of Bureaucracy, and Experiments as a Method for Analysis and Evaluation of Reforms (project 2011–2013). iims.hse.ru/en/csid/projects. Accessed August 25, 2017.

International City/County Management Association; National League of Cities. Economic Development Dataset 1999 – Full Dataset, bookstore.icma.org/Data_Sets_C42.cfm. Accessed August 25, 2017.

International City/County Management Association; National League of Cities. Economic Development Dataset 2004 – Full Dataset, bookstore.icma.org/Data_Sets_C42.cfm. Accessed August 25, 2017.

International City/County Management Association; National League of Cities. Economic Development Dataset 2009 – Full Dataset, bookstore.icma.org/Data_Sets_C42.cfm. Accessed August 25, 2017.

International Monetary Fund. 2014. Vietnam: 2014 Article IV Consultation – Staff Report. IMF Country Report No. 14/311. www.imf.org/external/pubs/ft/scr/2014/cr14311.pdf. Accessed August 26, 2017.

Isaacs, Rico and Sarah Whitmore. 2014. The Limited Agency and Life-Cycles of Personalized Dominant Parties in the Post-Soviet Space: The Cases of United Russia and Nur Otan. *Democratization* 21: 699–721.

James, Sebastian. 2007. The Effect of Tax Rates on Declared Income: An Analysis of Indian Taxpayer Response to Changes in Income Tax Rates. PhD dissertation, Harvard University.

References

James, Sebastian, 2009. Incentives and Investments: Evidence and Policy Implications. www.wbginvestmentclimate.org/uploads/IncentivesandInvestments.pdf. Accessed August 26, 2017.

Jandl, Thomas. 2014. State Versus State: The Principal-Agent Problem in Vietnam's Decentralizing Economic Reforms. In Jonathan London (ed.), *Politics in Contemporary Vietnam: Party, State, and Authority Relations*. London: Palgrave MacMillan, 65–83.

Jensen, Nathan M. 2017. Job Creation and Firm-Specific Location Incentives. *Journal of Public Policy* 37(1): 85–112.

Jensen, Nathan M., Edmund J. Malesky, Mariana Medina, and Ugur Ozdemir. 2014. Pass the Bucks: Investment Incentives as Political Credit-Claiming Devices. *International Studies Quarterly* 58: 433–447.

Jensen, Nathan M., Edmund J. Malesky, and Matthew Walsh. 2015. Competing for Global Capital or Local Voters? The Politics of Business Location Incentives. *Public Choice* 164: 331–356.

Jia, Ruixue, Masayuki Kudamatsu, and David Seim. 2015. Political Selection in China: The Complementary Roles of Connections and Performance. *Journal of the European Economic Association* 13: 631–668.

Johnson, Walter. 2015. Ferguson's Fortune 500 Company: Why the Missouri City – Despite Hosting a Multinational Corporation – Relied on Municipal Fees and Fines to Extract Revenue from its Poorest Residents. *Atlantic*. (April 26).

Jolley, G. Jason, Mandee Foushee Lancaster, and Jiang Gao. 2015. Tax Incentives and Business Climate: Executive Perceptions from Incented and Nonincented firms. *Economic Development Quarterly* 29: 180–186.

Kaiser, Borid. 2014. RDCV: Stata module to perform Sharp Regression Discontinuity Design with Cross Validation Bandwidth Selection. *Statistical Software Components* S457908, Boston College Department of Economics, revised November 7, 2015.

Katz, Ethan. 2001. Bias in Conditional and Unconditional Fixed Effects Logit Estimation. *Political Analysis* 9: 379–384.

Keefer, Philip. 2009. Inequality, Collective Action, and Democratization. *Political Science and Politics* 42: 661–666.

Keen, Michael and Mario Mansour. 2010. Revenue Mobilization in Sub-Saharan Africa: Challenges from Globalization II-Corporate Taxation. *Development Policy Review* 28: 573–596.

Kenyon, Daphne A., Adam H. Langley, and Bethany P. Paquin. 2012. Property Tax Incentive Pitfalls. *National Tax Journal* 65: 1011–1022.

King, Gary, Robert O. Keohane, and Sidney Verba. 1994. *Designing Social Inquiry: Scientific Inference in Qualitative Research*. Princeton, NJ: Princeton University Press.

Klemm, Alexander and Stefan Van Parys. 2012. Empirical Evidence on the Effects of Tax Incentives. *International Tax and Public Finance* 19: 393–423.

Kline, Patrick and Enrico Moretti. 2014. People, Places, and Public Policy: Some Simple Welfare Economics of Local Economic Development Programs. *Annual Review of Economics* 6: 629–662.

Konitzer, Andrew. 2005. *Voting for Russia's Governors*. New York: Cambridge University Press.

Konitzer, Andrew and Stephen Wegren. 2006. Federalism and Political Recentralization in the Russian Federation: United Russia as the Party of Power. *Publius* 36: 503–522.

Kono, Daniel. 2006. Optimal Obfuscation: Democracy and Trade Policy Transparency. *American Political Science Review* 100: 369–384.

Krause, Lawerence B. 1987. Thinking About Singapore. In Lawrence Krause, Ai Tee Koh, and Yuan Lee Tsao (eds.), *The Singapore Economy Reconsidered*. Singapore: Institute of Southeast Asian Studies.

Landry, Pierre F. 2008. *Decentralized Authoritarianism in China*. New York: Cambridge University Press.

Langfitt, Frank. 2009. Laid-Off Furniture Workers Try to Leap to Google. *NPR.org*. (December 16). www.npr.org/templates/story/story.php?storyId=121516133. Accessed August 26, 2017.

Larano, Cris. 2012. JG Summit Holdings, Inc.: Summit's Naphtha Cracking Plant to Start Operations November 2013. *Manila Times* (Philippines). (October 22). www.4-traders.com/JG-SUMMIT-HOLDINGS-INC-7862776/news/JG-Summit-Holdings-Inc-JG-Summit-s-Naphtha-Cracking-Plant-to-Start-Operations-November-2013-15411914/. Accessed August 26, 2017.

Lazarev, Valery. 2005. Economics of One-Party State: Promotion Incentives and Support for the Soviet Regime. *Comparative Economic Studies* 47: 346–363.

Le, Diep, Eli Miloslavsky, and Howard J. Shatz. 2003. State Foreign Office Database. Public Policy Institute of California (electronic database) (on file with authors).

Lee, David S. and Thomas Lemieux. 2010. Regression Discontinuity Designs in Economics. *Journal of Economic Literature* 48: 281–355.

Legislative Division of Post Audit. 2013. Performance Audit Report. Economic Development: Determining Which Economic Development Tools Are Most Important and Effective in Promoting Job Creation and Economic Growth in Kansas, Part 1. www.kslpa.org/assets/files/reports/R-13-010.pdf. Accessed August 26, 2017.

Legislative Division of Post Audit. 2014. Economic Development: Determining Which Economic Development Tools Are Most Important and Effective in Promoting Job Creation and Economic Growth in Kansas, Part 3. www.kslpa.org/assets/files/reports/r-14-011.pdf. Accessed August 26, 2017.

LeRoy, Greg. 2007. Nine Concrete Ways to Curtail the Economic War Among the States. In Ann Markusen (ed.), *Reining in the Competition for Capital*. Kalamazoo, MI: W.E. Upjohn Institute.

Li, Quan. 2006. Democracy, Autocracy, and Tax Incentives to Foreign Direct Investors: A Cross-National Analysis. *Journal of Politics* 68: 62–74.

Li, Quan. 2016. Fiscal Decentralization and Tax Incentives in the Developing World. *Review of International Political Economy* 23: 232–260.

Li, Hongbin and Li-An Zhou. 2005. Political Turnover and Economic Performance: The Incentive Role of Personnel Control in China. *Journal of Public Economics* 89:1743–1762.

Liang, Jiaqi. 2015. Who Maximizes (or Satisfices) in Performance Management? An Empirical Study of the Effects of Motivation-Related Institutional Contexts on Energy Efficiency Policy in China. *Public Performance and Management Review* 38: 284–315.

Lieb, David A. 2013. Analysis: Boeing Bid Could Impact Mo. Regardless. *St. Louis Post-Dispatch.* (December 15).

Lobao, Linda and David S. Kraybill. 2005. The Emerging Roles of County Governments in Metropolitan and Nonmetropolitan Areas: Findings from a National Survey. *Economic Development Quarterly* 19: 245–259.

Logan, Tim. 2013. What Boeing Wants: A look at the 777X Request for Proposals. *St. Louis Post Dispatch* (December 5).

Long, J. Scott and Jeremy Freese. 2005. *Regression Models for Categorical Outcomes Using Stata.* 2nd ed. College Station, TX: Stata.

Lü, Xiaobo and Landry, Pierre. F. 2014. Show Me the Money: Interjurisdiction Political Competition and Fiscal Extraction in China. *American Political Science Review* 108(3): 706–722.

Lupia, Arthur and Matthew D. McCubbins. 1998. *The Democratic Dilemma: Can Citizens Learn What They Need to Know?* New York: Cambridge University Press.

Magaloni, Beatriz. 2008. *Voting for Autocracy: Hegemonic Party Survival and its Demise in Mexico.* New York: Cambridge University Press.

Magaloni, Beatrice and Kricheli, Ruth. 2010. Political Order and One-Party Rule. *Annual Review of Political Science* 13: 123–143.

Magaloni, Beatriz, Jonathan Chu, and Eric Min. 2013. Autocracies of the World, 1950–2012 (Version 1.0). Dataset. Stanford University. http://cddrl.fsi.stanford.edu/research/autocracies_of_the_world_dataset. Accessed August 26, 2017.

Magaloni, Beatriz and Ruth Kricheli. 2010. Political Order and One-Party Rule. *Annual Review of Political Science* 13: 123–143.

Malesky, Edmund J. 2008a. Provincial Governance and Foreign Direct Investment in Vietnam. *Twenty Years of Foreign Investment in Vietnam.* Ho Chi Minh City: Knowledge Publishing House.

Malesky, Edmund J. 2008b. Straight Ahead on Red: How Foreign Direct Investment Empowers Subnational Leaders. *Journal of Politics* 70: 97–119.

Malesky, Edmund J. and Paul Schuler. 2011. The Single-Party Dictator's Dilemma: Information in Elections Without Opposition. *Legislative Studies Quarterly* 36: 491–530.

Malesky, Edmund J. 2015. The Vietnam Provincial Competitiveness Index: Measuring Economic Governance for Private Sector Development, 2014 Final Report. Hanoi: Vietnam Chamber of Commerce and Industry and United States Agency for International Development. www.pcivietnam.org. Accessed August 27, 2017.

Manion, Melanie. 1993. *Retirement of Revolutionaries in China: Public Policies, Social Norms, Private Interests.* Princeton, NJ: Princeton University Press.

Markusen, Ann and Katherine Nesse. 2007. Institutional and Political Determinants of Incentive Competition. In Ann Markusen (ed.), *Reining in the Competition for Capital.* Kalamazoo, MI: W.E. Upjohn Institute.

Marshall, Alfred. 1920. *Principles of Economics.* 8th ed. London: Macmillan.

Maskin, Eric, Yingyi Qian, and Chenggang Xu. 2000. Incentives, Information, and Organizational Form. *The Review of Economic Studies* 67: 359–378.

Maskin, Eric and Jean Tirole. 2004. The Politician and the Judge: Accountability in Government. *American Economic Review* 94: 1034–1054.

Mason, Susan and Kenneth P. Thomas. 2010. Tax Incremental Financing in Missouri: An Analysis of Determinants, Equity, and Path Dependency. *Economic Development Quarterly* 24: 169–179.

Massachusetts Department of Revenue. 2014. Report on the Impact of Massachusetts Film Industry Tax Incentives Through Calendar Year 2012. www.mass.gov/dor/docs/dor/news/reportcalendaryear2012.pdf. Accessed August 26, 2017.

Masunaga, Samantha. 2015. Applebee's Is Moving Its Headquarters to Glendale. *Los Angeles Times*. (September 4).

Mattera, Philip, Thomas Cafcas, Leigh McIlvaine, Andrew Seifter, and Kasia Tarczynska. 2012. Money-Back Guarantees for Taxpayers: Clawbacks and Other Enforcement Safeguards in State Economic Development Subsidy Programs. www.goodjobsfirst.org/moneyback. Accessed August 26, 2017.

Mattera, Philip, Kasia Tarczynska, and Greg LeRoy. 2013. Megadeals: The Largest Economic Development Subsidy Packages Ever Awarded by State and Local Governments in the United States. www.goodjobsfirst.org/sites/def ault/files/docs/pdf/megadeals_report.pdf. Accessed August 26, 2017.

Mattera, Philip, Kasia Tarczynska, Leigh McIlvaine, Thomas Cafcas, and Greg LeRoy. 2012. Paying Taxes to Their Bosses: How a Growing Number of States Subsidize Companies with the Withholding Taxes of Workers. www.goodjobs first.org/sites/default/files/docs/pdf/taxestotheboss.pdf. Accessed August 26, 2017.

Mauzy, Diane K. and Robert Stephen Milne. 2002. *Singapore Politics Under the People's Action Party*. New York: Routledge.

Mayhew, David. 1974. *Congress: The Electoral Connection*. New Haven, CT: Yale University Press.

McCrary, Justin. 2008. Manipulation of the Running Variable in the Regression Discontinuity Design: A Density Test. *Journal of Econometrics* 142: 698–714.

McCulloch, Neil and Edmund J. Malesky. 2014. What Determines the Quality of Subnational Economic Governance? Comparing Indonesia and Vietnam. In Hall Hill (ed.), *Indonesia Update: Regional Dynamics in a Decentralized Indonesia*. Canberra: Australia National University, ch. 9.

McDowall, David. 1980. Interrupted Time Series Designs. In Michael S. Lewis-Beck, Alan Bryman, and Tim Futing Liao (eds.), *The Sage Encyclopedia of Social Science Research Methods*. New York: Sage.

McKelvey, Richard D. and William Zavoina. 1975. A Statistical Model for the Analysis of Ordinal Level Dependent Variables. *Journal of Mathematical Sociology* 4: 103–120.

Mekong Private Sector Development Facility. 2004. Good Local Governance: A Key to Economic Growth. *Business Issues Bulletin* 3(6) (August). http://www-wds .worldbank.org/external/default/WDSContentServer/WDSP/IB/2006/08/02/000 310607_20060802145627/Rendered/PDF/368300VN0Local1ce0BIB161VN01 PUBLIC1.pdf. Accessed August 26, 2017.

Miller, Gerald J. 2011. *Government Budgeting and Financial Management in Practice*. Boca Raton, FL: CRC.

Miller, Rich. 2013. Google Expands in North Carolina, Will Boost Renewables. *Data Center Knowledge*. (April 19). www.datacenterknowledge.com/archives/2013/04/19/google-expands-in-north-carolina-will-boost-renewables/. Accessed August 26, 2017.

Misra, Tanvi. 2012. How Local Sales Taxes Target the Poor and Widen the Income Gap. *Atlantic*. (January 20).

Missouri Department of Economic Development. 2014. *Missouri Quality Jobs Program: Program Guidelines*. https://ded.mo.gov/programs/business/mo-quality-jobs-program. Accessed August 26, 2017.

Missouri Department of Revenue. 2015. Tax Increment Financing in Missouri. Local TIF Local Project Information and Financial Disclosure. dor.mo.gov/pdf/2014TIFAnnualReport.pdf. Accessed August 26, 2017.

Mitchell, Robert C. and Richard T. Carson. 1989. *Using Surveys to Value Public Goods: The Contingent Valuation Method*. Baltimore, MD: John Hopkins University Press.

Montjoy, Robert S. and Douglas J. Watson. 1993. Within-Region Variation in Acceptance of Council-Manager Government: Alabama and the Southeast. *State and Local Government Review* 25: 19–27.

Moran, Theodore. 1998. *Foreign Direct Investment and Development*. Washington, DC: Institute for International Economics.

Moran, Theodore H. 2002. *Beyond Sweatshops: Foreign Direct Investment and Globalization in Developing Countries*. Washington, DC: Brookings Institution.

Moran, Theodore. 2005. How Does FDI Affect Host Country Development? Using Industry Case Studies to Make Reliable Generalizations. In Theodore H. Moran, Edward M. Graham, and Magnus Blomström (eds.), *Does Foreign Direct Investment Promote Development?* Washington, DC: Institute for International Development.

Moran, Theodore, Edward M. Graham, and Magnus Blomström. 2005. *Does Foreign Direct Investment Promote Development?* New York: Peterson Institute for International Economics.

Morisset, Jacques and Neda Pirnia. 1999. How Tax Policy and Incentives Affect Foreign Direct Investment. World Bank Policy Research Working Paper 2509.

Morley, Hugh R. March 13, 2011. Panasonic Deal Stirs Criticism of N.J. Tax-Credit Programs. *NorthJersey.com*.

Morton, Rebecca and Charles Cameron. 1992. Elections and the Theory of Campaign Contributions: A Survey and Critical Analysis. *Economics & Politics* 4: 79–108.

Mrozek, Paul. 2013. Speaker Critical of Tax Incentive Packages for Retail Projects. *The Daily News*. May 31. http://thedailynewsonline.com/news/article_f0626b54-c9a8-11e2-a7c7-001a4bcf887a.html. Accessed June 15, 2014.

Munshi, Neil. 2013. US States Trade Tax Offers in Battle to Host Boeing. *Financial Times*. (December 13).

Mutz, Diana C. and Pemantle, Robin. 2015. Standards for Experimental Research: Encouraging a Better Understanding of Experimental Methods. *Journal of Experimental Political Science* 2(2): 192–215.

Myagkov, Mikhail, Peter Ordeshook, and Dimitri Shakin. 2009. *The Forensics of Electoral Fraud*. New York: Cambridge University Press.

Nash, Betty. 2011. When South Carolina Met BMW. *Region Focus* 9(2): 20–22.

National Education Association. 2003. Protecting Public Education: From Tax Giveaways to Corporations: Property Tax Abatements, Tax Increment Financing, and Funding for Schools. NEA Research Working Paper. files.eric.ed.gov/fulltext/ED480936.pdf. Accessed August 26, 2017.

Nelson, Kimberly. 2011. State-Level Autonomy and Municipal Government Structure: Influence on Form of Government Outcomes. *American Review of Public Administration* 41: 542–561.

Neumark, David and Jed Kolko. 2010. Do Enterprise Zones Create Jobs? Evidence from California's Enterprise Zone Program. *Journal of Urban Economics* 68: 1–19.

Neumark, David, Brandon Wall, and Junfu Zhang. 2011. Do Small Businesses Create More Jobs? New Evidence from the National Establishment Time Series. *Review of Economics and Statistics* 93: 16–29.

Newport, Frank. 2011. Americans Favor Jobs Plan Proposals, Including Taxing Rich. *Gallup*. (September 20). www.gallup.com/poll/155768/americans-focus-jobs-best-improve-economy.aspx. Accessed August 26, 2017.

Newport, Frank. 2012. Americans Focus on Jobs as Best Way to Improve US Economy. *Gallup*. (July 19). www.gallup.com/poll/149567/americans-favor-jobs-plan-proposals-including-taxing-rich.aspx. Accessed August 26, 2017.

New York State. 2015. Governor Cuomo Announces $181 Million to Fund Projects Generating Economic Opportunity Throughout New York State. (June 1). www.governor.ny.gov/news/governor-cuomo-announces-181-million-fund-projects-generating-economic-opportunity-throughout. (Governor Cuomo press release). Accessed August 26, 2017.

New York State. 2014. Governor Cuomo Announces $709.2 Million in Economic Development Resources Awarded in Fourth Round of Regional Council Initiative. (December 11). www.governor.ny.gov/news/governor-cuomo-announces-7092-million-economic-development-resources-awarded-fourth-round. (Governor Cuomo press release). Accessed August 26, 2017.

Nguyen Tan Dung. 2010. Decision No. 24/2010/NĐ-CP: Regulations on Hiring, Use, and Management of State Officials. Office of the Government, Hanoi, Vietnam. (March 15). http://thuvienphapluat.vn/van-ban/Bo-may-hanh-chinh/Nghi-dinh-24-2010-ND-CP-tuyen-dung-su-dung-quan-ly-cong-chuc-102412.aspx. (in Vietnamese). Accessed August 26, 2017.

Norton, Edward C., Hua Wang, and Chunrong Ai. 2004. Computing Interaction Effects and Standard Errors in Logit and Probit Models. *The Stata Journal* 4: 154–167.

Oates, Wallace E. 1972. *Fiscal Federalism*. New York: Harcourt Brace Jovanovich.

Oakley, Deirdre and Hui-Shien Tsao. 2006. A New Way of Revitalizing Distressed Urban Communities? Assessing the Impact of the Federal Empowerment Zone Program. *Journal of Urban Affairs* 25: 443–471.

Office of Missouri Governor Jay Nixon. 2012. Gov. Nixon Helps Automotive Parts Supplier Break Ground on New $42 Million Production Facility in Liberty. (June 25). http://governor.mo.gov/news/archive/gov-nixon-helps-automotive-parts-supplier-break-ground-new-42-million-production. Accessed August 26, 2017.

Office of Missouri Governor Jay Nixon. 2016. Building Missouri's Future. Accessed June 14, 2016. http://www.cuinc.org/wp-content/uploads/2016/06/Gov.-Jay-Nix-Website.htm. Accessed August 26, 2017.
Oman, Charles. 2000. Policy Competition for Foreign Direct Investment: A Study of Competition Among Governments to Attract FDI. Paris: Organisation for Economic Co-operation and Development.
Orlando Sentinel. 2009. We Think: Incentives Will Allow State to Become Competitive in Film Game. (January 2). www.orlandosentinel.com/opinion/orl-ed02109jan02-story.html. Accessed August 26, 2017.
Paiva, Roberto, Sergio F. Marques, Jefferson L. B. Sanches, and Frank de Meijer. 2012. Brazil: The State VAT Competition Reaches a New Stage. *Indirect Tax Briefing* 5 (August): 58–61. http://taxinsights.ey-vx.com/archive/archive-articles/brazil-the-state-vat-competition-reaches-a-new-stage.aspx. Accessed August 26, 2017.
Paquette, Daniel. 2017. "Trump Said He Would Save Jobs at Carrier. The Layoffs Start June 20," *The Washington Post Wong Blog* (May 24) https://www.washingtonpost.com/news/wonk/wp/2017/05/24/here-is-the-number-of-jobs-carrier-is-moving-to-mexico-after-trump-said-hed-save-them/?utm_term=.002e376d2399. Accessed August 5, 2017.
Patrick, Carlianne Elizabeth. 2014. Does Increasing Available Non-Tax Economic Development Incentives Result in More Jobs? *National Tax Journal* 67: 351–386.
Patton, Zach. February 8, 2007. Betting the Farm. *Governing.* http://www.governing.com/mag/March-2007.html. Accessed August 26, 2017.
Persson, Torten, Gérald Roland, and Guildo Tabellini. 1997. Separation of Powers and Political Accountability. *Quarterly Journal of Economics* 112: 1163–1202.
Peters, Alan H. 1993. Clawbacks and the Administration of Economic Development Policy in the Midwest. *Economic Development Quarterly* 7(4): 328–340.
Peters, Alan H. and Peter Fisher. 2004. The Failures of Economic Development Incentives. *Journal of the American Planning Association* 70: 27–37.
Petrocik, John R. 2009. Measuring Party Support: Leaners are Not Independents. *Electoral Studies* 28: 562–572.
Pew Center on the States. 2012. *Evidence Counts. Evaluating State Tax Incentives for Jobs and Growth.* Washington, DC: The Pew Foundation.
Khai, Pham Van. 2000. Decision No. 71/2000/NĐ-CP: Regulations Concerning the Working Period of Bureaucrats and Civil Servants at Retirement Age. Office of the Government, Hanoi, Vietnam. (November 23). http://thuvienphapluat.vn/van-ban/Bo-may-hanh-chinh/Nghi-dinh-71-2000-ND-CP-quy-dinh-viec-keo-dai-thoi-gian-cong-tac-cua-can-bo-cong-chuc-den-do-tuoi-nghi-huu-47037.asp. (in Vietnamese). Accessed August 26, 2017.
Khai, Pham Van. 2002. Official Letter 18/2002/CT-TTg: On the Implementation of the Party's on Official Work and Legal Decisions on the Retirement of Bureaucrats and Civil Servants of the State. Prime Minister's Office, Hanoi, Vietnam. (September 5). http://thuvienphapluat.vn/van-ban/Lao-dong-Tien-luong/Chi-thi-18-2002-CT-TTg-thuc-hien-nghiem-chinh-Quyet-dinh-Dang-co

ng-tac-can-bo-quy-dinh-phap-luat-nghi-huu-can-bo-cong-chuc-vien-chuc-nha-nuoc-49962.aspx. (in Vietnamese). Accessed August 26, 2017.

Khai, Pham Van. 2003. Decision No. 27/2003/QĐ-TTg: On the Time Period Allowed for Officials, Retiring Officials, and Civil Servants Exiting Service, Hanoi, Vietnam. (February 19). http://thuvienphapluat.vn/van-ban/Bo-may-hanh-chinh/Quyet-dinh-27-2003-QD-TTg-quy-che-bo-nhiem-bo-nhiem-lai-luan-chuyen-tu-chuc-mien-nhiem-can-bo-cong-chuc-lanh-dao/50527/noi-dung.aspx. (in Vietnamese). Accessed August 26, 2017.

Phillips, Joseph M. and Ernest P. Goss. 1995. The Effect of State and Local Taxes on Economic Development. *Southern Economic Journal* 62(2): 320–333.

Plümper, Thomas, Vera E. Troeger, and Hannes Winner. 2009. Why There is No Race to the Bottom in Capital Taxation. *International Studies Quarterly* 53: 761–786.

Pluta, Rick. 2013. Governor Hopes to Rely Less on State Incentives for Future Jobs. *Michigan Radio*. (January 24). michiganradio.org/post/governor-hopes-rely-less-state-incentives-future-jobs. Accessed August 26, 2017.

Png, Ivan. 2013. Climate Change in China: Communism is Cooler. Paper presented at the Department of Geography Seminar Series, National University of Singapore (April 19).

Polimetrix. 2005. American Public Opinion Poll, October 2005. http://hdl.handle.net/1902.1/14620. Accessed August 26, 2017.

Poole, Keith and Thomas Romer. 1985. Patterns of Political Election Contributions to the 1980 Campaign for the US House of Representatives. *Public Choice* 47: 63–112.

PricewaterhouseCoopers. 2016. Vietnam Pocket Tax Book 2016. Ho Chi Minh City, Vietnam. www.pwc.com/vn. Accessed August 26, 2017.

Pries, Ludger. 2006. Cost Competition or Innovation Competition? Lessons from the Case of the BMW Plant Location in Leipzg, Germany. *Transfer: European Review of Labour and Research* 12: 11–29.

Prilliman, Soledad Artiz and Kenneth J. Meier. 2014. Taxes, Incentives, and Economic Growth: Assessing the Impact of Pro-Business Taxes on U.S. State Economies. *Journal of Politics* 76(2): 364–379.

Rauch, James E. 1995. Bureaucracy, Infrastructure, and Economic Growth: Evidence from US Cities During the Progressive Era. *The American Economic Review* 85: 968–979.

Reese, Laura A. 2014. The Alchemy of Local Economic Development. *Economic Development Quarterly* 28: 206–219.

Reuter, Ora John. Forthcoming. *The Origins of Dominant Parties: Building Authoritarian Institutions in Post-Soviet Russia*. New York: Cambridge University Press.

Reuter, Ora John and Noah Buckley. 2015. Why Authoritarian Elections? An Elite-Based Theory with Evidence from Russian Mayoral Elections. Paper presented at the European Association for Comparative Economic Studies – Higher School of Economics Workshop, Moscow, Russia (June 29).

Reuter, Ora John and Graham Robertson. 2012. Subnational Appointments in Authoritarian Regimes: Evidence from Russian Gubernatorial Appointments. *Journal of Politics* 74: 1023–1037.

Reuter, Ora John and Rostilav Turovsky. 2014. Dominant Party Rule and Legislative Leadership in Authoritarian Regimes. *Party Politics* 20: 663–674.

Rice, Bradley Robert. 1977. *Progressive Cities: The Commission Movement in America, 1901–1920.* Austin: University of Texas Press.

Richter, Brian Kelleher, Krislert Samphantharak, and Jeffrey Timmons. 2009. Lobbying and Taxes. *American Journal of Political Science* 53: 893–909.

Rodríguez-Pose, Andrés and Glauco Arbix 2001. Strategies of Waste: Bidding Wars in the Brazilian Automotive Sector. *International Journal of Urban and Regional Research* 25: 134–154.

Rodrik, Dani. 1997. *Has Globalization Gone Too Far?* Washington, DC: Institute for International Economics.

Rudra, Nita. 2008. *Globalization and the Race to the Bottom in Developing Countries.* New York: Cambridge University Press.

Rundlett, Ashley and Milan W. Svolik. 2016. "Deliver the Vote! Micromotives and Macrobehavior in Electoral Fraud," *American Political Science Review* 110(1): 180–197.

Ryan, Kelsey. 2014. Incentive at Heart of Wichita Debate over Sales Tax Jobs Fund. *Wichita Eagle.* (October 25).

Schiesl, Martin J. 1977. *The Politics of Efficiency: Municipal Administration and Reform in America: 1880–1920.* Berkeley: University of California Press.

Schumacher-Matos, Edward. 2011. Planet Money Misfires on Local Economic Developers. *NPR.org.* (June 22). www.npr.org/blogs/ombudsman/2011/06/23/137349286/planet-money-misfires-on-local-economic-developers. Accessed August 26, 2017.

Schurmann, Franz. 1968. *Ideology and Organization in Communist China.* 2nd ed. Berkeley: University of California Press.

Schweich, Thomas A. 2012. Schweich Issues Audit of Missouri Department of Economic Development-Business and Community Service Division. http://app.auditor.mo.gov/AuditReports/CitzSummary.aspx?id=127. Accessed August 26, 2017.

Scott, Alwyn. 2013. Boeing 777x Aircraft: Will New Jet Be Built in South Carolina? *Christian Science Monitor.* (October 31).

Selznick, Philip. 1952. *The Organizational Weapon: A Study of Bolshevik Strategy and Tactics.* Washington, DC: RAND Corporation.

Sharafutdinova, Gulnaz. 2010. Subnational Governance in Russia: How Putin Changed the Contract with His Agents and the Problems It Created for Medvedev. *Publius* 40: 672–696.

Sharp, Elaine B. and Kevin Mullinix. 2012. Holding Their Feet to the Fire: Explaining Variation in City Governments' Use of Controls on Economic Development. *Economic Development Quarterly* 26: 138–150.

Shevtsova, Liliya. 2007. *Russia: Lost in Transition.* Washington, DC: Carnegie Endowment for International Peace.

Shih, Victor, Christopher Adolph, and Mingxing Liu. 2012. Getting Ahead in the Communist Party: Explaining the Advancement of Central Committee Members in China. *American Political Science Review* 106: 166–187.

Sinnaeve, Adina. 2007. How the EU Manages Subsidy Competition. In Ann Markusen (ed.), *Reining in the Competition for Capital*. Kalamazoo, MI: W.E. Upjohn Institute.

Slater, Dan. 2003. Iron Cage in an Iron Fist: Authoritarian Institutions and the Personalization of Power in Malaysia. *Comparative Politics* 36: 81–101.

Slemrod, Joel. 2006. The Role of Misconceptions in Support for Regressive Tax Reform. *National Tax Journal* 59: 57–75.

Smart, Michael and Daniel M. Sturm. 2013. Term Limits and Electoral Accountability. *Journal of Public Economics* 107: 93–102.

Smith, Benjamin. 2005. Life of the Party: The Origins of Regime Breakdown and Persistence Under Single-Party Rule. *World Politics* 57: 421–451.

Smith, Richard. 2016. Did the Community Renal Tax Incentives Pirate Businesses from Other Places? *Economic Development Quarterly* 30: 146–61.

Snyder, James M. 1990. Campaign Contributions as Investments: The House of Representatives 1980–1986. *Journal of Political Economy* 98: 1195–1227.

Spielman, Fran. 2015. Chicago to Get $250 Million as Emanuel Winds Down 7 Downtown TIF Districts. *Chicago Sun-Times*. (July 12).

State of Mississippi. 2016. Edison Chouest Offshore Locating Shipbuilding Operations, TopShip, LLC, in Gulfport, Miss. (February 8). www.governorbryant.com/edison-chouest-offshore-locating-shipbuilding-operations-topship-llc-in-gulfport-miss/. (Governor Bryant press release). Accessed August 26, 2017.

State of New Jersey. 2016. Lt. Governor Guadagno Attends Axtria Inc. Grand Opening. (February 23). http://www.freep.com/story/news/local/union-county/2016/02/23/guadagno-axtria-inc/80808552/. (Governor Christie press release). Accessed August 26, 2017.

Story, Louis. 2012. As Companies Seek Tax Deals, Governments Pay High Price. *New York Times*. (December 1).

Suits, Daniel B. 1977. Measurement of Tax Progressivity. *The American Economic Review* 67(4): 747–752.

Sullivan, Daniel Monroe. 2002. Local Governments as Risk-Takers and Risk-Reducers: An Examination of Business Subsidies and Subsidy Controls. *Economic Development Quarterly* 16(2): 115–126.

Sullivan, Daniel Monroe and Gary Green. 1999. Business Subsidies and Municipal Controls. *Journal of Urban Affairs* 21(3): 267–279.

Svolik, Milan. 2012. *The Politics of Authoritarian Rule*. New York: Cambridge University Press.

Swank, Duane. 2002. *Global Capital, Political Institutions, and Policy Change in Developed Welfare States*. New York: Cambridge University Press.

Swank, Duane. 2006. Tax Policy in an Era of Internationalization: Explaining the Spread of Neoliberalism. *International Organization* 60: 847–882.

Swank, Duane and Sven Steimo. 2002. The New Political Economy of Taxation in Advanced Capitalist Democracies. *American Journal of Political Science* 46: 642–655.

Szakonyi, David and Eugenia Nazrullaevay. 2015. Policy Unfamiliarity: Political Uncertainty and Private Investment in Hybrid Regimes. Dataset. Supplied directly to authors.

Talton, Jon. 2014. Seattle Needs to Get off the Bench in the Global-Investment Game *Seattle Times*. (April 12).
Tavares-Lehmann, Anna-Teresa. 2016. "Types of Investment Incentives." In Anna-Teresa Tavares-Lehman, Lisa Sachs, Lise Johnson, and Perrine Toldano (eds.), *Rethinking Investment Incentives: Trends and Policy Options*. New York: Columbia University Press.
Tavits, Margit. 2009. *Presidents with Prime Ministers: Do Direct Elections Matter?* Oxford: Oxford University Press.
Teorell, Jan, Carl Dahlström, and Stefan Dahlberg. 2011.The QoG Expert Survey Dataset University of Gothenburg, The Quality of Government Institute.
Terbush, Jon. 2011. Rick Perry's Job Creation Numbers May Be Artificially Inflated. *Business Insider*. (October 11).
Texans for Public Justice. 2010. Phantom Jobs: The Texas Enterprise Fund's Broken Promises. info.tpj.org/watchyourassets/enterprise3/index.html. Accessed August 26, 2017.
Texans for Public Justice. 2011. Perry's Piggybank: Texas Enterprise Fund Recipients Gave $7 Million to Rick Perry and His Republican Governors Association. (October). info.tpj.org/reports/pdf/PerryPiggybankTEF.pdf. Accessed August 26, 2017.
TexasAhead. 2016. Type A and B Economic Development Corporations Overview. Accessed June 14, 2016. texasahead.org/tax_programs/typeab/. Accessed August 26, 2017.
Thai Press Reports. January 6, 2006. Government Moves on Illegal Incentives (on file with authors).
Thomas, Kenneth P. 2007. *Investment Incentives: Growing Use, Uncertain Benefits, Uneven Controls*. Geneva, Switzerland: Global Subsidies Initiative of the International Institute for Sustainable Development.
Thomas, Kenneth P. 2011. *Investment Incentives and the Global Competition for Capital*. New York: Palgrave Macmillian.
Thomas, Kenneth and Fiona Wishlade. 2009. Locational Tournaments in the U.S. and the EU. Paper presented at the Biennial Conference of the European Studies Association, Los Angeles, CA. (23–25 April). www.unc.edu/euce/eus a2009/papers/thomas_10H.pdf. Accessed August 26, 2017.
Tiebout, Charles. 1956. A Pure Theory of Local Expenditures. *The Journal of Political Economy* 64: 416–426.
Today's Zaman (Turkey). May 18, 2012. Hyundai to Invest $607 Mln, Double Its Production in Turkey. www.cihan.com.tr/en/hyundai-to-invest-607-mln-double-its-production-in-turkey-704920.htm. Accessed August 26, 2017.
Tullock, Gordon, 1958. *A General Theory of Politics*. Charlottesville: University of Virginia.
Tullock, Gordon. 1972. The Purchase of Politicians. *Western Economic Journal* 10: 354–355.
Tullock, Gordon; Charles K. Rowley (ed.). 2005. *The Selected Works of Gordon Tullock*. Vol. IV, *The Economics of Politics*. Indianapolis, IN: Liberty Fund.
UNCTAD. 1996. Incentives and Foreign Direct Investment. Current Studies, Series A, No. 30, New York: United Nations Conference on Trade and Development.

UNCTAD. 2002. *World Investment Report.* New York: United Nations Conference on Trade and Development. http://unctad.org/en/docs/wir2002_en.pdf. Accessed August 26, 2017.

Utah Office of the Legislative Auditor General. 2013. A Performance Audit of Utah Science Technology and Research Initiative. Report to the Utah Legislature No. 2013–12.

Vietnam Chamber of Commerce and Industry VCCI 2015. Annual Provincial Competitiveness Index – Foreign Investment Survey (PCI-FDI). http://eng.pcivietnam.org/phieu-khao-sat-pci-c18.html. Accessed August 26, 217.

Vietnam National Assembly. 2005. Law No. 59/2005/QH11: Investment Law, Hanoi, Vietnam. (November 29). http://thuvienphapluat.vn/van-ban/Doanh-nghiep/Luat-dau-tu-2005-59-2005-QH11-6916.aspx. (in Vietnamese). Accessed August 26, 2017.

Vietnam National Assembly. 2014. Law No. 67/2014/QH13: Investment Law. Hanoi, Vietnam. (November 26). http://thuvienphapluat.vn/van-ban/Dau-tu/Luat-Dau-tu-2014-259729.aspx. (in Vietnamese). Accessed August 26, 2017.

Vlaicu, Razvan and Alexander Whalley. 2016. Hierarchical Accountability in Government. *Journal of Public Economics* 134: 85–99.

Volden, Craig 2002. The Politics of Competitive Federalism: A Race to the Bottom in Welfare Benefits? *American Journal of Political Science* 46(2): 352–363.

Vo Van Kiet. 1994. Official Letter No. 668-TTg: A Few Issues in the Implementation of Retirement Law for Civil Servants and Bureaucrats. Prime Ministers Office, Hanoi, Vietnam. (November 11). http://thuvienphapluat.vn/van-ban/Bao-hiem/Chi-thi-668-TTG-thuc-hien-che-do-nghi-huu-can-bo-cong-chuc-38913.aspx. (in Vietnamese). Accessed August 26, 2017.

Vu Long. 2005. State Hits out at Illegal Investment Incentives. *Vietnam Investment Review* 1 (May 23).

Vu Thanh Tu Anh, Le Viet Thai, and Vo Tat Thang. 2007. Provincial Extralegal Investment Incentives in the Context of Decentralization in Viet Nam: Mutually Beneficial or a Race to the Bottom. Policy Dialogue Paper, United Nations Development Program. www.undp.org/content/dam/vietnam/docs/Publications/9716_071205_provincentives.pdf. Accessed August 26, 2017.

Wagner, Richard E. 1976. Revenue Structure, Fiscal Illusion, and Budgetary Choice. *Public Choice* 25: 45–61.

Walker, Robert and David Greenstreet. 1991. The Effect of Government Incentives and Assistance on Location and Job Growth in Manufacturing. *Regional Studies* 25: 13–30.

Wallace, Jeremy L. 2016. Juking the Stats? Authoritarian Information Problems in China. *British Journal of Political Science* 46: 11–29.

Warne, Russell T. 2014. A Primer on Multivariate Analysis of Variance (MANOVA) for Behavioral Scientists. *Practical Assessment, Research & Evaluation* 19: 1–10.

Wassmer, Robert W. and John E. Anderson. 2001. Bidding for Business: New Evidence on the Effect of Locally Offered Economic Development Incentives in a Metropolitan Area. *Economic Development Quarterly* 15(2): 132–148.

Weber, Rachel. 2003. Equity and Entrepreneurialism: The Impact of Tax Increment Financing on School Finance. *Urban Affairs Review* 38: 619–644.

Weeks, Jessica. 2008. Autocratic Audience Costs: Regime Type and Signaling Resolve. *International Organization* 62: 35–64.

Weeks, Jessica. 2014. *Dictators at War and Peace*. Ithaca, NY: Cornell University Press.

Weingast, Barry R. and Mark J. Moran. 1983. Bureaucratic Discretion or Congressional Control? Regulatory Policymaking by the Federal Trade Commission. *Journal of Political Economy* 91: 765–800.

Wells, Louis T., Nancy J. Allen, Jacques Morisset, and Neda Pirnia. 2001. Using Tax Incentives to Compete for Foreign Investment: Are They Worth the Costs? Foreign Investment Advisory Service, Occasional Paper No. 15. Accessed August 26, 2017.

Wichita Eagle. 2011. Applebee's to move headquarters, 390 jobs to Kansas City, Mo. from Lenexa. *Wichita Eagle*. (May 27). www.kansas.com/news/arti cle1064938.html. Accessed August 26, 2017.

Wildasin, David E. 1989. Interjurisdictional Capital Mobility: Fiscal Externality and a Corrective Subsidy. *Journal of Urban Economics* 25: 193–212.

Wilson, John Douglas. 1986. A theory of interregional tax competition. *Journal of Urban Economics* 19: 296–315.

Wilson, John Douglas and David E. Wildasin. 2004. Capital Tax Competition: Bane or Boon? *Journal of Public Economics* 88: 1065–1091.

Wishlade, Fiona. 2008. The Control of Regional Aid to Large Investment Projects: Workable Compromise or Arbitrary Restraint? *European State Aid Law Quarterly* 3: 495–506.

Wolfers, Justin. 2002. Are Voters Rational? Evidence from Gubernatorial Elections. Working Paper No. 1730, Graduate School of Business, Stanford University.

Wright, Joseph. 2008. Do Authoritarian Institutions Constrain? How Legislatures Affect Economic Growth and Investment. *American Journal of Political Science* 52: 322–343.

Xu, Chenggang. 2011. The Fundamental Institutions of China's Reforms and Development. *Journal of Economic Literature* 49: 1076–1151.

Zee, Howell H., Janet G. Stotsky, and Eduardo Ley. 2002. Tax Incentives for Business Investment: A Primary for Policy Makers in Developing Countries. *World Development* 30: 1497–1516.

Zheng, Yu. 2012. When World's Workshop Meets Its Office: Comparative Advantage, Institutions, and Foreign Investment in China and India. East Asia Institute Fellows Program Working Paper Series No. 34, Seoul, Republic of Korea.

Zheng, Yu. 2014. *Governance and Foreign Investment in China, India, and Taiwan: Credibility, Flexibility, and International Business*. Ann Arbor: University of Michigan Press.

Zodrow, George R. and Peter Mieszkowski. 1986. Pigou, Tiebout, Property Taxation, and the Underprovision of Public Goods. *Journal of Urban Economics* 19: 356–370.

Index

777X, 222

Abbott, Greg, 26
Advantage Illinois, 194
Aldrich, John H., 114
American Community Survey, 186
American Enterprise Institute, 20
American Federation of Labor and Congress of Industrial Organizations (AFL-CIO), 202
American Federation of Teachers, 194, 202
anchoring vignettes experiments, 100
Anderson, John E., 50
Ansolabehere, Stephen, 84
Applebees, 3
appropriation clauses, 184
Arbix, Glauco, 52, 101
Arceneaux, Kevin, 98
Argentina, 37
Arkansas, 193
  Booneville, 193
  Camden, 193
  Crossett, 193
  Eldorado, 193
  Newport, 193
  Russellville, 193
Atlantic Monthly, 179
Australia, 145
Authoritarian, 122, 123, 125, 157, 165, 228
Axtria Inc, 22

Barlow, David, 44
Bartik, Timothy J., 50
Basinger, Scott J., 30, 115
Batangas City, 37
Binh Duong, 122
BlackRock Private Equity Partners, 97
Blame Avoidance, 23, 101
Blomstrom, Magnus, 52
BMW, 7, 29
Bobonis, Gustavo J., 47, 50
Boeing, 5, 45, 222

Bondonio, Daniele, 50
Brazil, 29, 38, 101
Bristol, 95
British Aerospace, 8
British Petroleum, 84
Bronzini, Raffaello, 47, 49
Brown, Jerry, 195
Brown, Michael, 179
Buettner, Thiess, 52
Bulgaria, 35
Buss, Terry F., 49
Busso, Matias, 50

cadre promotion, 128
California, 50, 195
California Professional Firefighters association, 196
California Redevelopment Association, 196
California Teachers' Association, 196
Campaign Contributions, 6, 11, 83, 86
Canada, 37, 58, 205, 208, 229
Canes-Wrone, Brandice, 62
Carrier, 18
causal inference, 98, 160
Central Committee, 123
Charles, Cameron, 84
Chicago, 69, 195, 222
China, 36, 145
Chinese Party Organization Committee, 127
Chrysler, 8, 194
clawback provisions, 199, 213, 221, 228
Clinton, Hillary, 18
Coarsened Exact Matching, 57, 200, 218
Cohen, Jeffrey E., 98
Comprehensive Annual Reports, 201, 214
conceptualization, 141
Connecticut, 95
Consumer Expenditure Survey, 186
contingency funds, 97
contingent valuation designs, 100

254

Index

Cooperative Congressional Election Survey, 99
Corporate Income Tax, 3, 33, 132
Corporate Welfare, 1, 19, 58, 194
Corruption, 6, 11, 27, 83
Corzine, Jon, 97
Credit Claiming, 8, 13, 23, 27, 101, 109, 116, 122, 129, 157, 166, 205, 228
credit clauses, 184
Credit Income Tax, 32
Cross-National Analysis, 32, 63, 124, 141, 167, 228, 230
Cuomo, Andrew, 22, 26
Czech Republic, 35

Dairy Queen, 51
Davies, Ronald B., 30
Davine, Harold, 115
de Blasio, Guido, 47, 49
deal-closing funds, 98
Delaware, 187
Department of Planning and Investment, 122
diff-in-diff, 108, 160
Digital Domain Media Group, 5
DineEquity, 3
Distributional Effects, 179
Dung, Nguyen Tan, 142

Easson, Alex, 9, 46, 48
East-West Gateway, 181
Eckel, Carsten, 30
Effective Average Tax Rate, 32
Emanuel, Rahm, 195
Emerson Electric, 179
Enterprise Zones, 31, 50
Entropy Balancing, 57, 70, 74, 77
ESPN, 95
Estonia, 35
European Union, 29, 35, 117, 145

Federalism, 37
fence breaking, 122
Ferguson, 179, 197
Film Tax Credit, 195
FOIA, 216
Ford Foundation, 202
framing effect, 99

Gaines, Brian J., 100
gambling-for-resurrection strategy, 114
Geddes, Barbara, 126, 136, 158
General Department of Taxation, 122
Georgia, 46

Georgia Economic Developers Association, 203
Germany, 49
Good Jobs First, 198
Google, 41, 45
Gordon, Sanford C., 85
Goss, Ernest Preston, 50
Government Accounting Oversight Board (GASB), 199, 201
Government Finance Officers Association, 203
Greenbaum, Robert T., 50
Greenstone, Michael, 48
Grimmer, Justin, 20
Grossman, Gene M., 84
Guanajuato, 38
gubernatorial appointments, 159
Guisinger, Alexandra, 98
Gura, David, 44

Hagen, Ken, 64
Hainmueller, Jens, 74
Hallerberg, Mark, 30
Hanson, Andrew, 51, 180
Harrington, Joseph E., 21, 62
Hays, Jude C., 30
Head, Keith, 52
Helpman, Elhanan, 84
Honda, 38
Hungary, 29, 35

Illinois, 194
Illinois Jobs Now!, 194
import duties, 132
Incentive Environment Index, 183
Incentives. See Location-Specific Incentives
IncentivesMonitor, 186, 208
Independent Budget Office New York City, 202
India, 37
Indianapolis, 18
Indonesia, 14, 37
inequality, 182
  racial, 179
  tax, 180, 183, 187
  wage, 182
information asymmetry, 96, 123, 224
Institute on Taxation and Economic Policy (ITEP), 186
International City/County Management Association, 67, 184, 203
International Economic Development Council, 203
International House of Pancakes, 3

256   Index

International Standard Industrial Coding (ISIC), 149
interrupted time-series, 158, 160
IRS Individual Public Use Tax Files, 186
Israel, 37

Jalisco, 38
James, Sebastian, 53
Japan, 145
Java, 37
Jensen, Nathan M., 55
JG Summit Holdings, 36
Jindal, Piyush, 45
Jintao, Hu, 130
Johnson, Walter, 179
Jordan, 48, 53

Kansas, 41, 52, 92, 200, 214, 223
Kansas City Border War, 1, 53, 54, 92
Kansas City Development Corporation, 2
Kansas City, Kansas, 1, 53, 92
Kansas City, Missouri, 1, 53, 92
Keen, Michael, 31, 52
Kentucky, 52
Kia Motors, 46
King, James D., 98
Klemm, Alexander, 5, 31, 32, 33, 35, 36, 37, 38, 47, 132, 139
Kokko, Ari, 52
Kolko, Jed, 51
Kono, Daniel, 207
Kraybill, David S., 69
Kuwait Petroleum Corporation, 37

Latvia, 35
Lenoir, 41, 42, 44, 45
LeRoy, Greg, 51
LexisNexis, 115
Liberal Party, 212
licensing fees, 132
Likert scale, 102
Lithuania, 35
Lobao, Linda, 69
Local Development, 13, 22, 26, 45, 49, 54, 67, 79, 128
Local Parliament Project, 208
Location-Specific Incentives, 1, 45, 182
  and municipal regime type, 68
  discretionary allotments, 37, 86
  effectiveness of, 46, 48
  increase in, 30
  infrastructure improvements, 2, 4, 37, 53, 60, 122
  job creation through, 49
  relocation funds, 2, 37

statutory requirements, 37
subsidized land, 2, 37, 122
tax relief, 3, 5, 22, 31, 46, 49, 52, 122
worker retraining grants, 2
logit, 191
Louisiana, 45

Magaloni, Beatriz, 126, 136, 158
Malloy, Daniel P., 95
Mansour, Mario, 31, 52
Markusen, Ann, 9, 31
Massachusetts, 195
McCrary density test, 144, 151
Mekong Private Sector Development Facility, 122
Memphis Firefighters Association, 202
Mercedes-Benz, 4
meritocracy, 127, 128, 157
Mexico, 37, 38
Michigan, 25, 50
Ministry of Finance, 122
Minnesota, 52
Minnesota State Legislature, 202
Missouri, 92, 179, 200, 214
  Ferguson, 179, 197
  Ozark, 215
  Ripley, 215
  St. Louis, 181
Missouri Quality Jobs Program, 2, 200, 213, 217
Missouri Works Program, 215
Moeller, Enoch, 42
Moran, Theodore, 54
Moretti, Enrico, 48
Morisset, Jacques, 48, 52
Morton, Rebecca, 84
Moscow, 161
Mozambique, 48, 53
multivariate analysis of variance, 150
Mutz, Diana C., 102

National Association of Counties, 204
National Association of State Auditors, Comptrollers and Treasurers, 203
National Education Association, 194
National League of Cities, 67, 203
natural experiment, 151
Nebraska, 50
Nelson, Kimberly, 68, 77
Nesse, Katherine, 9, 31
Neumark, David, 51
New Jersey, 22, 97
New York, 22, 69
New York Times, 198
Nicaragua, 53

Nissan, 5
Nixon, Jay, 12, 26, 92
North Carolina, 41
North Korea, 126
Northrop Grumman, 45
Norton, Edward C., 109
Nova Scotia, 38

Oakley, Deirdre, 51
Ohio, 50, 204, 224
Oklahoma, 52
omitted variable bias, 105, 135
Ontario, 38, 208
Opel, 36
operationalization, 141
Ordered Probit, 104, 105
Organization for Economic Co-operation and Development, 38

Patrick, Carlianne Elizabeth, 49, 183
Patton, Zach, 44
Pauken, Tom, 26
Pennsylvania, 97
perception bias, 138
Perry, Rick, 26, 83, 86, 92, 226
personalism, 124, 130, 158, 165, 228
Pew Charitable Trusts, 230
Pew Foundation, 217
Phillips, Joseph M., 50
Pirnia, Neda, 48, 52
Plainsboro, 97
Poland, 35
Polimetrix, 102
Political Pandering, 5, 8, 20, 23, 166
  upward, 14, 157, 167, 227
Polity IV, 136
probit, 152
Promoting Employment Across Kansas, 1, 6, 54, 200, 214, 223
property tax, 97, 132
Provincial Competitiveness Index (PCI), 145
Provincial People's Committee chairmen (PCOMs), 142
public-private partnerships, 184
Putin, Vladimir, 17, 124, 126, 158

Quality of Government Institute, 138
Quebec, 38, 58, 208
Quinn, Pat, 194

Race-to-the-Bottom, 6
regional decentralized authoritarianism, 128

Regression Discontinuity, 16, 47, 141, 142, 143, 147, 152
regressive tax, 180, 183, 184, 204
Richter, Brian Kelleher, 85
Robin, Pemantle, 102
Rodríguez-Pose, Andrés, 52, 101
Rohlin, Shawn, 51, 180
Romania, 35
Roots, 8
Rover Group, 8
Ruf, Martin, 52
Russia, 124, 126, 158, 165, 228

Seaboard Corporation, 52
Seattle, 222
Serbia, 36, 48, 53, 101
Shatz, Howard J., 47, 50
shooting, 179
Singapore, 145
single-party, 124, 125, 157, 167, 228
Skoda, 35
Skudutis, Tom, 12
Sly, James, 3
Snyder, Rick, 25
South Africa, 224
South Carolina, 29, 45
South Korea, 145
St. Louis Economic Development Partnership, 179
St. Petersburg, 161
Standard Industrial Classification (SIC), 217
stock clauses, 184
Stockholm, 138
Strain, Michael, 20
Suharto, Muhammad, 130
Survey Experiment, 67, 98, 99, 102, 105, 117, 120, 205, 229
Svolik, Milan, 126, 130, 158
Swank, Duane, 30
Sweden, 138

Taiwan, 145
Tax Foundation, 45
tax holidays, 97, 207
Tax Increment Financing, 4, 179, 194
term limits, 142
Texas, 83, 86, 92, 192
Texas Development Corporation Act, 193
Texas Enterprise Fund, 1, 83, 85, 86, 98, 226
Thailand, 48
The American Panel Survey (TAPS), 205
Thomas, Kenneth P., 39
transparency, 199, 201, 202, 205, 208, 229

Trump, Donald, 18, 20
Tsao, Hui-Shien, 51
Tullock, Gordon, 5, 62, 84
Turkey, 35

Ukraine, 35
United Arab Emirates, 5
United Kingdom, 8, 13, 116
United Russia, 158, 159
United States, 4, 13, 37, 44, 47, 48, 49, 59, 62, 145, 205, 229
unobserved heterogeneity, 98
upward accountability, 124
Urban Transit Hub Tax Credit, 97
US Census, 185, 186
US Conference of Mayors, 204
US Country Commercial Guides on incentives, 132
Utah, 224

value added tax, 132
Van Parys, Stefan, 5, 31, 32, 33, 35, 36, 37, 38, 47, 132, 139

Vietnam, 122, 139, 141, 157, 228
Vietnamese Chamber of Commerce and Industry, 145
Vietnamese Communist Party, 142
Vlaicu, Razvan, 65
Volkswagen, 35

Walden, Michael, 43
Washington, 187, 222
Washington State, 5
Washington University, 205
Wassmer, Robert W., 50
Weber, 128, 138
Wells, Louis T., 14, 47
Whalley, Alexander, 65
Wilson, Darren, 179

YouGov UK, 117
YouGovPolimetrix, 99

Zedong, Mao, 130
Zee, Howell H., 49
Zheng, Yu, 128